MARKETING GREEN
BUILDING SERVICES

MARKETING GREEN
BUILDING SERVICES
STRATEGIES FOR SUCCESS

Jerry Yudelson

AMSTERDAM • BOSTON • HEIDELBERG • LONDON • NEW YORK • OXFORD
PARIS • SAN DIEGO • SAN FRANCISCO • SINGAPORE • SYDNEY • TOKYO
Architectural Press is an imprint of Elsevier

ELSEVIER

Architectural
Press

Architectural Press is an imprint of Elsevier
Linacre House, Jordan Hill, Oxford OX2 8DP, UK
30 Corporate Drive, Burlington, MA 01803, USA

First Edition 2008

British Library Cataloguing in Publication Data
A catalogue record for this book is available from the British Library

Library of Congress Catalog Number: 2007931726

ISBN 978-07506-8474-3

For information on all Architectural Press publications
visit our website at www.architecturalpress.com

Typeset by Charon Tec Ltd (A Macmillan Company), Chennai, India
www.charontec.com

Printed and bound in China

Working together to grow
libraries in developing countries

www.elsevier.com | www.bookaid.org | www.sabre.org

ELSEVIER   BOOK AID
            International   Sabre Foundation

CONTENTS

LIST OF ILLUSTRATIONS AND PHOTOS

LIST OF TABLES

PREFACE AND ACKNOWLEDGMENTS

This book raises and attempts to answer several key questions: How is green building marketing similar to all other types of architectural and engineering services marketing, and how is it remarkably different? What available tools and techniques from conventional marketing can we use to greater effect in marketing green design services? What is the size of the market for green buildings? How can we estimate the future growth of this market? Who are the winners thus far in the green building services marketing derby? How should a design firm position itself to succeed in this growing marketplace?

To quote Tom Watson, the marketing genius behind IBM's early success, "Nothing happens until a sale is made." Green building designers and advocates need a firm grounding in marketing theory and contemporary marketing strategy and tactics to be effective in this rapidly changing marketplace. Conventional marketers and sales people need to understand what the green building client really wants, to be more effective in presenting green design features and sustainable strategies to this buyer.

PURPOSE OF THIS BOOK

This book presents the special features of marketing green buildings. It is designed for "insiders," people such as yourself whose livelihood depends on successfully marketing design services to serve green building projects. There are thousands of us out there, trying to transform the building industry into a more environmentally responsible activity, and we're doing it one presentation, one meeting, one design, one project, one new product put into use, at a time.

ORGANIZATION OF THIS BOOK

Like Caesar's Gaul, this book is divided into three parts. Part 1 surveys the green building marketplace, primarily in the US and Canada, using the most up-to-date information obtainable from those countries Green Building Councils. With a thorough grounding in the actual market dynamics, Part 2 takes a step back and asks how marketing theory, strategy and tactics, could be useful in marketing green design services. Part 3 then puts this information into the form of "seven keys" for marketing sustainable design services to your current and prospective client base. In the Part 1, Chapter 1 gives a brief overview of the current status of green buildings, including defining terms and examining drivers and barriers in the market. Chapter 2 examines green building market growth overall, then for each major sector of the building industry. This chapter also presents an overview of the various green building rating programs, especially those in the US, Canada, the UK and Australia. Chapter 3 presents the business case for green buildings, circa 2007. Chapter 4 looks at costs of green buildings, since higher costs can be a significant factor in holding back green building growth. Chapter 5 looks at the characteristics of green buildings in selected vertical markets. Chapter 6 examines specialty markets for sustainable design services, including urban planning, mixed-use development and commercial interiors. Chapter 7 looks at the current state and likely future success of various green building technologies, with a special focus on solar power. Chapter 8 presents case studies of successful green building marketing at design firms and also looks at these marketing efforts from the client's point of view. In Part 2, Chapter 9 reviews classical marketing strategies for emerging markets such as green building and in particular shows how to use the theory of "diffusion of innovations," which has characterized similar innovative marketing efforts around the world. Chapter 10 deals with the tactical issues of marketing green building services, assisted by successfully positioning the firm in the marketplace. Chapter 11 looks at green building marketing from a larger strategic viewpoint, and shows how to change the "DNA" of a firm to meet the challenges of this new market. Part 3 presents "six strategic insights" for green building marketing. Chapter 12 presents the seven keys a firm can use to enhance its green building marketing. Chapter 13 looks to the future of green building and architectural design, toward major changes in the LEED green building rating system, the growth of other rating systems, emerging technologies and new points of focus for this emerging industry. Appendix 1 briefly lists some valuable resources, while Appendix 2 compares the four major LEED rating systems in detail, so that the green building marketer can see what challenges and opportunities they present for the firm. Appendix 3 presents a list of the most common acronyms used in this book.

SUMMARY

Throughout this document, I rely on empirical data, most of it publicly available from the US and Canada Green Building Councils, from papers presented at green building conferences, from trade journals and from my own analyses of these data. I have also used a number of proprietary surveys from respected trade journals and professional organizations, as well as personal interviews to round out the picture of green building marketing given in this book. These survey results are all accessible, so that you can see for yourself what hundreds of green building firms, architectural and construction firm principals, and buyers think about selling and buying various sustainable design services.

I welcome dialog with readers and users of this information about how we can bring about a successful transformation of the building industry, to one that produces what most people say they want from it: energy and resource efficient, environmentally sound, healthy, comfortable and productive places to live, work, study and play. I encourage readers to send me their responses, so that, together, we can improve the state of marketing green buildings, to bring about a healthier future for all. Please go to my web page, www.greenbuildconsult.com, to find the appropriate email address to contact me.

No preface would be complete without thanking the many people who helped put this book together. My editorial associate, Gretel Hakanson, and my graphic designer, David Ziegler-Voll of Creative Tornado, both provided invaluable assistance. My wife Jessica put up with the obsessions (and late nights) that come with writing any book. I especially want to thank Randy Pollock, a principal and CMO at Walter P. Moore Inc., Houston, Texas and Andrea Norman, the director of marketing and business development at RSP Architects and Temple, Arizona, for kindly agreeing to review the draft manuscript and to Craig Park of HDR, Inc. for writing the foreword. I also offer my deep appreciation for those who shared their experiences of green design and construction marketing with us, by way of telephone and email interviews: Jim Broughton, TAS; Jonah Cohen, Thomas Hacker Associates; Richard Cook, Cook + Fox; Leland D. Cott, Bruner/Cott; John Echlin, SERA Architects; Rebecca Flora, Green Building Alliance; Jim Goldman, Turner Construction Company; Bert Gregory, Mithun; Mark Gudenas, Swinerton Builders; Kimberly Hickson, BNIM Architects; Steven Kendrick, LPA Architects; Jerry Lea, Hines; Craig Park, Leo A Daly; Russell Perry, SmithGroup; J. Rossi, Burt Hill; Paul Shahriari, GreenMind Inc.; Leith Sharp, Harvard University; Kirsten Sibilia, FXFOWLE Architects; and William Viehman, Perkins+Will. Together they represent a range of experience and expertise that is truly staggering. Without their contribution, this book would not have its particular relevance and richness.

Jerry Yudelson
Tucson, Arizona
May 2007

FOREWORD

There is a sea change in environmental consciousness happening worldwide: Green is "the new black." As awareness of global warming, diminishing natural resources and energy costs increases, the demand for sustainable design and construction is also increasing – at an unprecedented rate. Demand for green building is not merely a passing fad. We are entering a pivotal time in history where new, fundamental changes in design and construction are being created. How well we're prepared for the changes will determine our future success.

But first – why should we care? Because sustainable design for buildings offers the largest single potential for global energy efficiency. Buildings are *the* major source of demand for energy and materials that produce by-product green-house gases (GHG). Studies show that the building sector accounts for over 40 percent of world's energy requirements. And more than 20 percent of the present energy consumption and carbon dioxide generation could be saved by applying acknowledged standards to new and refurbished buildings. Furthermore we could be carbon neutral, using no fossil fuel GHG emitting energy to build and operate our buildings, with only a little more effort.

Exciting times for sure. But why is this so important? The impact of green design on the building industry is being felt everywhere – from urban planning to interiors, from commercial buildings to homes. With productions such as Al Gore's film *An Inconvenient Truth*, the PBS series *design e^2: The Economies of Being Environmentally Conscious* narrated by Brad Pitt, and Ed Begley Jr.'s personal eco-stories *Living with Ed* on cable-TV, the public's perception of the importance of green design is dramatically increasing. Demand is sure to follow.

Equally important, investors in buildings of all types (and the related design, engineering and construction-related services they require) are now, more than ever, willing to buy good green design. They recognize the intrinsic value of sustainable practice in the projects they create. It is no longer just an issue of "How much more will it cost?" but more likely "Sustainable design *must* be used because it adds value to my investment." Quite simply, being "green" makes good business sense.

And so, you ask, "How can the building industry professional keep up with, and profit from, this change?" The answer is simple: "Read this book!"

In *The Architect's Guide to Marketing Green Building Services*, Jerry Yudelson has assembled a compendium of best practices for marketing sustainable design services. He shows you how to strengthen the message you take to the marketplace. And he makes the often arcane aspects of sustainable design highly accessible to the nontechnical reader.

I was honored when Jerry asked me to write the foreword for this book. In my own published research, I address the importance of marketing traditional professional services that relies on three factors: *expertise* (the technical ability to perform the service), *excellence* (the ability to differentiate the service through marketing based on doing it well) and *experience* (the ability to deliver the service in a memorable way to both the client and your staff) to ensure that the buyer returns, and hopefully tells a few other potential customers about your service along the way. I also acknowledge that the difficult part of marketing professional services is differentiation. Developing a unique brand requires identifying your specialization and promoting it effectively. Jerry addresses these issues with a comprehensive "how to" for green services.

Today, being "green" can be an important differentiator for your firm. *Marketing Green Building Services* shows you how. Starting with the impact of the industry standard, US Green Building Council's *Leadership in Energy and Environmental Design* (LEED®) accreditation for professionals and rating system and certification program for buildings, Jerry sets forth the basic criteria necessary to succeed. In his business case descriptions, he provides guidelines for enhanced proactive communications. And in his case studies, he offers success stories of some of the leading firms in sustainable design and construction. In addition, one of the important highlights of this book is how to focus on client-oriented needs, values and metrics of satisfaction. As client needs evolve, so must the practice.

Marketing Green Building Services also extends marketing sustainable design into the future. As one of the pioneers in sustainable engineering, Jerry has been at the forefront of developing green initiatives. Through his network of professional relationships, he has been in a unique position to both "learn what works," and "see what's coming." In this book, he looks to the future, focusing on trends in both market adoption and acceptance, and toward the next steps in advancing proactive sustainable design.

Embracing the tenets of the "2010 Imperative" and "2030 Challenge," (see http://architecture2030.com) *Marketing Green Building Services* is a must read for building-related ecological literacy. These international initiatives are supported by the American Institute of Architects (AIA), the US Green Building Council (USGBC), the American Society of Heating, Refrigeration and Air-Conditioning Engineers (ASHRAE), the Society of Building Science Educators

(SBSE) and the Association of Collegiate Schools of Architecture (ACSA), among many others.

The 2010/2030 programs are designed to have a pronounced impact on global warming and world resource depletion by improving ecological knowledge in design education and in application in school design, and more importantly, by reducing carbon usage and greenhouse gas emissions in all new buildings, developments and major renovations.

Marketing Green Building Services provides the fundamentals for the professional practice that can lead to a significant reduction in our carbon footprint and help achieve the goal of preserving and improving our environment. In the spirit of producing positive and proactive environmental results, Jerry's writing is an important, relevant and timely call to action for implementing sustainable design as a key feature of your practice.

As Kermit the Frog once said, "*It's not easy being green.*" In both marketing and sustainable design literature, theory is everywhere, but practical, pragmatic and proven guidance is hard to find. *Marketing Green Building Services* breaks the mold with a perfect mix of background, applications and evidence that you can use today, making it easy to guide your firm's marketing efforts to a successful, profitable and sustainable future.

Craig Park, FSMPS, Assoc. AIA
Chief Marketing Officer, LEO A DALY
Omaha, Nebraska

July 2007

INTRODUCTION

THE FUTURE OF GREEN BUILDINGS

Hurricane Katrina in 2005, a 50 percent increase in oil prices since 2004 and Al Gore's Academy Award-winning documentary, "An Inconvenient Truth," taken together, have put an end to the public's "age of innocence" about the power of natural forces, the continued availability of cheap oil and the inevitability of climate change. As a result, we've seen a "sea change" in consumer attitudes toward everything green, including green homes and green buildings. There is a momentum that will sweep across the entire design, development and construction industry over the next three to five years that each firm must prepare for, or risk being left at a considerable competitive disadvantage. This book shows your firm how to respond to this tidal wave of public concern and professional opportunity.

These and other outside events have led building owners, buyers and developers to become increasingly concerned with long-term operating costs for energy. These forces include the growing realization of the problem of global warming (through greenhouse gas emissions); environmental hazards of mold, chemical allergies and other indoor air quality issues, along with attendant lawsuits; current oil price escalations; and a more or less permanent drought throughout the Western United States. Beginning in 2004, the rapid (and seemingly permanent) rise in oil prices strongly affected the psychology of consumers, building owners, developers and public officials, who are beginning to realize for the first time since the early 1980s that energy prices are likely to be much higher for the foreseeable future than in the recent past.[1]

The greenhouse gas issue and the resulting human-induced climate change will be the key factor in driving major reductions in buildings' energy use, which will bring about a revolution in passive solar design, incorporation of daylighting and use of natural ventilation approaches in much of the US. Over the next three years, we will see architects and engineers routinely aiming at 50 percent reductions in building energy use (from current baselines). The Conference Board is a national business group for very large corporations. Indicating the seriousness with which the business community views the issue of greenhouse gas emissions and associated global climate change, the Conference Board's environmental expert stated as early as 2004: "Given the increasing costs of, and uncertainties surrounding the reliability of traditional energy sources and growing pressures for higher standards of citizenship and contributions to global sustainability, businesses that ignore the debate over climate change do so at their peril."[2]

SOCIAL AND CULTURAL CHANGE

As more stakeholder groups become knowledgable about green buildings, they are demanding such projects for their schools and campuses, healthcare institutions, museums, libraries and public buildings. This grassroots support is especially manifested in public and nonprofit buildings, but it will become increasingly evident as public support and understanding for the concept of sustainability grow. On college campuses, sustainability is rapidly becoming a galvanizing issue for students and faculty, so the push for green building projects in higher education will gain considerable momentum by 2008 to 2009.[3]

TECHNOLOGICAL CHANGES

Many green building measures, such as underfloor air distribution systems, photovoltaics, rainwater harvesting, onsite waste treatment and green roofs, are becoming mainstream technologies and are building a strong track record in design and use. As a result, these measures are gaining a strong, supportive infrastructure of salespeople and suppliers, a better cost history, an understanding of how to bid and install them, and a growing number of advocates among architects and engineers who are learning to design and specify such systems. The construction industry infrastructure is quite mature and highly complex, and it is important that green building marketers master its intricacies to get new green building designs, technologies and products into that marketplace.

We are beginning to see venture capital (or private equity) come into the green building and renewable energy arena for the first time in many years. According to one source, venture capital investments in "clean technology" totaled more than nine percent of all new investment in 2006, up from about four percent in 2005.[4] This new money will in turn spur technological innovations that will drive down the cost of green building technologies and make them more feasible for the average project.

Technological innovation thrives when an industry such as green building is growing rapidly, costs are coming down, competition is growing, capital is freely available and consumer demand is growing. Throw in the potential for this new technology to be made in China and other low-cost countries and add the concern over climate change, and we should be seeing a host of green building technology innovations in the next three to five years.

ECONOMIC CHANGES

Today's relatively low interest rates may persist for several more years due to high levels of productivity and worldwide supply overcapacity in many industries. Lower interest rates have the effect of encouraging capital investments that yield long-term operating cost savings, because the present value of future savings is larger in today's dollars than in a higher-interest-rate environment. In addition, the relative lack of investment in energy-supply infrastructure in recent years may have the effect of guaranteeing higher future energy prices. As a result, the return on capital investments for energy and water conservation becomes more favorable with each passing year. It is fairly easy to justify a five-year, or even ten-year, payback (return of initial investment in annual energy savings) for energy conservation and efficiency investments, at least on rational economic grounds, because of the value they add to buildings by generating higher net operating income. In turn, these developments will lead buildings by 2010 to be built 30 to 50 percent more efficient than current codes.

POLITICAL AND LEGAL CHANGES

More cities and states are adopting incentive programs for green buildings, including direct financial incentives. These incentives have generated private-sector investment in such diverse places as Washington, Oregon, California, New York and British Columbia. The federal Energy Policy Act of 2005 provides significant new tax credits for solar systems placed in service through the end of 2008. If the cost of oil and gas remains high, it is likely that these incentives will be extended beyond calendar year 2008. Developers and design professionals should take advantage of them for projects now underway that will be completed by the end of 2008. The new Democratic Congress is likely to extend the Energy Policy Act for a number of years before 2007 is up, ensuring that these incentives will help drive the use of solar and energy conservation technology in green buildings.

INDUSTRY PRACTICES

In just about every area of the country and every sector of the marketplace, design contracts are awarded on qualifications, rather than fee or price. Fees are negotiated after a selection is made. It is becoming increasingly difficult for firms to qualify for a "short list" of finalists for any important public or institutional project without having a strong green building orientation, knowledge of green building products and some successful projects under their belts. Several of the larger design firms we interviewed for this book believe that 2007 will mark the year in which firms begin to compete solely on sustainable design results, rather than just on good intentions, qualified people and projects in the pipeline. Competitive pressures alone are driving more firms toward green building projects, even if some of their principals are not really "believers" in sustainable design. It is also leading firms to hire younger professionals who are green building advocates and become a positive influence within their firms.

CERTIFICATION PROGRAMS

We profile a number of building certification programs in this book, including the well-established Energy Star label for commercial buildings in the US. However, in the commercial and institutional marketplace for green buildings (those that go beyond just energy conservation), the LEED rating system of the US Green Building Council is basically the only game in town and is the certification method that most drives green building demand. In 2006, more than 1,100 projects registered for LEED certification for the first time, totaling more than 130 million square feet of space, more than 5 percent of the entire building construction industry.

Several other certification programs are being used to handle subsets of the LEED rating system, for example, schools, healthcare and laboratories. Rating systems for green buildings also use methods for evaluating building products, indoor air quality, reductions in carbon dioxide emissions, cool roofs, green roofs, and other similar technologies and building systems. State-level homebuilder, nonprofit, and utility rating systems and incentive programs also serve the residential green building market.

THE MARKETING DILEMMA

Given this ferment in the marketplace for green buildings, one would expect most firms to have responded strongly by now. However, that is not the case; most leading architecture and engineering firms are having trouble getting more than 25 percent of their technical staff to become LEED Accredited Professionals, the basic accreditation now possessed by more than 36,000 design and construction industry professionals.[5] And many firms are not yet re-orienting themselves in the way I believe necessary for long-term success, as the entire design profession moves toward sustainable design as an overriding concern. This book discusses that dilemma and what to do about it.

I interviewed a number of leading marketers and design firm principals for this book. Steven Kendrick is an Architect and Principal of a leading California-based design firm, LPA Inc., ranked 28th nationally in 2005 among architect/engineering firms.[6] He is a strong proponent of sustainable design and talked of his firm's approach:

> "We've updated our practice to focus on sustainable design. In 2006, we were challenged by the president of our firm to have everybody become LEED Accredited Professionals, and for a firm of over 200 that's quite a challenge. At this point [March 2007], 75% of our staff is LEED Accredited.

We don't look at sustainable design as a separate market. We apply sustainable design to all of the market segments that we're involved with from our private work to all of our public work.

We've had some clients now that have seen what we're doing with sustainable design who are now coming to us, even if they don't have a project at the moment, and asking us how they can get a sustainable quotient into their next project. We're also seeing some recruitment benefits from our sustainable focus. We've been able to bring a few people in who have achieved their LEED accreditation at other firms. Then they see what we're doing in sustainable design and they've come over here, because [at LPA] it's driven top-down and not bottom-up.

If sustainability is not in the firm's DNA and they don't start at the beginning at the grass roots level and just apply things to projects to make them sustainable, it's going to cost more and they'll never understand what's possible.[7]

How things change

A 2006 book by a Silicon Valley maven, Pip Coburn, presents compelling evidence why some technologies succeed in the marketplace while others never get off the ground.[8] While the book primarily deals with the fate of new computing and electronic technologies for both consumer and business markets, the lessons it presents are broadly applicable to green building adoptions and to green building marketing.

In essence, the book documents two critical factors in the success of new technologies. One, the "Total Perceived Pain of Adoption" (TPPA) and the other, the degree of "Crisis" involved. The first critical factor, TPPA, deals with the full costs of understanding and deploying new technology. In Coburn's view, the problem with most new technologies is that they're developed by technologists (scientists and engineers, computer programmers and geeks) whose main interest is in doing with technology whatever "cool" things can be done. Their primary worldview is that anyone who doesn't see things their way is "un-cool" or a "dummy."

The second factor, Crisis, is equally important. Most new technologies don't get mainstream acceptance unless there's a "crisis" of some kind with current technology.

Without a genuine crisis of performance or economics, most new technologies can't overcome people's genuine concerns with the economic and technical risks of new approaches.

What's needed for the rapid adoption of new technologies is the combination of both factors: TPPA needs to be relatively low (i.e., pain of adoption needs to be far less than the gain from adoption) and the sense of organizational or personal crisis needs to be high. In this respect, Coburn's approach is entirely consistent with other classic works on the theory of innovation adoption, presented in Chapter 9. Things don't change just because new things are available; people need good reasons to make significant changes in business and personal affairs.

Think about some of the new technologies that you or your colleagues have adopted in the past few years. Quickly, Blackberries come to mind. The TPPA factor is not large, since the Blackberry™ is basically a marriage of a Palm Pilot, on the market for more than 10 years, and a cell phone of similar vintage. The Crisis factor lies in the need for increasingly mobile workers to stay in touch with the home office and with each other. *Voilá*, the Blackberry (or "Crackberry," to those addicted to it). Think of how you feel getting a return email, usually quite short, with the tag line, "sent from my wireless email Blackberry." Pretty left out, right? The TPPA is also not large because the cost of failure is small: just a few hundred dollars and a return to your previous "out of touch" existence.

Now think about the adoption cycle for green buildings. What about the TPPA and the Crisis factors? In the summer of 2006, I attended a conference hosted by three major professional associations in higher education. One of the presentations dealt with the use of LEED and green building approaches by 11 campuses in the Boston area, a location that many times is a "hotbed" of new ideas and quite receptive to new technology and green buildings. Of these 11 institutions of higher education, only three were actually members of the US Green Building Council, and less than half had completed even one LEED-certified building through early 2006. What became clear from the presentation was that neither the TPPA factor nor the Crisis factor is yet at work in green building adoption for higher education in that region.

Chapter 5 suggests that higher education adoption of green building practices is still in the "innovator" stage (less than three percent of new buildings or major renovations actively pursue LEED certification), but is rapidly moving into the "early adopter" stage (with LEED accounting for 3 to 16 percent of total new building or renovation projects), primarily because of campus pressure from below (students and faculty) and sometimes from above (presidents and chancellors).

But let's return to the Boston-area campuses, for example. As we stated earlier, the TPPA factor needs to be low, not high, for green building adoption to occur. Campuses that make green building investments have to see them as fairly easy and cost effective. What are the facts? Chapter 4 cites a 2005 national survey of some 665 design and construction industry executives, including owners, showed that they thought the additional cost of "going green" ranged from 13 to 18 percent, a killer in today's high-cost construction environment. Most of the Boston-area facilities would probably concur, yet a

2006 project at Harvard University delivered a LEED Platinum project with no additional cost.[9]

There is still the perception, true or not, that "LEED costs too much" for the benefits received. If users think LEED costs too much, what can be done to lower the perceived costs of LEED projects, other than actual experience? The job of the design firm is to deliver green projects on conventional budgets, so that clients will no longer fear "budget busting" results. Many are starting to do so, but it appears that TPPA is still thought too high by most potential users to justify using it on a regular basis.

What about the Crisis factor? Is there a crisis (problem) for which green buildings are a logical and compelling answer? In the opinion of many, such as New Mexico architect Edward Mazria, the need to get new buildings to be 90 percent or more efficient, compared with 2003 standards by 2030 (and 60 percent more efficient by 2010), is compelling, in terms of their cumulative global environmental impact. However, such large-scale "crises" seldom enter into day-to-day decision-making among design and construction teams and building owners or developers. What might constitute a Crisis for a facility director, project manager or architect is when the president of the university makes a public commitment to LEED Silver for all new projects. Then it's hard not to see a reason to go forward with a LEED project. Absent that imperative, most people try to achieve less lofty goals, such as basic certification (still about 40 percent of all LEED certifications), or to "design to LEED standards" without certifying at all (probably at least a third of projects that have sustainability goals). But whenever I hear this, I ask people to think of what our government's revenues would be like if we all just decided to pay our taxes "according to Internal Revenue Service (IRS) guidelines," without having to justify the amount to the IRS!

How should design and construction firms promote the rapid growth and adoption of green buildings and new green building technologies? Now the answer is relatively easy. *Lower the TPPA, the Total Perceived Pain of Adoption*, by continuing to work to make green buildings easier to build with a more certain outcome; in addition firms should publish case studies that reveal design team processes and choices that result in *lower* total capital costs for high-performance projects. One engineering firm did just that, publishing a case study of the engineering design of the world's largest LEED Platinum project. By making this widely available, it has distributed more than 9,000 copies of their report, a clear testament to the hunger for this information.[10] You just might agree that sending 9,000 copies of a quality case study of a high-performance green project around the world, upon written request, would qualify as a sound marketing move! And in fact, the firm reports that it is now working on more than 60 LEED-registered projects, almost triple the number before the report was published.

As for Crisis, there's not much that green building advocates can do to increase the sense of crisis in energy and water costs for buildings and the continuing interest of user groups in more sustainable approaches for building design and corporate responsibility. Global warming concerns and $70 per barrel oil already do that job quite nicely. Unfortunately, the crisis is not yet pointed enough for most project teams to take action for high-level LEED buildings, unless some CEO or university president or political leader makes it their priority.

If you're among the many trying to figure out how to succeed in the world of green building marketing, take it as your task to figure out how to decrease TPPA and increase the understanding of Crisis. Your clients will reward you beyond your expectations.

NOTES

1. In its Annual Energy Outlook for 2006, the US Energy Information Administration increased its 2025 price projection for oil by more than 63 percent from the 2005 outlook (www.eia.doe.gov/oiaf/aeo/key.html). In December 2005 position statement, the American Institute of Architects called for increasing building energy efficiency by 50 percent over 2003 levels by the year 2010 (www.aia.org/siteobjects/files/hpb_position_statements.pdf).

2. Green Biz Newsletter [online], www.greenbiz.com/news, September 13, 2004 issue (accessed April 24, 2007).

3. See, for example, the Association for the Advancement of Sustainability in Higher Education [online], www.aashe.org, a new campus sustainability initiative.

4. Clean Edge [online], www.cleanedge.com/reports-trends2007.php (accessed April 24, 2007).

5. US Green Building Council, LEED Faculty Newsletter, April 2007.

6. "Giants 300," annual survey, *Building Design & Construction*, July 2006, p. 59.

7. Interview with Steven Kendrick, LPA Inc., April 2007.

8. Pip Coburn (2006) *The Change Function: Why Some Technologies Take Off While Others Crash and Burn*. New York: Portfolio/Penguin.

9. Personal communication, Leith Sharp, Director, Harvard Green Campus Initiative, March 2006.

10. Case study is available at www.interfaceengineering.com; April numbers for report distribution and LEED-registered projects furnished courtesy of Interface Engineering. The author of this book was the editor of the case study.

PART

1   THE GREEN BUILDING
    MARKET

1 WHAT IS A GREEN BUILDING?

Green buildings and sustainable design have been major movements in the design, development and construction industry since about 2000, with an accelerating interest since 2005. In September 2006, for example, the first new building at the *Ground Zero* site in New York City, 7 World Trade Center (7 WTC), was completed as a LEED (Leadership in Energy and Environmental Design) Gold-rated green building. The developer, Silverstein Properties, committed to producing future buildings at this important symbolic site as LEED Gold-certified properties. Figure 1.1 shows the 52-story, $700 million, 1,700,000 square foot (156,000 sqm) 7 WTC building.[1]

Future buildings at the WTC site will also be built to a design standard that is 20 percent more efficient than the New York Energy Conservation Construction Code. At the LEED award ceremony in September 2006, New York state Governor George Pataki announced an agreement with Silverstein Properties that calls for the Freedom Tower and each of the WTC Office Towers to utilize cutting-edge fuel cell technology to increase efficiency and provide secure clean on-site power generation. These fuel cell installations, totaling 4.8 megawatts of power generation, will together constitute one of the largest fuel cell installations in the world.[2]

GREEN BUILDING CHARACTERISTICS

In Chapter 2, we deal with the growth of the green building movement. But first, we need to get more specific about what we actually mean by the term "green building." A green building is one that considers and reduces its impact on the environment and human health. A green building is designed to use less energy and water and consider the life cycle of the materials used. This is achieved through better site development practices, design, construction, operation, maintenance, removal and possible reuse of materials.

In the US and Canada, a commercial green building is generally considered to be one certified by the LEED green building rating system of the US Green Building Council (USGBC) or Canada Green Building Council.

▲ **1.1**   The 52-story 7 World Trade Center, the first new building at "Ground Zero" is certified LEED-NC Gold. Copyirght © David Sunberg/Esto, reprinted with permission.

More than 98 percent of the certified green buildings in both countries come from this system.[3]

In September 2006, the US General Services Administration (GSA) reported to Congress that it would use only the LEED system for assessing the government's own projects.[4] However, in the commercial and institutional arena, if a building is not rated and certified by an independent third party with an open process for creating and maintaining a rating system, it can't really be called a green building, since there's no other standard definition. If someone tells you they are "following LEED" but not bothering to apply for certification of the final building, you should rightly wonder if they will really achieve the results they claim. If they say they are doing "sustainable design," you have a right to ask, "Against what standard are you measuring your design, and how are you going to demonstrate it?"

Commercial and institutional buildings

A green building is one using design and construction practices that significantly reduce or eliminate the negative impact of buildings on the environment and occupants. In the LEED system, these practices cover building location, water and energy use, environmentally preferable purchasing, improved indoor environmental quality and a "continuous improvement" approach to green building innovations. The LEED rating system is a publicly available document;[5] though owned by the USGBC, it has an extensive committee structure charged with keeping it current and improving it over time. The current version is known as "LEED version 2.2."

Table 1.1 shows the six major categories in the LEED rating system for new and renovated commercial buildings, mid-rise and high-rise residential towers, existing building evaluations and commercial tenant improvements. At first thought, many people think of a green building as one that is lower in energy use and uses recycled-content materials. Looking at the entire LEED rating system, one can see that the categories of concern are much broader and more comprehensive. The design, development and construction industry in the US and Canada has embraced this system over all other competitors. In this regard, one can say confidently that marketers need to understand only the LEED system to see how they can promote their firms' green building activities.

Figure 1.2 shows the Artists for Humanity EpiCenter project in Boston, a LEED Platinum-certified building renovation typical of the projects underway in many cities. Completed in 2004, this four-story, 23,500 square foot (2180 sqm) building, includes several notable green design aspects:[6]

- A 49-kilowatt roof-mounted, grid-connected photovoltaic (PV) array, currently the largest PV array in Boston, provides solar power for the building.

Table 1.1   LEED system categories of concern

Category of Concern	Issues Evaluated by the LEED System
1. Sustainable sites	Site selection, land use, transportation, site impacts of construction, stormwater management, urban heat island effect and nighttime light pollution.
2. Water efficiency	Water conservation in landscape irrigation and building fixtures
3. Energy use reduction and atmosphere protection	Energy-conserving building operations, renewable energy systems, building commissioning, reduced use of ozone-depleting chemicals in HVAC systems, energy monitoring and green power use
4. Materials and resource conservation	Use of existing buildings; facilitating recycling by building occupants; construction waste recycling; use of salvaged materials, recycled-content materials, locally and regionally produced materials, agricultural-based materials and certified wood products.
5. Indoor environmental quality	Improved ventilation and indoor air quality; use of nontoxic finishes and furniture; green housekeeping; daylighting and views to the outdoors; thermal comfort; and individual control of lighting and HVAC systems.
6. Innovation and design process	Exemplary performance in exceeding LEED standards and use of innovative approaches to green design; use of LEED Accredited Professionals.

▶ **1.2** Designed by Arrowstreet, the Artists for Humanity Epicenter in Boston is certified LEED-NC Platinum. Copyright © Richard Mandelkorn. Courtesy Arrowstreet, reprinted with permission.

- A super-efficient building envelope, including operable, low-emissivity, high-performance windows, reduces heating and cooling loads.
- Natural ventilation is used instead of mechanical cooling.
- South-facing windows provide passive-solar heat gain and daylighting.
- Open, unobstructed interior spaces allow for effective daylighting.
- Energy-efficient lighting is coupled with daylight dimming and automated controls to reduce lighting energy use.
- The efficient air-handling system includes a heat-recovery system, to capture some of the energy in outgoing ventilation air.
- Many building materials were salvaged; others have high recycled content.
- Rainwater is harvested and stored for landscape irrigation.

THE LEED RATING SYSTEMS

The essence of LEED, and its particular genius, is a point-based rating system that allows vastly different green building measures to be compared with one resulting aggregate score. LEED accomplishes this by rating all buildings across five categories of concern using key environmental attributes in each category. The five major issues for rating green buildings are creating sustainable sites, conserving water, conserving energy, using materials and resources efficiently and ensuring good indoor environmental quality.

LEED is also an amalgamation of "best practices" from a wide variety of disciplines including architecture, engineering, interior design, landscape architecture and construction. It is a mixture of performance standards (e.g., save 20 percent of the energy use of a typical building) and prescriptive standards (e.g., use paints with less than 50 g/l of volatile organic compounds, VOCs), but leans more toward the performance approach. In other words, LEED believes that best practices are better shown by results (outcomes) not by efforts alone (inputs).

Each LEED rating system has a different number of total points, so that scores can only be compared within each system; however the method for rewarding achievement is identical, so that a LEED Gold project for new construction represents in some way the same level of achievement (and level of difficulty) as a LEED Gold project for commercial interiors (tenant improvements). LEED project attainments are rewarded as follows:

- Certified > 40 percent of the basic or "core" points in the system
- Silver > 50 percent of the core points
- Gold > 60 percent of the core points
- Platinum > 80 percent of the core points

The LEED rating system is a form of an "eco-label" that describes the environmental attributes of the project. Prior to the advent of LEED, there was no labeling of buildings other than for their energy use, such as the federal government's Energy Star program.[7] While useful in presenting a building's energy use compared with all other buildings of the same type in a given region, Energy Star gives an incomplete picture of a building's overall environmental impact.

The irony here is that a $20 million building has less labeling than a $2 box of animal crackers, in terms of its "nutritional" benefits and its basic ingredients. Owners of commercial and institutional buildings have less knowledge of what is in the building they just built or bought than you might think, because the construction process is pretty messy: there are usually many substitutions and changes during the construction process, and there is seldom money left over to document what is actually in the building. To understand a building's ingredients and its expected performance (including operating costs for energy and water), an "eco-label" such as the LEED rating is especially valuable both to building owners and to occupants who may naturally be more concerned about how healthy the building is, rather than how much water it saves.

Complicating this rather straightforward percentage method is the addition of a sixth category with up to five "bonus" points for "innovation and design process" (see Table 1.1). In addition to securing a certain number of points, each rating system has "prerequisites" that each project must meet, no matter what level of attainment it achieves. For example, a LEED-certified building has to have a nonsmoking policy or must incorporate advanced design methods for containing environmental tobacco smoke and exhausting it from the building without contaminating the air.

The four major LEED rating systems use this scoring method. See Appendix 2 for a comparison of the credits in each system. The other two systems currently under evaluation through field testing use a somewhat different approach (LEED for Homes, LEED-H and LEED for Neighborhood Design, LEED-ND). Because most commercial design firms don't do tract housing, this book doesn't discuss the LEED-H rating system, in a pilot evaluation phase in 2007 (or other residential evaluation systems). The LEED for Neighborhood Development rating system is covered in Chapter 6, as part of the urban planning market segment. LEED-ND began a pilot evaluation phase in early 2007, with more than 200 participating projects. Table 1.2 shows the four major systems that account for the vast majority of LEED-registered and certified projects as of early 2007.

LEED is a self-assessed, third-party verified rating system. A design team estimates the particular credits for which a project qualifies and submits its documentation to the USGBC, which assigns the review to an independent reviewer. The reviewer agrees with you and awards the point claimed, disagrees and disallows the point, or asks for further information or clarification. As with all such systems, there is a one-step appeal process.

Table 1.2 Four major LEED rating systems

Rating System	Coverage
LEED for New Construction (LEED-NC)	New buildings and major renovations; housing more than three stories
LEED for Commercial Interiors (LEED-CI)	Tenant improvements and remodels that do not involve building shell and structure
LEED for Core and Shell (LEED-CS)	New buildings in which the developer or owner controls less than 50% of improvements
LEED for Existing Buildings (LEED-EB)	Buildings more than 2 years old in which no major renovations are contemplated

LEED for New Construction

The most widely known and used LEED system is LEED for New Construction (LEED-NC), which is useful for all new buildings (except Core and Shell developments), major renovations and housing of four stories and above. Table 1.1 captures the essence of the LEED-NC rating system's major issues. Through the end of 2006, about 77 percent of LEED projects were registered and/or certified under the LEED-NC assessment method (see Chapter 2). LEED-NC can also be used for projects on college and corporate campuses, in which common systems (parking, transportation and utilities) often supply a number of buildings. Figure 1.3 shows the distribution of credits in LEED-NC among the five major categories of concern.

A LEED-NC rating is typically awarded after a building is completed and occupied, since it requires a final checkout process known as "building commissioning" before the award can be made. Under the current LEED version 2.2, certain credits known as "design phase" credits can be assessed at the end of design and prior to construction, but no final certification is made until all credits are reviewed after substantial completion of the project.

LEED for Core and Shell buildings

LEED for Core and Shell (LEED-CS) is a system employed typically by speculative developers who control less than 50 percent of a building's tenant improvements. They may complete 40 percent of the space for a lead tenant, for example, and then rent the rest of the building to other tenants who will take smaller spaces. LEED-CS allows a developer to pre-certify a design, then use the LEED rating to attract tenants and, in some cases, financing. Once the building is finished, the developer submits documentation to secure a final LEED rating.

The benefit of the LEED-CS system stems from the fact that a developer cannot wait until a building is finished to begin marketing a LEED rating to prospective tenants. By allowing a pre-certification using a system very similar to LEED-NC,

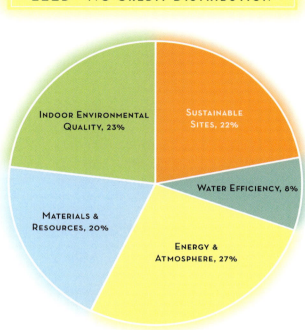

LEED - NC Credit Distribution

- Indoor Environmental Quality, 23%
- Sustainable Sites, 22%
- Water Efficiency, 8%
- Energy & Atmosphere, 27%
- Materials & Resources, 20%

▲ **1.3** LEED-NC credit distribution.

the USGBC assists the developer and encourages more green buildings. Not only that, LEED-CS awards a point for creating tenant guidelines that encourage each tenant to use the LEED-CI (LEED for commercial interiors) system to build out their interior spaces. If that happens, the result is similar to a LEED-NC building, and everyone is happy! Because a developer doesn't control the final build-out, LEED-CS has fewer total points than LEED-NC.

In Atlanta, Hines certified their 1180 Peachtree building as LEED-CS Gold. The 670,000 square foot building was sold by Hines in September 2006.[8] Both the Hines' LEED-Silver One South Dearborn building in Chicago and the 1180 Peachtree building sold in 2006 after completion of construction and leasing activity. Jerry Lea of Hines comments about the benefits of the rating system: "Both buildings got the highest sales price (dollars per square foot) for buildings ever sold in those two markets. Is it because they were green? ... I think there is some correlation that green buildings help you lease the space, and that helps sell them."[9]

LEED for Commercial Interiors

LEED-CI is designed mainly for situations in which the base building systems are not changed and which a tenant only takes up a few floors in a much larger building. In this situation, the ability to affect energy and water use, or open space, landscaping or stormwater management is either much smaller, or non-existent. Thus, other green building measures are incorporated into the evaluation system. These measures include choices that tenants can make about lighting design, energy-using equipment, lighting control systems, sub-metering, furniture and furnishings, paints, carpet and composite wood products, and length of tenancy.

The Rocky Mountain Institute (RMI) offices in Boulder, Colorado are a good example of a LEED-CI Platinum effort, as shown in Figure 1.4. Completed in 2005 and occupying 2,700 square feet (250 sqm) of third-floor commercial office space, this project shows what can be done with any office space. An open office floor plan, which allows light from south- and west-facing windows to infiltrate 75 percent of regularly occupied space, along with the installation of T5 HO fluorescent lamps, dimmable ballasts, and photocell and occupancy sensors reduced energy consumption for lighting by 70 percent. All remaining energy use and employee travel are 100 percent offset through the purchase of renewable energy certificates (RECs). Water-pressure-assist technology in toilets and water-free urinals

▲ **1.4** Designed by Shears Adkins/RMI, the Rocky Mountain Institute's Boulder office is certified LEED-CI Platinum. Photography by Michael Myers. Courtesy of Rocky Mountain Institute.

minimize wastewater volumes, while 0.5 gallon per minute water faucets with on-off sensors help reduce overall water use by 54 percent.[10]

LEED for Existing Buildings

LEED for Existing Buildings (LEED-EB) was originally proposed and designed to be a method for assuring on-going accountability of LEED-NC buildings over time. It has become instead a stand-alone rating system for building owners who want to benchmark their operations against a nationally recognized standard. LEED-EB addresses many issues not dealt with in new construction, including upgrades, operations and maintenance practices, environmentally preferable purchasing policies, green housekeeping, continuous monitoring of energy use, retrofitting water fixtures to cut use, re-lamping and a host of other measures. Figure 1.5 shows Girvetz Hall at the University of California, Santa Barbara, the first

▼ **1.5** Girvetz Hall was the first building at UCSB to go through the LEED-EB process; it is certified at the Silver level. Photography by Hyun Yu in 2005. Courtesy of UC Santa Barbara.

project on campus certified under the LEED-EB program. Some commercial building owners have decided that LEED-EB is a valuable tool for organizing their sustainability upgrades. By early 2007, five projects had received a LEED-EB Platinum rating, all in California, two occupied by State agencies and three by a large corporate owner.

OTHER GREEN BUILDING RATING SYSTEMS

In addition to LEED, there are other commercial and institutional green building rating systems. One system is called "Green Globes," a program of the non-profit Green Building Initiative. The Green Globes rating system is web based and supposedly easier for teams to use, but currently has less than 2 percent of the market for commercial and institutional buildings.[11] However, Green Globes has its adherents, mostly because it is said to be lower cost than LEED for the certification process. Because the system relies only on a self-assessment, critics contend that it lacks the rigor and therefore the credibility of an independent third-party validated system.

Green Globes has been approved for use in meeting green building requirements in six states; Arkansas, Connecticut, Hawaii, Maryland, Pennsylvania and Wisconsin. Along with the USGBC, the Green Building Initiative is an accredited US standards development organization. A 2006 study by the University of Minnesota compared the credits offered by the two systems and found 80 percent of the available points in Green Globes are addressed in the LEED-NC version 2.2 (the current standard) and that 85 percent of the points in LEED-NC version 2.2 are addressed in Green Globes.[12] In essence, the standards are virtually identical, but LEED has market dominance and will likely keep it in the years ahead.

Three non-US rating systems have substantial support in their respective markets: the Japanese CASBEE system, the European GB Tool and the British BREEAM.[13] However, only LEED is supported by the US federal government. The GSA report mentioned earlier in this chapter compared LEED with Green Globes and these three other systems for rating the "greenness" of a building design and construction project. Although the study found each of the rating systems has merits, GSA concluded that LEED "continues to be the most appropriate and credible sustainable building rating system available for evaluation of GSA projects."[14]

TYPICAL GREEN BUILDING MEASURES

While there's no such thing as a "typical" green building, there are specific design and construction measures which are used in many green buildings. If you are a designer, understanding these measures will help you work with green builders, building owners, developers, facility managers, government officials, business clients, nonprofit executives or just interested stakeholders in a green building program.

Based on an analysis of the first 450 LEED-NC-certified projects, the following technical measures that one might associate with a typical green building project are actually likely to be used in less than a third of all green building projects (see Tables 7.1 and 7.2 for details on all such measures):

- Solar PV systems.
- High-efficiency ventilation and underfloor air distribution systems.
- Operable windows and greater control over thermal comfort by occupants.
- Use of certified wood products.
- Rapidly renewable materials such as cork and bamboo flooring.

Most of these systems and approaches aren't common because they have fewer opportunities, experience supply-chain difficulties or require greater initial cost (such as solar PV systems).

However, there are other opportunities to use green products in LEED systems, in particular, by using furniture and furnishings that have salvaged or reclaimed materials (such as partitions), high-recycled-content materials (such as recycled plastics), use agricultural products such as wheatboard and strawboard, cotton or wool, contain 100 percent certified wood from sustainably managed forests and are made from formaldehyde-free composite wood products.

THE CASE FOR HIGH-PERFORMANCE BUILDINGS

Owners and developers of commercial and institutional buildings across North America are discovering that it is often possible to have "champagne on a beer budget" by building high-performance buildings on conventional budgets. Many developers, building owners and facility managers are advancing the state of the art in commercial buildings through new tools, techniques and creative use of financial and regulatory incentives. For the past 10 years, in ever increasing numbers, we have begun to see development of commercial structures for owner-built, built-to-suit and speculative purposes, using green building techniques and technologies.

Measuring high performance

Typically, green buildings are measured against "code" buildings, in other words, structures that qualify for a building permit, but don't go beyond the minimum requirements. Typically a project has to score some minimum number of points above the code threshold to qualify for a green or certified or high-performance rating.

In seven years, since the introduction of LEED in the spring of 2000, it has become for all practical purposes the "de facto" US national standard. LEED is primarily a performance standard, in other words, it generally allows one to choose how to meet certain benchmark numbers – saving 20 percent on energy use vs. code, for example – without requiring specific measures. In this way, LEED is a flexible tool for new construction or major renovations in almost all commercial buildings across North America. As a design tool, LEED has proven its value to help organize the work of design teams tasked with creating green buildings.

By the end of December 2006, LEED-NC had captured about 10 percent of the total new building market, with nearly 4,000 registered projects encompassing nearly 500 million square feet of new and renovated space. Currently, about 100 new projects per month register for evaluation under the LEED-NC system and 30–40 are certified. Since a project only gets "certified" under the LEED-NC system once it is completed and ready for occupancy, many projects are just coming up to the finish line of completing the documentation for a LEED rating.

LEED provides for four levels of certification: "plain vanilla" Certified, Silver, Gold and Platinum. In 2003 and 2004, three projects in southern California achieved the Platinum rating; however, all three were projects for nonprofit organizations or government agencies. One was for a local utility, one was for a county park with the Audubon Society and one was for the Natural Resources Defense Council. As of the end of 2006, more than 500 projects had completed the certification process under LEED-NC. I project more than 300 new buildings will be certified under LEED-NC in 2007 and perhaps as many as 500 total LEED projects, including certifications from all four major LEED rating systems.

To LEED or lead?

What are the differences between using the other organizations' guidelines and using the LEED certification process? In one sense, they are complementary: using other guidelines can typically take a project more than halfway toward LEED certification. However, LEED focuses on a broader range of issues than most other green building or energy-efficiency guidelines. For example, if owners' points of focus are primarily on energy use, reducing carbon dioxide emissions (linked to global warming) and improving indoor air quality, then a variety of advanced building guidelines can take them there efficiently. These improvements lead to reducing operating costs and improved occupant health, productivity and comfort. *However, at this time, only LEED and Energy Star have marketplace acceptance at this point as "brand names" that indicate a high level of performance against measurable criteria.*

LEED and other building evaluation systems encourage an "integrated design" process, in which the building engineers (mechanical, electrical, structural and lighting) are brought into the design process with the architectural and interiors team at an early stage, often during programming and conceptual design. Integrated design explores, for example, building orientation, massing and materials choices as critical issues in energy use and indoor air quality, and attempts to influence these decisions before the basic architectural design is fully developed.

For example, the Advanced Building guidelines from the New Buildings Institute (www.newbuildings.org) brings together more than 30 criteria for building designers to define and implement high performance in building envelope, lighting, HVAC (heating, ventilating and air-conditioning) systems, power systems and controls. Each of these elements is critical in determining building performance, and they often interact in surprising ways. The developers of this tool documented energy savings of 20–27 percent in 15 major climatic regions of the United States, using sophisticated modeling techniques, for energy-conservation and energy-efficiency investments that have a 3-year payback or less.[15] LEED-NC version 2.2 provides one energy-efficiency credit point for meeting the prescriptive requirements of the E-Benchmark tool version 1.1.

What is the usefulness of these other guidelines? Because not all projects with sustainability goals decide to pursue LEED certification or actually follow through with certification after the initial LEED registration, it is useful for designers to have other tools to ensure that their buildings are energy efficient and have healthy levels of indoor air quality.

In the case of government buildings, nearly 40 percent of the total market (in terms of number of projects) and 35 percent (in total area), there has been substantial acceptance of LEED as a standard for both developing better buildings and demonstrating public commitment to higher levels of environmental responsibility. For example, the city of Seattle adopted a policy in 2001 that all new public buildings over 5,000 square feet had to be LEED Silver certified. By 2007, a number of other cities and several states had adopted similar policies, including Chicago (LEED certified), Boston (LEED Silver certified), Vancouver, British Columbia (LEED Gold certified), and the States of California, Arizona and Washington (LEED Silver certified).

Pennsylvania developers learned how to competitively specify and bid public office space that required the achievement of a LEED "Gold" rating; the 35,000 square feet. The Cambria office project in Ebensburg, built for $90 per square foot, became the first LEED Gold-certified project in the United States in late 2001. Other states, cities and colleges are trying similar performance-based LEED contracting, as they strive to meet their real estate needs without putting out the upfront capital.

Designing high-performance buildings

What are the design and operating characteristics of high-performance buildings? They save 25–30 percent or more of conventional building energy use by incorporating high-efficiency systems and conservation measures in the basic building envelope, HVAC plant and lighting systems. These systems and efficiency measures can include extra insulation, high-quality glazing and solar control measures; Energy Star appliances such as copiers, computer monitors and printers; building orientation and massing to utilize passive solar heating and cooling design; high-efficiency lighting (often using T5 high-output lamps in many applications); carbon dioxide monitors that monitor room occupancy and adjust ventilation accordingly, so that energy is not wasted in ventilating unoccupied space; occupancy sensors — which turn off lights and equipment when rooms are unoccupied; and higher-efficiency HVAC systems, variable speed fans and motor drives, to produce the same comfort level with less input energy; and many similar techniques.

High-performance buildings are "commissioned," through the use of performance testing and verification before the end of construction, for all key energy-using and water-using systems. Typically, commissioning involves creating a plan for all systems to be tested, performing functional testing while the mechanical and control contractors are still on the job, and providing the owner with a written report on the performance of all key systems and components. Green building commissioning involves third-party peer reviews during design, to see if design intent has actually been realized in the detailed construction documents. Finally, most commissioning programs also involve operator training and documentation of that training for future operators.

Think of commissioning as analogous to the "sea trials" a ship undergoes before it is handed over to the eventual owners. No ship would be put into use without such trials, which may expose flaws in design or construction, and no building should commence operations without a full "shakedown cruise" of all the building systems that use energy and affect comfort, health and productivity. Often, the documentation provided by the commissioning process can be helpful later on in troubleshooting problems with building operations.

High-performance buildings achieve higher levels of indoor air quality through a careful choice of less-toxic paints, sealants, adhesives, carpets, and coatings for the base building and tenant improvements, often in conjunction with building systems that provide higher levels of filtration and carbon dioxide monitors to regulate ventilation according to occupancy. With so many building occupants having breathing problems and chemical sensitivities, it just makes good business sense to provide a healthy building. Documentation of these measures can often help provide extra backup when fighting claims of "sick building syndrome." This benefit of "risk management" is an often overlooked aspect of green building guidelines, but can often be useful to demonstrate to prospective tenants or occupants, the often "invisible" measures taken by building designers and contractors to provide a safe and healthy indoor environment.

Healthy buildings incorporate daylighting and views to the outdoors not only for occupant comfort, health and productivity gains, but also to reduce energy costs. There is a growing body of evidence that daylighting, operable windows and views to the outdoors can increase productivity from 5 to 15 percent and reduce illness, absenteeism and employee turnover for many companies. Throw in higher levels of building controls that allow for such things as carbon dioxide monitoring and ventilation adjustments, for example, and one has an effective program addressing the "people problem" (see Chapter 11) that can be sold to prospective tenants and other stakeholders. For owner-occupied buildings, such benefits alone are often enough to justify the extra costs of these projects. Considering that 60 percent or more of the operating costs of service companies (which most are) relate to employee salaries and benefits, it just makes good business sense to pay attention to productivity, comfort and health in building design and operations.

Drivers of green building market growth

There are a number of important trends favoring the continued rapid growth of green buildings through 2012. Table 1.3 shows important drivers for green building growth.

The commercial and institutional green building market continues to grow at more than 50 percent per year (see Figure 2.2). In 2006, cumulative LEED-NC

Table 1.3   Drivers for green building growth

Driver	Expected Importance to 2012
1. Higher oil and natural gas prices	Significant
2. Energy Policy Act of 2005	Diminishing over time, as economics of renewable energy improves
3. Movement back into the cities	Moderate impact, but opens up new markets for urban infill with green projects
4. Changes in cultural patterns, to favor more environmentally friendly lifestyles	Moderate impact, a long-standing trend that will increase the market for green commercial buildings
5. New local government, utility and state government tax incentives for green buildings and renewable energy	Significant influence on all types of commercial projects
6. Growing evidence for the business case benefits of green buildings	Significant driver; productivity gains and utility savings can easily outweigh most cost increases
7. Local government incentives and mandates for green buildings	Small at this time, but potentially huge impact on private sector's willingness to "go green"
8. Growing awareness of the role played by buildings in carbon dioxide emissions	Potentially large impact on measures to reduce building energy use
9. Growing pressure on companies to conduct sustainable operations	Potentially moderate impact on the demand for green offices and tenant improvements

registered projects and project area grew by more than 40 percent and LEED-NC-certified projects grew by more than 50 percent. LEED statistics indicate considerable growth potential ahead for commercial green buildings as well as high-rise and mid-rise residential projects (a dozen or more of the LEED-NC-certified projects in fact are mid-rise to high-rise multi-family residential units, both rental and for sale).

The growth of the market tends to feed on itself: as more green projects are built and costs are reduced, leading to more cost-effective projects, the scales tip in favor of building even more green building projects. Greater publicity for green buildings leads to more pressure on companies to specify green design for their next building project. For these and many other reasons, the exponential growth of the green building market, should continue for the foreseeable future, at least through 2012 (see Chapter 13).

In 2006, the LEED rating system registered more than 1,100 new projects, totaling nearly 140 million square feet of space. I predict that the total number of LEED registered projects will increase more than threefold from year-end 2006 through year-end 2010, continuing to increase at more than 30 percent per year even through 2012.[16] Growth in LEED-certified projects means that people everywhere will continue to see more information about green buildings in their cities and towns.

The national Energy Policy Act of 2005 (EPACT) contains increased incentives for residential solar electric and water-heating systems, as shown in Table 1.4. Prolonged oil prices above $50 per barrel have changed the psychology of American consumers and businesses for the first time in a generation.

The new reality of energy is that it is a "seller's market," and prices are likely to climb as new supplies become harder to find, extract and develop. Over time, this will likely translate into higher electricity and gas prices for residential use and more interest in investing in conservation.

Table 1.4 National Energy Policy Act of 2005 provisions[17]

Affected Technology	Tax Credit
PVs	30% (unlimited)
Solar thermal systems	30% (unlimited)
Microturbines	10% (up to $200 per kilowatt credit)
Energy conservation investments for HVAC, envelope, lighting and water-heating systems	$1.80 per sq.ft. (federal tax deduction if exceeding 50% savings vs. ASHRAE 90.1-2001 standard); up to $0.60 per sq.ft. for lighting retrofits alone.

The US Environmental Protection Agency's Energy Star program, the most well known to consumers, will also be used to promote energy-efficient and zero-net-energy, or *carbon neutral* commercial and institutional buildings. By 2008, we will begin seeing buildings routinely cut energy use 50 percent or more below 2003 levels through integrated design and innovative technological approaches. With the growing awareness of the carbon dioxide problem and the contribution of buildings and urban settlement patterns to global warming, architects and others in the design and construction industry have begun to propose positive actions. One sign of this is the position statement adopted by the American Institute of Architects (AIA) in December 2005, calling for a minimum 50 percent reduction in building energy consumption by 2010.[18] In its statement, the AIA supported "the development and use of rating systems and standards that promote the design and construction" of more resource-efficient communities.

Government incentives and mandates

No discussion of the drivers for green building growth would be complete without mentioning the strong role that government is playing in promoting green buildings, not only for its own use, but also increasingly as incentives or requirements for private sector building activity. Table 1.5 shows the large number of government programs that exist to promote green buildings as of April 2007.

More cities that have subscribed to climate change initiatives will begin to require green buildings from commercial and residential projects, especially large developments with major infrastructure impacts. For example, by early 2007, 367 mayors from both political parties representing over 55 million Americans in all 50 states and Washington, DC had signed on to the US Mayor's Climate Protection Agreement. Mayors of seven of the ten largest US cities had signed along with mid-size and smaller cities.[20] Mayors who sign on to the agreement are making a commitment to reduce greenhouse gas emissions in their own cities and communities to 7 percent below 1990 levels by 2012 through actions like increasing energy efficiency, reducing vehicle miles traveled, maintaining healthy urban forests, reducing sprawl and promoting use of clean, renewable energy resources. In 2006, Washington, DC, required all new commercial buildings over 50,000 square feet to submit a LEED checklist by 2009 to receive a building permit.[21] Also in 2006, Boston amended its building code to require all buildings, public and private, over 50,000 square feet (4500 sqm) to be LEED certified or prove that they could meet the LEED standards.[22] Beginning in 2004, many states, large universities and many cities began to require LEED Silver level (or better) achievements from their own construction projects. Many universities have instituted LEED Gold requirements for large capital projects, among them Arizona State University.[23]

Table 1.5 Government initiatives for green buildings (selected)[19]

Governments and government agencies that have passed legislation, executive orders, ordinances, policies or other incentives for buildings to meet LEED criteria:

Federal initiatives

Departments of Energy, Interior, State and Defense: Environmental Protection Agency, US GSA

State Initiatives

Arizona	Illinois	Nevada	Pennsylvania
Arkansas	Maine	New Jersey	Rhode Island
California	Maryland	New Mexico	Washington
Colorado	Massachusetts	New York	
Connecticut	Michigan	Oregon	

County Government Initiatives

Alameda County, CA	King County, WA
Cook County, IL	Sarasota County, FL
County of San Mateo, CA	Suffolk County, NY

Local Government Initiatives

Acton, MA	Calgary, AB	Long Beach, CA	Sacramento
Albuquerque	Chicago	Los Angeles	Salt Lake City
Arlington, MA	Cranford, NJ	New York	San Diego
Arlington, VA	Dallas, TX	Normal, IL	San Francisco
Atlanta	Eugene, OR	Oakland, CA	San Jose, CA
Austin, TX	Frisco, TX	Omaha	Santa Monica
Berkeley, CA	Gainesville, FL	Pasadena, CA	Scottsdale, AZ
Boston	Grand Rapids, MI	Phoenix	Seattle
Boulder, CO	Houston	Pleasanton, CA	Vancouver, BC
Bowie, MD	Issaquah, WA	Portland, OR	Washington, DC
Calabasas, CA	Kansas City, MO	Princeton, NJ	

The larger picture

Reducing carbon dioxide emissions from the buildings sector is critical. Energy-efficient design and operations of buildings, along with on-site renewable energy production are a strong part of the answer for Americans to reduce their "carbon footprint." Figure 1.6 shows the divergence between carbon dioxide emissions between now and 2050 with a "business as usual" scenario and a strong carbon release mitigation program. You can see how important green buildings are to the efforts to bring carbon dioxide emissions back to 1990 levels, as required by the Kyoto Protocol.

Triggers to green building

The top triggers for green building among building owners are shown in Table 1.6, in terms of the percentage of all building owners surveyed that mentioned a particular motivation.[24] From this list, it is easy to see that the prime motivator for owners is reducing energy costs. As a result of the new awareness of

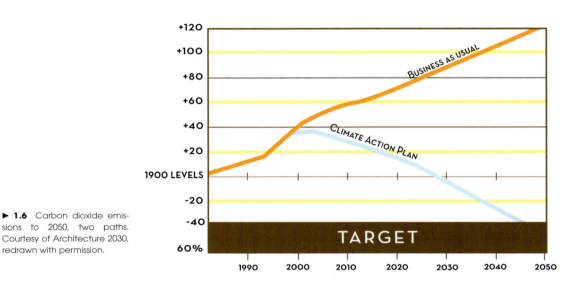

U.S. Building Sector CO2 Emissions

BUSINESS AS USUAL

CLIMATE ACTION PLAN

TARGET

► **1.6** Carbon dioxide emissions to 2050, two paths. Courtesy of Architecture 2030, redrawn with permission.

Table 1.6 Triggers to green building[25]

Key Issues	Motivations
Energy cost increases/utility rebates	74
Achieving superior energy performance	68
Lower life-cycle operating costs	64
Have a positive environmental impact	60
Easier to get LEED certification now	54
Secure a competitive advantage	53
Respond to government regulations	53
Secure productivity benefits	53

McGraw-Hill Construction. Green Building SmartMarket Report, 2007. Education Green Building Issue. Reprinted with permission.

rising energy costs for electricity, oil and natural gas, we expect more building owners and developers to be urging their design teams to cut energy use 30 percent or more below the ASHRAE 90.1-2004 standard found in LEED version 2.2.

BARRIERS TO GREEN BUILDING MARKET GROWTH

Still, there are barriers to the widespread adoption of green building techniques, technologies and systems, some of them related to real-life experience and the rest to a lingering perception in the building industry that green buildings add extra cost (see Chapter 4). Senior executives representing architectural and engineering firms, consultants, developers, building owners, corporate owner–occupants and educational institutions have positive attitudes about the benefits and costs of green construction, according to the 2005 *Green Building Market Barometer*, a survey conducted by Turner Construction Company.[26] For example, 57 percent of the 665 executives surveyed said their companies are involved with green buildings; 83 percent said their green building workload has increased since 2002; and 87 percent said they expected green building activity to continue. Additionally, 34 percent of those not currently working with green construction said their organization would be likely to do so over the next 3 years. However, despite an overwhelming sense that green buildings provided considerable benefits, these same executives thought that green buildings cost 13–18 percent more than standard buildings!

Another survey of the building industry, published in 2006 revealed similar findings:[27]

- 57 percent of 872 building owners and developers said it was hard to justify greater initial costs;
- 56 percent said green buildings added significantly to first cost;
- 52 percent said the market was not willing to pay a premium;
- 36 percent said the process was too complicated, with too much paperwork;
- 30 percent said the market was not comfortable with new ideas or new technologies;
- only 14 percent did not see sustainable design as a market barrier.

Jim Goldman is a Project Executive with Turner Construction in Seattle and was co-chair of the national committee for LEED-NC. A significant barrier, says Goldman, "is the amount of time within the building cycle that is allowed to make critical design decisions. When using an integrated design process, a critical methodology when designing green buildings, it can take additional time to get to the optimal design solution rather than the industry 'rule of thumb' standard solution," and time is often in short supply. Goldman also says cost is always a barrier, both construction cost and the costs of services for studying green options and for certifying the projects.[28]

NOTES

1 Robin Pogrebin, "Architecture: How Green is My Tower?" *New York Times*, April 16, 2006.

2   Oikos Green Building News [online], http://oikos.com/news/2006/10.html (accessed April 26, 2007).

3   Author's analysis, based on reported certifications for new construction projects at the end of 2006. At that time, LEED had certified about 513 systems, Green Globes less than 10, or 2% of the total.

4   General Services Administration, Report to Congress, September 2006 [online], https://www.usgbc.org/ShowFile.aspx?DocumentID=1916 (accessed March 6, 2007).

5   US Green Building Council [online], www.usgbc.org/leed.

6   American Institute of Architects [online], www.aiatopten.org/hpb/overview.cfm?ProjectID=736 (accessed April 26, 2007).

7   Energy Star program [online], www.energystar.gov (accessed April 26, 2007).

8   www.hines.com/property/detail.aspx?id=507 (accessed March 20, 2007).

9   Interview with Jerry Lea, Hines, March 2006.

10 Project information provided by Rocky Mountain Institute, www.rmi.org.

11 Green Building Initiative [online], www.thegbi.org. As of April 2007, GBI reported only eight projects certified under the Green Globes standard vs. more than 600 certified by the LEED for New Construction standard at the same time, http://www.oregonlive.com/oregonian/stories/index.ssf?/base/business/1176436580204130.xml&coll=7&thispage=2.

12 "Green Buildings and the Bottom Line," *Building Design & Construction Magazine*, Supplement, pp. 56–57, November 2006, www.bdcnetwork.com.

13 US Green Building Council [online], https://www.usgbc.org/ShowFile.aspx?DocumentID=1916 (accessed April 22, 2007).

14 US Green Building Council [online], https://www.usgbc.org/ShowFile.aspx?DocumentID=1916 (accessed April 3, 2007).

15 For a somewhat technical description of this approach, see Peter Jacobs and Cathy Higgins, "Integrated Design for Small Commercial Buildings: An Idea Whose Time Has Come," *HPAC Engineering*, July 2004, 44–53.

16 This is a far more conservative estimate than that of the USGBC's CEO Rick Fedrizzi, who announced a goal of 100,000 registered projects by 2010, at the organization's annual conference in November 2006.

17 Florida Solar Energy Center [online], www.fsec.ucf.edu/EPAct-05.htm (accessed April 22, 2007).

18 American Institute of Architects [online], December 19, 2005 press release, viewable at www.aia.org.

19 www.govpro.com/ArchiveSearch/Article/27938 (accessed March 30, 2007).

20 City of Seattle, Mayor's Office [online], http://www.seattle.gov/mayor/climate/PDF/USCM_Faq_1-18-07.pdf (accessed April 26, 2007).

21 Construction Weblinks [online], www.constructionweblinks.com/Resources/Industry_Reports__Newsletters/Apr_16_2007/wash.html (accessed April 26, 2007).

22 McGraw-Hill [online], www.construction.com/greensource/news/2007/070312Boston.asp (accessed April 26, 2007).

23 Association for the Advancement of Sustainability in Higher Education (AASHE) [online], www.aashe.org/resources/pdf/AASHEdigest2006.pdf (accessed April 26, 2007).

24 *Green Building Smart Market Report*, McGraw-Hill Construction, 2005, 44 pp., available at www.construction.com.

25 *Education Green Building SmartMarket Report*, 2007, McGraw-Hill Construction Research & Analytics [online], www.construction.com/greensource/resources/smartmarket.asp (accessed April 25, 2007).

26 Turner Construction Company [online], www.turnerconstruction.com/greensurvey 05.pdf (accessed March 6, 2007).

27 Rob Cassidy, "Green Buildings and the Bottom Line," *Building Design & Construction Magazine*, November 2006 supplement, www.bdcmag.com, p. 8 (accessed March 6, 2007). Reprinted with permission from Building Design+Construction. Copyright 2007 Reed Business Information. All rights reserved.

28 Interview with James Goldman, Turner Construction Company, March 2007.

2   TODAY'S GREEN BUILDING MARKET

Who are the winners in today's green building market? Which firms have developed clear game plans and achieved obvious successes in marketing green building services and green building projects? More than seven years after the introduction of the LEED rating system and nearly 15 years after the creation of the US Green Building Council (USGBC), certain patterns are emerging, and it is becoming possible to identify design firms that have taken and are likely to keep a leading role in the business of green building. They are putting their professionals through LEED trainings, certifying their projects at ever-higher levels of LEED certification and making strong internal commitments to sustainable design. Here are a few examples of what is a strong national trend in the US and increasingly so in Canada, Australia and Western Europe.

GREEN BUILDING MARKET LEADERS

Among the large architectural firms, giant HOK (ranked first of the largest architect/engineer firms in the US, based on 2005 billings)[1] stands out for its early commitment to green buildings, sharing of resources with others similarly committed in the late 1990s and authorship of one of the leading texts on green buildings.[2] A clear indicator of a firm's commitment is the number of LEED Accredited Professionals (LEED APs) among its staff. HOK had more than 450 LEED APs on its staff as of mid-2007. The largest architectural firm in the US, Gensler, had the second-highest total, 575 LEED APs among its professional staff, 23 percent of the total staff, as of July 2007.[3]

The third largest US architectural firm, Perkins+Will had 753 LEED APs as of mid-2006 (the highest total in the country), 61 percent of the firm's total staff. The firm's chief marketing officer, William Viehman, comments that "Sustainable design is an integral part of our practice. We generated several firm-wide initiatives about five years ago (2002), one of which was to establish a leadership position in sustainable design. It started out as a responsible and professional thing to do, and we had encouragement to do it at all levels." According to Viehman, in the current marketplace for large institutional projects (more than half of the firm's client base), "Knowledge of sustainable design is now the price of admission. Talking about it is less a point of differentiation than it was 18 months ago. In virtually every competitive selection process, you go into it expecting to have some conversation about sustainability, and you know all of your competitors will too. The differentiating point now is clearly on results, what you have achieved in sustainable design in past projects."[4]

Among smaller architectural firms of less than 200 or 250 employees, a number of regional firms stand out, including BNIM Architects in Kansas City, Missouri; Mithun architects and planners in Seattle, Washington (see case study in Chapter 10); LPA Architects in Irvine, California; and Overland Partners in San Antonio, Texas, to name just a few. Each of these firms is led by one or more principals strongly committed to sustainable design, participated in some of the earliest green building efforts of the late 1990s, and has stayed abreast of the green building industry by making an aggressive commitment to innovation in this area. Not all firms and all principals of these firms share this passion, but those who do have also been able to attract talented and dedicated project architects and designers to their firms to implement their visions.

Kirsten Sibilia is a marketing director for FXFOWLE Architects in New York City, a firm regarded for the past 10 years as a national leader in sustainable design. She says, "We're finding more and more clients who are willing to push the green envelope and want to know what's new, different and innovative. That sentiment comes from corporate, nonprofit and institutional clients. Some of these clients realize that a green building will help them. But I would say at least half of our clients come to us looking to do something new and different because they believe in environmental responsibility."[5] FXFOWLE is reaping the benefit of having established a leadership position in an emerging industry, once it starts growing fast.

At BNIM, a firm established in Kansas City in 1970, sustainability has long been a passion of firm principal Bob Berkebile. As one of the founders of the AIA Committee on the Environment and an early supporter of the USGBC, Berkebile was involved in many of the leading projects of the 1990s and early 2000s. As a result of his visibility and accomplishments, many other talented and committed designers have joined BNIM. Kimberly Hickson, Principal in charge of the Houston office for BNIM says,

> Bob brings a global perspective to every situation and has the remarkable ability to make everyone he encounters more aware of environmental issues. His knowledge, authenticity and ability to connect with people have been partly responsible for our reputation as a green firm. Our collective passion and commitment plays a part as well. We have a Platinum-rated building because of a committed team, not just one

person. Our goal is to have 100 percent of the firm certified as LEED APs. About a year ago we starting pushing to have the firm principals become LEED AP certified, and now we are about 80 percent of the way there.[6]

In the engineering field, some large national and international firms, including Flack+Kurtz in New York (with 350 employees, it ranked as the 17th largest US engineering firm in 2006), Arup in London/New York/Los Angeles (73 offices, 7,000 employees), and to some degree Syska & Hennessy in New York (600 employees, the third largest US building engineering firm) have been able to carve out a niche as the preferred engineers for major projects by design firms.[7]

Smaller size, relatively few offices and an efficient cost structure have also allowed a number of regional firms to flourish in serving the needs of sustainable design-oriented architects. In Canada, Keen Engineering carved out an enviable niche as the green engineering firm of choice; after extending its reach to a growing number of projects in the US, Keen was acquired by Stantec Consulting in late 2005. Before its sale, Keen also showed the greatest commitment to the LEED process of any architectural or engineering firm, with 140 LEED APs in a staff of about 200.[8]

Among large national construction firms, Turner Construction Company in New York, the country's largest commercial builder, stands out for its commitment to getting LEED professional accreditation for its employees. In mid-2007, Turner counted 260 employees as LEED APs, about 4.5 percent of its total staff of nearly 6,000.[9] At mid-year 2007, DPR Construction (Redwood City, California), had 185 LEED APs, 27 percent of its total staff of 665.[10] No other construction firm showed more than 125 LEED APs at mid-year 2007, so these two companies must be acknowledged as the market leaders in this regard (see Table 9.5).

There are also specialized green building consulting firms; they are all generally smaller than 15–20 people, having "co-evolved" with the rise of the green building movement. None of the really large consulting engineering or pure management or technical consulting firms appears yet to have taken a significant consulting interest in the green design business. Some of the leading green building consulting firms are CTG Energetics in Irvine, California; Paladino & Associates in Seattle; Green Building Services, Portland; 7group in Pennsylvania – a federation of independent consultants; O'Brien and Company in Seattle; Simon and Associates in San Francisco; Architectural Energy Group and RMI, both of Boulder, Colorado.

What do these design, construction and consulting firms have in common? They are technical leaders in sustainable design. They have been early entrants into the field. They have the size, scope and – in some cases – prime location to be at the nexus of sustainable design developments. They have worked on many of the landmark projects in this emerging industry. They are attractive companies to work for and as a result have attracted talented designers, consultants and project managers – a must in the intense and highly competitive architecture, engineering and construction industry. They excel at public relations, and they participate in a variety of industry forums and associations, often in a leadership role. We will explore many of these attributes in later chapters, as we discuss how firms should tailor their marketing offerings to benefit from the rapid growth of the green building industry.

Consider these facts: there were more than 35,000 LEED APs as of January 2007 and nearly 45,000 people had participated in LEED training workshops.[11] There were more than 6,000 LEED-registered projects, and 700 of these projects have been certified as of April 2007.[12] So, it is not surprising that green building industry leaders have yet to emerge – firms with 20 or 30 LEED-certified projects under their belt. Many of the larger firms have in fact done fine green building projects without going through LEED certification, and many smaller firms have consistently won the "Top 10" annual awards from the AIA Committee on the Environment, with or without acquiring LEED certification.

Since LEED is still a relatively new certification, only seven years old in the spring of 2007, and since it can take a year or more after completion of construction to achieve project certification, it is not surprising that few firms have yet to take a strong market lead in this industry.

One other factor is also important: by and large, architecture, engineering and building construction is a regional and even local industry; in general, it has been the small- and medium-sized firms, looking for a market edge and more likely to be influenced by a few passionate designers, who have seized the initiative in green design. The larger architecture, engineering and construction firms, with superior technical resources and strong client relationships, are now playing "catch up," a fact that will dominate the green building market in the future. Smaller firms will obviously be able to compete in certain market segments and geographic regions, but they may have to lower their sights in general toward smaller projects with LEED goals. Occasionally small firms can win larger projects based on design competitions, often by teaming with larger national firms (and the reverse is also true). Competitions, such as those offered by the *Design Excellence* program of the US GSA, allow smaller firms to take an occasional marketing gamble to get a larger project.[13]

LEED will continue to evolve: its stated goal is to serve primarily the top 25 percent of all building projects, and the "bar" for certification will keep getting raised higher as more projects meet the current standards.

GREEN BUILDING MARKET SURVEYS

A July 2006 Internet-based survey of more than 700 building owners, developers, architects, contractors, engineers and consultants, commissioned by Turner Construction Company, provided revealing data about the state of the green building market. Looking ahead three years, 93 percent of executives working with green buildings expect their workload of green building projects to increase, more than half expecting the load to rise substantially. Of those executives currently involved with green building projects, 88 percent have seen a rise in green building activity the past three years, and 40 percent say a substantial rise.[14]

About 75 percent of executives at organizations involved with green buildings reported a higher return on investment (ROI) from these buildings vs. 47 percent among executives not involved with green buildings. It is not clear from the survey what "hard" data these expected returns are based on, other than projected energy efficiency savings.

More importantly, of executives involved with green buildings, 91 percent believed that such buildings lead to higher health and well-being of building occupants, as did 78 percent of executives not involved with green buildings. In other words, when health and well-being are considered, the business case for green buildings is stronger than one based strictly on economic criteria. This is likely the case, because green buildings are associated in most people's minds with daylighting, views to the outdoors for everyone and higher levels of indoor air quality, whereas most people are less aware of projected levels of energy and resource savings associated with green buildings.

Greater experience with green buildings leads to more positive views of their impact on health and well-being. Of those executives involved with six or more green building projects, 65 percent had a positive view of their impact on these issues, against only 39 percent of executives involved with only one or two green building projects.

Given these positive views of green buildings, it is surprising that the largest obstacles of widespread adoption of green building approaches are perceived higher costs (70 percent of all respondents cited this issue), lack of awareness regarding benefits (63 percent) and lack of interest in life cycle cost assessment (53 percent), owing to short-term budget considerations.

LEED PROJECT TRENDS IN 2007

Figure 2.1 shows the growth of LEED-registered and certified projects and registered project area between 2000 and the end of 2006. Tables 2.1 and 2.2

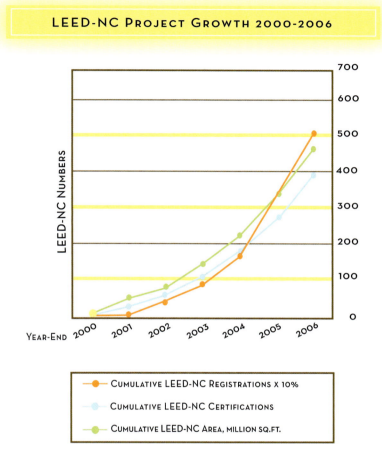

LEED-NC PROJECT GROWTH 2000-2006

Legend:
- Cumulative LEED-NC Registrations x 10%
- Cumulative LEED-NC Certifications
- Cumulative LEED-NC Area, million sq.ft.

▶ **2.1**   Green building activity, 2000–2006.

show the growth of LEED-certified and registered projects between 2002 and early 2007. From these data, we can begin to see some clear trends emerging.

Cumulative LEED certifications grew by 67 percent in 2006. Cumulative LEED project registrations grew by 50 percent in 2006. Clearly, LEED projects continue to grow much faster than the building industry itself and represent a major trend that is likely to continue for a long time. Data for the first 3 months of 2007 show this trend actually accelerating; from these data, one can project LEED registrations in 2007 to increase nearly 70 percent over 2006 year-end totals, and certifications to increase even more.

Table 2.1   Growth of LEED certifications, all rating systems, 2002–2007

Years/Program	LEED-NC	LEED-CI	LEED-EB	LEED-CS	Total
2002	38	–	–	–	**38**
2003	44	0	2	–	**46**
2004	85	21	13	–	**119**
2005	163	19	11	8	**201**
2006	183	52	11	19	**265**
Total	**513**	**92**	**37**	**27**	**669**
2007 (3 months)	87	18	5	2	112
	600	110	42	29	781

Source: USGBC data, provided to the author, April 2007. All data year-end.

Table 2.2   Growth of LEED registrations, all rating systems, 2002–2007

Year/Program	LEED-NC	LEED-CI	LEED-EB	LEED-CS	Total
2002	349	4	6	1	**360**
2003	471	48	39	10	**568**
2004	697	54	43	51	**845**
2005	966	127	63	80	**1,236**
2006	1,137	229	93	183	**1,642**
Total	**3,895**	**462**	**244**	**325**	**4,926**
2007 (3 months)	677	117	112	153	1,059
	4,572	579	356	478	5,985

Source: USGBC data, provided to the author, April 2007. All data year-end.

The green building industry in the US has seen significant expansion in this decade. By the end of 2006, the LEED-NC green building rating system – a good indicator of green building activity – had captured about 10 percent of the market for new commercial and institutional buildings, with nearly 4,000 registered projects encompassing more than 560 million square feet of new and renovated green building space. LEED-NC project registrations in 2006 topped 1,100 for the first time, adding more than 130 million gross square feet of project area.

Many states and municipalities have adopted green building policies, incentives, laws and regulations, as support for green building spreads across the country. At the federal level, the EPACT provides increased incentives for energy conservation in new and existing buildings. Most observers expect Congress to extend EPACT beyond its scheduled expiration at the end of 2008.

Professional organizations continue to promote green development and sustainable design find that it is both good business and responsible corporate citizenship. Moreover, they are keeping up with the larger trend that is accelerating green building adoption. As we discussed earlier, some large architectural firms now have more than 500 LEED APs on staff, and others are rapidly adding to their totals, with some firms having the goal of 100 percent of technical staff possessing the LEED AP credential.

As a sign of the rapid adoption of green design and products by the mainstream construction industry, the USGBC's annual *Greenbuild* conference – the largest conference and trade show of its kind in the world – attracted more than 13,000 participants to Denver in November 2006 and expects to attract 20,000 people to the 2007 show in Chicago.

In 2005, the AIA, the leading voice for American architects, adopted an ambitious policy statement supporting sustainable design, declaring that by 2010 current consumption levels in new buildings should decrease by 50 percent, compared with 2005 averages and should be reduced in 10 percent increments every 5 years thereafter.[15] The AIA has continued to push forward with moving the profession toward sustainability as a core value of architecture, making sustainable design the theme of its 2007 national conference.

Changing public perceptions are strongly influencing this move toward green development. For all the reasons described in Chapter 3, the strong business case for green buildings is gaining increased recognition, especially as global political and environmental conditions prompt rising concerns about the future. Many schools, interpretive centers and educational nonprofits are responding to this concern by building LEED-certified projects. Figure 2.2 shows the Global Ecology Center at Stanford University, operated by the Carnegie Institution, a LEED-NC Gold-certified project. The project features a "stack effect" ventilation tower that draws cool air into the building through ground-level openings, and then exhausts the heated air through the tower.

Oil prices have increased dramatically since 2004, and the current geopolitical situation intensifies the prospect of uncertain supplies in the coming years. The price per barrel surged above $50 in 2005 – and to $65 in April 2007 – and threatens to stay at that level. Growing evidence for human-induced global warming also had made people uneasy about dwindling natural resources and more aware of the impact of buildings on energy, water and land resources. Both factors have prompted a stronger public acceptance of the need for conserving fossil fuel-generated energy in buildings and in urban design in general.

The lifestyle preferences of twenty-first century consumers also bring new demand for green buildings. More people – especially among the huge wave

▲ 2.2 The Global Ecology Center at Stanford University, built by DPR Construction, features a 45 feet cooling tower with a structural steel "wind catcher" directs the downward movement of cooler air. The air descends through the tower, passing through a cold-water mister about a third of the way down, and into the main lobby. Courtesy of DPR Construction.

of retiring baby boomers – are choosing to "re-urbanize" in healthy, environmentally friendly settings. Consumers in the LOHAS (Lifestyles of Health and Sustainability) category constitute more than a quarter of the US population. These educated consumers make conscientious purchasing and investing decisions based on social and cultural values. They represent a marketplace of more than $200 billion for sustainable goods and services, with an estimated $76.47 billion to spend in the sustainable economy market sector on green building, renewable energy and other items.[16]

CURRENT MARKET IMPACT OF GREEN BUILDINGS

As with most market dynamics, growth is distributed unevenly throughout the US, with leadership roles tending to fall on the West Coast, the Mid-Atlantic and Northeast.

Geography

Geographically, the top six states for LEED-NC project registrations are California, New York, Washington, Pennsylvania, Illinois and Oregon (see Table 9.3 for further details). On a per-capita basis, smaller states such as Oregon and Washington lead the way. Oregon has about 3 times the national average project registrations per capita, and Washington has about 2.7 times the average. California, in contrast, is just 1.25 times the national average in registered projects per capita, a surprising fact given that state's strong environmental advocacy on many other issues. The West Coast has more than one-third of all LEED-NC project registrations in the country, but only about 16 percent of the total US population. Other areas of strong LEED project activity include the upper Great Lakes area, Texas and the New England–New York–mid-Atlantic states. In terms of LEED-certified projects, Table 2.3 shows the states with 10 or more such projects, as of March 2007. While New York and Illinois have many registered projects, many of those are recent and have not yet received certification. This is an indicator that marketers can expect rapid growth in LEED project certifications in those two states by the end of 2008.

Types of registered projects

LEED registrations by project type are a bit harder to discern, because USGBC data groups many projects into a "multiple-use" category that is not well defined. With this caveat, the project types with the largest number of LEED-NC registrations are the following, excluding multiple use:

* Commercial offices (13 percent)
* Schools and colleges (13 percent)
* Public order/safety (4 percent)
* Multi-family residential (5 percent).[17]

LEED is now widespread in the commercial office category and fairly widespread in schools and colleges. A large number of mostly public projects represent the next level of activity (assembly, interpretive center, library and public order/safety such as police and fire stations, as well as courthouses). Obviously, the public sector also represents much of the commercial office project type as well. Two interesting areas for future growth are multi-family residential, in which marketing advantages are gradually appearing, and industrial, likely driven by corporate sustainability policies.

Types of certified projects

In this segment, the classifications are easier to understand, possibly because they are fewer in number and more readily correspond to our practical experience. Table 2.4 shows the main project types that had received LEED certification by early 2007. Commercial offices and multiple-use projects

Table 2.3   LEED-certified projects, by state, all LEED rating systems (10 or more)

States	Number of LEED Certified Projects	Percentage of Total Certified Projects*
California	89	12.6
Pennsylvania	65	9.2
Washington	56	8.4
Oregon	44	6.2
Michigan	38	5.4
Massachusetts	35	4.9
Georgia	32	4.5
Colorado	29	4.1
Illinois	28	4.0
New York	23	3.2
Texas	23	3.2
Ohio	16	2.3
New Jersey	15	2.1
Virginia	15	2.1
Arizona	14	2.0
Florida	14	2.0
Maryland	14	2.0
Missouri	12	1.7
Wisconsin	12	1.7
Washington, DC	11	1.6
North Carolina	11	1.6
Utah	11	1.6
South Carolina	10	1.4

Source: USGBC LEED-NC Technical Review Workshop Notebook. Data as of March 20, 2007.

*Based on a total of 708 US-certified projects.

(many of which are offices with ground-floor retail) make up more than 52 percent of total certified projects.

Green building owners

The main types of owners of green buildings are private sector (for-profit companies), nonprofit (including private schools, colleges and universities, healthcare facilities and various NGOs – nongovernmental organizations), all levels of government and individuals. Table 2.5 shows the number of certified projects by type of owner, again as of March 2007.

From Table 2.6, we know that government and institutional users (including education and healthcare) dominated the first five years of LEED-NC-project

Table 2.4   LEED-certified projects, by project type, all LEED rating systems

Project Type	Gross sq.ft. (millions)	Number of Projects*	Percentage of Total Projects
Commercial office	23.9	203	26.6
Multi-use	24.2	195	25.6
Industrial/public works	5.6	28	3.7
Higher education	4.0	51	6.7
Multi-unit residential	3.5	24	3.1
K-12 education	3.3	32	5.2
Laboratory	2.3	17	2.2
Retail	1.8	19	2.5
Healthcare	1.2	14	1.8

Source: USGBC LEED-NC Technical Review Workshop Notebook. Data as of March 20, 2007.

*Based on 762 total certified projects.

Table 2.5   LEED-certified projects, by owner type, all LEED rating systems

Owner Type	Gross sq.ft. (millions)	Number of Projects*	Percentage of Total Area	Percentage of Total Projects	Average Size Projects Area (Gross sq.ft.)
Profit corporation	45.3	317	47.7	41.6	143,000
Nonprofit corporation	10.6	129	11.2	16.9	82,000
Local government	13.4	122	14.1	16.0	110,000
State government	9.2	76	9.7	10.0	121,000
Other	7.2	63	7.6	8.3	114,000
Federal government	4.2	40	4.4	5.2	106,000
Individual	4.9	15	5.2	2.0	327,000
Total All Projects	**94.9**	**762**			**124,500**

Source: USGBC LEED-NC Technical Review Workshop Notebook. Data as of March 20, 2007.

*Based on 762 total certified projects.

registrations, with 64 percent of the total registrations and 54 percent of the total registered project area (excluding other/individual project registrations for which no owner type is specified). Indeed, government-owned projects represented close to half (44 percent) of all LEED-NC-registered projects through 2005, indicating the prevalence of two driving forces in the green building marketplace: a long-term ownership and operations perspective, and environmental policy considerations. (These two considerations probably also are driving current nonprofit and corporate sector LEED registrations.)

By early 2007, however, the situation had changed dramatically. Table 2.5 shows that private-sector LEED-certified buildings (from all systems) now account for almost half of all project area and nearly 42 percent of the total number. By contrast, government projects (at all three levels of government) comprised only 28 percent of all project area and 31 percent of the total project count. Counting nonprofits along with governmental projects (both represent institutional markets) would make these totals 38 percent of project area but 47 percent of total projects, on a par with the private sector.

What opportunities does this situation create for a design, construction or development firm? One implication is that an intense focus on government and institutional projects may be less warranted, although these projects are likely to have strong policies driving their use of the LEED rating system for project evaluation. A second implication is that the fastest growing group of potential clients comprises private-sector companies with sustainability or environmental stewardship policies and aspirations. What might have been true a few years ago is no longer the case. Corporate and facilities managers are no longer divorced from larger corporate goals; their concerns have moved from a primary focus on lowering real estate costs for building projects, to an intense interest in green buildings, but they are still concerned about projects that have higher initial costs.

Toyota Motor Sales USA's corporate manager for real estate and facilities, Sanford Smith says, "goals for reducing energy consumption and carbon emissions are set in the corporate 2007–2011 Action Plan."[18] In describing the role of green buildings in the larger corporate context, Smith says, "by utilizing a sustainable approach, we can harness the power of design to establish and build on the notion of a life cycle culture shared among everyone." Toyota's projects include a Gold certification for the Torrance, California office headquarters complex, LEED Silver vehicle distribution center in Portland, OR and a LEED-CI Silver-certified public affairs leased space in Washington, DC.

This private-sector attitude is changing rapidly, however, as the business case for productivity increases and other soft benefits in green buildings (see Chapter 3), particularly the effects of daylighting, higher indoor air quality levels and views to the outdoors, start to be more appreciated. Since 2005, the percentage of total LEED registrations by private owners has increased from about 26 to 47 percent, indicating that this client group is growing much faster than LEED registrations as a whole.

Higher education
According to LEED statistics, higher education project registrations made up about 6.5 percent of the total number of LEED-registered projects in early

2007, totaling more than 250 university projects. Assume for a moment that there are about 3,000 colleges in the US, each starting just one new building project per year. In this case, LEED projects would represent less than five percent of the college and university market.

As of March 2007, there were only 51 LEED-certified higher education projects in the country (Table 2.4); representing 6.7 percent of all certifications, so market penetration in this sector is just beginning. I surveyed the campus environment in 2004 and found that at least 50 percent of the LEED projects at that time existed because of support from top leadership.[19] With the growing concern on campus over human-induced climate change, campus leadership has become even more attuned to green building issues since that time.[20]

Higher education also represents a good market for designers who are allied with developers, because most campuses do not have the funds to build all the facilities they need and are increasingly turning to developers for funding, project management, ownership and operations. Most campuses still expect to be in business 50 or 100 years from now, so they make excellent captive tenants. For design firms, this means often that the route to gaining more business in higher education can be through the development world.

Private sector
LEED-registered projects in the private sector have widely varying ownership types and perspectives. Many of the initial projects have come from large corporations that have strong environmental stewardship goals and values and wanted to "walk the talk" in their (typically large) building projects. These companies include Ford, Toyota, Honda, The Gap, Goldman Sachs and PNC Bank. In addition, many small business owners (including architects designing their own facilities) have strong environmental values that they have illustrated by greening their own, typically smaller, projects. Finally, a few speculative developers have decided that LEED is the right thing to do and have found that LEED goals and registration can confer marketing advantages. Table 2.2 shows that the number of LEED-CS project registrations will soon exceed 500. At an average project size of 350,000 square feet (32,000 sqm), LEED-CS Development registered projects will soon encompass 175 million square feet (16 million sqm).

Figure 2.3 shows the LEED-NC Gold-certified headquarters building of Melink Corporation in Ohio. We are beginning to see a trend of many companies involved with the construction industry, including architects, engineers, contractors and product manufacturers, building LEED-certified offices for their own use. This process also helps them become more familiar with LEED requirements and the costs of certification.

▲ **2.3** Designed to be 50 percent more energy-efficient than a conventional building, Melink's Corporate Headquarters in Milford, Ohio is LEED-NC Gold certified. Courtesy of Melink Corporation.

Table 2.6   Growth of LEED-NC-registered projects by owner type, 2003–2005

Owner Type	July 2003 Projects	July 2004 Projects	September 2005 Projects	February 2007 Projects	Percentage of Total Projects, 2007
For-profit corporation	237	372	579	2,532	47
Local government	227	345	494	772	14
Nonprofit corporation	138	272	441	876	16
State government	100	174	260	441	8
Federal government	81	142	188	293	6
Other	51	109	179	324	6
Individual	7	14	36	129	2
Total projects	**841**	**1,428**	**2,177**	**5,367**	**100**

Source: USGBC, April 2007, September 2005, July 2004 and July 2003 tallies.*

*The USGBC registered project database was significantly corrupted; these numbers are not totally reliable.

Growth by owner type

Through early 2007, the greatest growth in projects by owner type occurred in the nonprofit sector, followed by the private sector; federal, state and local government projects grew more slowly than the average (Table 2.6). By early 2007, less than 40 percent of the registered projects were in the government sector, and the growth rate in that sector has been below average. The percentage of for-profit LEED-registered projects is increasing, as is that of nonprofit projects. By early 2007, for-profit owners accounted for 42 percent of the total number of projects but about 48 percent of all LEED project areas, as these projects tend to be about 50 percent larger than those of government and nonprofits.

Growth by project size

For-profit companies tend to build larger projects – an average of about 151,000 square feet (based on their first 579 registered projects) – compared with an average of 100,000 square feet for all other projects (Table 2.7). At about $150 per square foot ($1633 per sqm), the estimated construction cost each project would be about $23 million. Federal projects represent the next largest average project size, at about 125,000 square feet each (based on 188 projects). State government projects on average are about 91,000 square feet, while the nonprofit sector builds the smallest projects on average. This difference is somewhat logical, given that local governments and nonprofits tend to build museums, recreation and cultural centers, libraries, fire and police stations, animal care facilities and similar smaller projects. By contrast, the for-profit and federal government sectors tend to build larger office buildings (134,000 square feet), laboratories (139,000 square feet), multiple-use (111,000 square feet) and similar facilities (Table 2.8).

Table 2.7 Growth of LEED-NC-registered projects by area, 2003–2007

Owner Type	July 2003 (000 sq.ft.)	July 2005 (000 sq.ft.)	Average Project Size (000 sq.ft.), 2004	Average Project Size (000 sq.ft.), 2005	Percentage of Total Project Area, 2005	Average Project Size (000 sq.ft.), February 2007
For-profit Corporation	37,399	87,697	157.4	151.4	35	95.5
Local Government	24,381	45,237	94.3	91.6	18	92.5
Nonprofit Corporation	14,583	35,574	90.8	80.7	14	80.7
State Government	16,397	29,827	134.6	114.7	12	90.5
Federal Government	12,666	24,817	152.7	132.0	10	125.4
Other	5,938	21,791	138.5	121.7	9	108.8
Individual	410	2,547	55.4	70.8	1	118.1
Total Project Area	**111,774**	**247,493**				
Average Project Size (000 sq.ft.)	132.9		123.8	113.7	100.0	

Source: USGBC, April 2007, September 2005, July 2004 and July 2003 tallies.

Growth by building type

The largest category of LEED-registered buildings is multiple-use facilities, which might contain offices, parking and ground-floor retail (Table 2.8). These buildings accounted for nearly 19 percent of all LEED-registered projects as of early 2007. Among LEED-registered projects, the faster-growing building types

Table 2.8   Growth of LEED-NC-registered projects by building type, 2003–2007

Building Type	July 2003	September 2005	February 2007	Percentage of Total Projects, 2007*	Average Size (000) sq.ft., 2005
Multiple use	160	672	1,710	18.6	111
Commercial office	151	318	500	13.0	134
Higher education	84	155	251	6.5	79
K-12 education	52	133	228	6.0	121
Multi-unit residential	32	97	191	4.9	147
Public order/safety	49	104	156	4.0	96
Industrial	33	71	106	2.7	140
Healthcare	19	45	103	2.7	276
Library	33	76	97	2.5	49
Interpretive center	45	77	90	2.4	28
Laboratory	27	52	64	1.7	140
Assembly	14	31	44	1.2	169
Recreation	11	30	42	1.1	43
Finance and communications	9	25	32	<1.0	24
Retail	4	19	37	<1.0	72
Military base	3	17	33	<1.0	57
Transportation stations	9	16	29	<1.0	310
Animal care	7	12	15	<1.0	41
Restaurant			9	<1.0	
Hotel/resort			19	<1.0	
Community development			23	<1.0	
Stadium/arena			8	<1.0	
Special needs			5	<1.0	
Single-family home			4	<1.0	
Daycare			21	<1.0	
All other	99	235	1,550	N/A	N/A
Total	**841**	**2,185**	**5,367**	**100.0**	**113**

Source: USGBC, April 2007, September 2005, July 2004 and July 2003 tallies.

*Excluding "all other" from the totals.

are multiple use, corporate offices, K-12 education, retail, multi-unit residential and healthcare. Figure 2.4 shows a corporate office in Salt Lake City, built by Big-D Construction for its own use and certified as a LEED-NC Gold project.

It is interesting that the growth of commercial office projects by project area during 2005 to 2007 was only half the growth by numbers reflecting a smaller project size for new LEED registrants. This difference probably reflects the growth of smaller office buildings in the nonprofit and local government sectors as well as the increase in smaller private–owner buildings. The average size of new private-sector projects registered under LEED by mid-2005 was 151,000 square feet, showing that the private sector continues to build large projects. Not all are commercial or corporate offices; they include large multifamily housing projects, laboratories, health care and industrial facilities.

▼ **2.4** Rennovated according to Utah's historical preservation methods, Big D Construction's Headquarters in Salt Lake City is certified LEED-NC Gold. Photography by Kevin at Perrenoud Productions. Courtesy of Big-D Construction.

LEED RATING SYSTEM USE

Table 2.9 shows the use of all four major LEED rating systems as of the end of March 2007. Notable are 733 total certified projects representing nearly 90 million square feet of space and the 5,308 total registered projects, representing 766 million square feet of space, about one-third the annual commercial construction area in the US. Note also the relatively large number of LEED-CS and LEED-CI projects, portending well for the future influence of LEED in these market segments.

USE OF CERTIFICATION PROGRAMS FOR GREEN BUILDING PROJECTS

There are numerous certification programs for green buildings in the US and Canada, including the six LEED rating programs from the USGBC, Green Globes, Green Guide for Health Care – GGHC (technically an evaluation method and not a formal rating system), Energy Star, the Collaborative for High Performance Schools (CHPS) and LEED for Schools. A new standard for minimum energy performance will be unveiled toward the end of 2007, called *Standard 189*; this will become the minimum performance standard for all mechanical engineering design, and it is a development architects also need to monitor. In this section, we will present practical information on the use of various LEED certification programs, along with GGHC, Energy Star, CHPS and Standard 189. (The release of LEED for Schools, a customized version of the LEED-NC rating system, is expected by mid-2007.)

LEED for New Construction

As of April 2007, LEED-NC version 2.0 had certified 535 US projects and 17 Canadian projects, along with one project in Spain, three in China, one in United Arab Emirates and three in India. The US projects represent 96 percent of all

Table 2.9 LEED rating system use, all systems, early 2007

Rating System	Project Status	Number of Projects	Million Gross sq.ft.	Average Size, sq.ft. (sqm)
New Construction	Registered	4,144 (78% of total)	560	135,000 (12,000)
	Certified	560 (76% of total)	60	93,000 (8,500)
Commercial Interiors	Registered	511	28	55,000 (5,000)
	Certified	103	5	48,500 (4,450)
Core and Shell	Registered	393	97	247,000 (22,600)
	Certified	28	9	321,000 (29,400)
Existing Buildings	Registered	260	81	311,500 (28,500)
	Certified	42	15	357,000 (32,750)

Source: USGBC. Data current as of March 31, 2007.

LEED-certified projects. Table 2.10 shows the attainment levels in the LEED version 2.0 and 2.1 rating systems. Taken together, 60 percent of all LEED-NC-certified projects (in the US only) have chosen to achieve a higher level than basic certified status, but (this is important for marketers) the number certifying at the basic Certified and Silver levels actually decreased between the 2000 and 2002 effective period of LEED-NC version 2.0 and the version 2.1, in effect for 2003–2005. This may mean that building teams were having a harder time meeting budget constraints during that time, as construction costs escalated rapidly, or it may simply mean that less experienced teams were not able to attain higher levels of certification for their first few LEED-NC projects.

LEED for Commercial Interiors

LEED-CI was introduced in November of 2004 as version 2.0, following a two-year pilot program of version 1.0. Through April of 2007, of the first 94 certified LEED-CI projects in the US, Table 2.11 shows the distribution of attainment levels. For LEED-CI, about 70 percent of the projects seek an attainment level beyond basic certified. From Table 2.11, one can see that the trend is toward higher attainment levels since version 2.0 was introduced. This may indicate that the market is getting more comfortable with the LEED-CI

Table 2.10 LEED-NC-certified project attainment levels (US projects only)

Attainment	LEED-NC Version 2.0	Percentage of Total	LEED-NC Version 2.1	Percentage of Total	Percentage of All Projects
Certified	86	37.7	128	41.3	39.8
Silver	66	28.9	104	33.5	31.6
Gold	68	29.8	70	22.6	25.7
Platinum	8	3.5	8	2.6	3.0
Total	**228**	**100**	**310**	**100**	**100**

Source: USGBC web site data, April 14, 2007.

Table 2.11 LEED-CI-certified project attainment levels (US projects only)

Attainment	LEED-CI version 1.0	Percentage of Total	LEED-CI Version 2.0	Percentage of Total	Percentage of All Projects
Certified	17	33.3	11	25.6	29.8
Silver	18	35.3	13	30.2	33.0
Gold	15	29.4	15	34.9	31.9
Platinum	1	2.0	4	9.3	5.3
Total	**51**	**100**	**43**	**100**	**100**

Source: USGBC web site data, April 14, 2007.

rating system and should signal to architects and interior designers that a client will likely expect a higher certification level than basic certified. The difficulty with most commercial interiors projects is that they happen so fast, typically only 90 to 120 days. This implies that achieving LEED Silver certification will be easiest when there is a readily available palette of green materials, products systems and approaches as part of a firm's standard approach to a project.

LEED for Existing Buildings

LEED-EB has been a more difficult system to "sell" to building owners because of its complexity (it has 80 core points vs. only 64 for LEED-NC) and because the business-case benefits are not as clear as in a new building or commercial interiors. LEED-EB was introduced in version 2.0 in November of 2004, at the same time as LEED-CI, after a two-year pilot evaluation period. However, through early 2007, more than twice as many projects had registered for certification under LEED-CI as under LEED-EB, perhaps because it is an easier system to use. Nevertheless, as of early 2007, more than 260 projects (representing more than 80 million square feet (7.4 million sqm) of buildings had registered for LEED-EB certification, and 44 projects had been certified. Table 2.12 shows the distribution of certification levels among the 44 projects in both the pilot evaluation and the LEED-EB 2.0 system. More than two-thirds attained a higher level than basic certified.

In terms of professional services potential, the primary beneficiaries of LEED-EB are likely to be mechanical and electrical engineers (and possibly energy services companies), since LEED-EB focuses heavily on energy use, water use and indoor environmental quality. However, the LEED-EB standard is focused on the environmental and human impacts of building operating practices, including chemical use, recycling, commuting, purchasing and similar continuing activities of building owners and operators. To the degree that projects focus on lighting design changes, daylighting, improving views and similar measures, architects are likely to find some work coming their way from LEED-EB projects, particularly if they have an active green building consulting program.

Table 2.12 LEED-EB-certified project attainment levels (US projects only)

Attainment Level	LEED-EB, All Versions	Percentage of Total
Certified	14	31.8
Silver	9	20.5
Gold	16	36.4
Platinum	5	11.4
Total	**44**	**100**

Source: USGBC web site data, April 14, 2007.

The USGBC expects the primary user group for LEED-EB to be facilities managers, who will use the rating system to benchmark and assess the environmental responsibility of their operations and maintenance practices. The rating system may also see considerable use by owners of multiple buildings on the same campus or site, such as facilities managers and sustainability committees at colleges and universities. For example, in 2006 the University of California, Santa Barbara campus committed to assess 25 existing facilities over the ensuing five years. Moreover, once corporate CEOs and CFOs of companies find out the high rates of financial returns and large publicity benefits of LEED-EB projects, I also expect to see more direct involvement of senior executives in pushing LEED-EB projects forward.

LEED-CS Development

LEED-CS is the most recent rating system, appearing in a version 2.0 form in the summer of 2006, following a two-year pilot evaluation period. Table 2.13 shows the attainment levels for the first 22 projects. Interestingly, in contrast to the other systems, very few projects have settled for the basic "certified" level; in fact, a greater percentage have secured Gold and Platinum than any other system. One guess is that this version allows "pre-certification" of a design, so that a developer can use the award level for marketing purposes. Gold and Platinum certifications certainly sound better as marketing inducements that just "certified" or even "silver." The second guess is that LEED-CS is an easier level of attainment, not only because it has fewer points than LEED-NC, but also because some of the opportunities for achieving high levels of energy efficiency, for example, are more accessible in a Core and Shell building.

Green Guide for Health Care

The GGHC is an important, LEED-based tool for hospitals and healthcare. Unlike LEED certification, GGHC covers both healthcare design/construction and operations and is individually self-assessed (but not third-party-verified.) However, even a self-assessment starts to bring elements to design and operations that will change how healthcare projects are designed, if for no other

Table 2.13 LEED-CS-certified project attainment levels (US projects only)

Attainment Level	LEED-CS, Version 1.0	Percentage of Total
Certified	2	9.1
Silver	8	36.4
Gold	10	45.4
Platinum	2	9.1
Total	**22**	**100**

Source: USGBC web site data, April 14, 2007.

reason than that designers and facilities managers now have a recognized checklist that they can apply to projects, with each item based on a sound healthcare policy. The GGHC includes 12 prerequisites (vs. LEED-NC's 7) and 97 total points (vs. LEED-NC's 69), so it is a more complex (and comprehensive) rating system. Participants in the pilot program for using GGHC included 115 facilities with more than 30 million square feet of space, located across the US and Canada. A new version, GGHC version 2.2, was released in January of 2007.[21]

Energy Star

Energy Star is a program developed in the early 1990s by the US Environmental Protection Agency (EPA) to set appliance efficiency standards. By 2005, the label had strong name recognition among consumers, making it easily one of the federal government's few successful attempts at creating a consumer brand. A recent EPA analysis showed that Energy Star buildings save $0.50 per square foot, compared with average performing buildings and operate 35 percent more efficiently. These buildings tend to continue saving this amount of energy over a four-year measuring period.

In 2005, Energy Star claims to have saved $4.6 billion in operating costs in buildings, eliminated the need for 150 billion kilowatt hours of electrical power use, provided the equivalent of 28,000 megawatts of electric power plant capacity – the equivalent of 28 large coal-fired power plants – and, from building alone, prevented 15 million metric tons (carbon equivalents) of greenhouse gas emissions.[22]

In the buildings sector, Energy Star has evaluated more than 26,000 commercial and institutional buildings for energy performance. Eligible building types for an Energy Star rating currently include offices (general, bank branch, courthouse, financial centers), K-12 schools, hospitals, hotels, supermarkets, dormitories and medical offices. The Energy Star program provides energy-use evaluations of building types that now include 38 percent of hospitals, 25 percent of office buildings, 24 percent of supermarkets, 15 percent of schools and 14 percent of hotels. This corresponds to 20 percent of the square footage of all commercial buildings representing a huge database of building energy use with which engineers can compare their designs.

EPA has awarded the Energy Star designation for energy efficiency to more than 3,200 buildings. These buildings represent more than 575 million square feet (about the same amount as the end of 2006 LEED-registered project area), save an estimated $600 million annually in lower energy bills, and prevent almost 11 billion pounds of greenhouse gas emissions, equal to emissions from almost 900,000 vehicles. The top performing buildings for 2006 include about 320 supermarkets, 320 office buildings and 200 K-12 schools. Almost

90 banks, courthouses, financial centers, hospitals, hotels, and – for the first time – dormitories also earned the ENERGY STAR, the most recognized national symbol for energy efficient buildings.[23]

An important note for marketers: EPA now allows design teams to put a "Designed to meet ENERGY STAR" on all project drawings, offering a great marketing opportunity. By the end of 2005, more than 70 firms had signed up and qualified to use this label.

Collaborative for High Performance Schools

The CHPS program provides in-depth technical resources, a green school building benchmark system and self-certification program for school districts. CHPS is widely known for helping school districts build a new generation of healthy, efficient, sustainable schools. More than 20 California school districts have adopted CHPS as their rating and evaluation system, as a mandatory design standard for all new construction, including the state's largest districts (e.g., Los Angeles, San Diego and San Francisco), as of the end of 2006.[24]

The benchmark system, known as the "CHPS Criteria," is a system of credits and prerequisites that provides a nationally accepted standard for what constitutes a high-performance school, and incorporates ideas that are unique to children's learning environments, including acoustics, superior indoor air quality measures and using schools as teaching tools.

Created in 2000, CHPS was originally created for use in California; since that time it has been regionally adapted in Massachusetts, Washington and New York, and it is currently being adapted by additional New England states. Since its inception in California, CHPS has not only expanded geographically but also in the programs it offers and in 2007 introduced the "CHPS Verified" program. This program combines project management, the CHPS building Criteria and a third-party assessment to ensure that the school project is designed and built to the highest-performance standards. A school is recognized as CHPS Verified by an independent, third party.[25]

Standard 189

Standard 189 is the product of a committee established by the US Green Building Council (USGBC); the American Society of Heating, Refrigerating and Air-Conditioning Engineers (ASHRAE); and the Illuminating Engineering Society of North America (IESNA). The three organizations are collaborating to develop this baseline green building standard that will bring green building practices into mainstream building design and construction. The standard is being written so that it may be incorporated into local building codes in the future.

Standard 189, *Standard for the Design of High-Performance Green Buildings except Low-Rise Residential Buildings*, will provide minimum requirements for the design of sustainable buildings to balance environmental responsibility, resource efficiency, occupant comfort and well-being, and community sensitivity. Using USGBC's LEED Green Building Rating System as a key resource, Standard 189 will be ANSI-accredited (American National Standards Institute). The intent of USGBC is to make attainment of Standard 189 a prerequisite for LEED certification, with the goal of reducing overall carbon emissions from green buildings by 50 percent as soon as possible. LEED will continue to serve market leaders and innovators by promoting the highest levels of building performance. Standard 189 is anticipated to begin pilot testing in late 2007.

NOTES

1   "Giants 300" survey, *Building Design & Construction Magazine*, July 2006, p. 43 [online], www.bdcnetwork.com.
2   Sandra Mendler, William Odell and Mary Ann Lazarus (2006) *The HOK Guidebook to Sustainable Design*, 2nd edn. 2006, Hoboken, New Jersey: John Wiley & Sons, Inc.
3   Dave Barista, "25,000 LEED Accredited Professionals and Counting," *Building Design & Construction*, July 2006, p. S5. LEED APs must take and pass a national exam in the LEED system.
4   Interview with William Viehman, Perkins+Will, April 2007.
5   Interview with Kirsten Sibilia, FXFOWLE Architects, April 2007.
6   Interview with Kimberly Hickson, BNIM Architects, April 2007.
7   "Giants 300" survey, op. cit.
8   Personal communication, Kevin Hydes, President, Keen Engineering, Ltd., Vancouver, BC.
9   Turner Construction Company [online], www.turnerconstruction.com/greenbuildings/content.asp?d=5808 (accessed April 22, 2007).
10 Personal communication, Ted van der Linden, DPR Construction, April 2007.
11 US Green Building Council data sheet, April 2007.
12 Ibid.
13 US General Services Administration [online], www.gsa.gov/designexcellence (accessed April 22, 2007).
14 Turner Construction Company [online], www.turnerconstruction.com/greensurvey05.pdf (accessed April 22, 2007).
15 Architectural Record [online], http://archrecord.construction.com/news/daily/archives/051227aia.asp (accessed April 22, 2007).
16 Natural Marketing Institute [online], http://www.lohas.com, provides descriptions of this growing market.
17 US Green Building Council, *Member Update,* September 2005.

18 Michael Reilly, "A Conversation with Sanford L. Smith," *The Marketer*, bimonthly from the Society for Marketing Professional Services, April 2007, p. 7.

19 Yudelson Associates, proprietary web-based survey with about 200 respondents, completed in summer, 2004.

20 See for example, the Annual Bulletin of the Association for the Advancement of Sustainability in Higher Education [online], www.aashe. org, for a list of campus sustainability activities including green building projects.

21 GGHC Newsletter, January/February 2007, www.gghc.org.

22 Energy Star [online], www.energystar.gov/ia/news/downloads/annual_report2005.pdf (accessed April 22, 2007).

23 Energy Star program [online], www.energystar.gov/index.cfm?c=news. nr_news#annual (accessed April 22, 2007).

24 Collaborative for High Performance Schools [online], www.chps.net (accessed April 22, 2007).

25 CHPS [online], www.chps.net/announcements/nwsltrApril07.htm (accessed April 22, 2007).

3 THE BUSINESS CASE FOR GREEN BUILDINGS

The business case for commercial green buildings in 2007 can be simply stated: if your next project is not a green building, one that is certified by a national third-party rating system, it will be functionally outdated the day it is completed and very likely to underperform the market as time passes.[1] That bold statement was echoed by a well-known real estate expert, who bluntly claimed that trillions of dollars of commercial property around the world would soon drop in value because green buildings are going mainstream and would render those properties obsolete.[2] In a meeting in Sydney, Australia, in February 2007, the head of Australia's Property Council, representing the entire development industry, claimed that no large developer in that country would ever start another project that wasn't going to be at least LEED Silver (Australia 4 Green Stars) certified.[3]

Within two years, the business case for green buildings is going to be part of "business as usual." Jerry Lea of the Houston-based national developer Hines, a strong proponent and developer of Energy Star and LEED buildings, says, "I think sustainable is here to stay. I think the definition of 'Class A' buildings very soon will include sustainable design and probably LEED certification."[4] Richard Cook, a prominent architect in New York City, says, "In five years, it will be clear that buildings not reaching the highest standard of sustainability will become obsolete."[5]

INCENTIVES AND IMPEDIMENTS TO GREEN BUILDINGS

Still, there are barriers to the widespread adoption of green building techniques, technologies and systems, some of them related to real-life experience and the rest to perception in the building industry that green buildings still add extra cost. This is surprising because senior executives representing architectural/engineering firms, consultants, developers, building owners, corporate owner–occupants and educational institutions have held positive attitudes about the benefits and costs of green construction for sometime.[6]

Given these positive views, it is surprising that the top obstacles to widespread adoption of green building approaches continue to be perceived higher costs and lack of awareness of the full range of benefits of green construction.

Other factors discouraging green construction remain the perceived complexity and cost of LEED documentation, short-term budget horizons on the part of clients and long payback for some energy-efficiency and renewable energy measures, the difficulty in quantifying benefits and sometimes the more complex methods, systems and technologies construction involved.

Overcoming impediments to green buildings

Architects, engineers, builders and developers are working hard to bring costs into line with benefits, in five specific ways. There are many ways in which design and construction decisions influence the costs of green buildings (see Chapter 4). Over the next three years, the green building industry is likely to focus on lowering the cost barrier, in several ways:

*   Working aggressively to lower the costs of green building through accumulating their own project experience and strengthening their focus on integrated design approaches that might lower some costs (such as HVAC systems) while increasing others (such as building insulation and better glazing), but with a net positive cost-reduction impact.
*   Developing communication and marketing strategies that make good use of available research that demonstrates the benefits of green buildings, to justify the economic and market risks inherent in trying something new. We'll see some of that research in what follows.
*   Finding ways to finance green building improvements to reduce or eliminate the first-cost penalty that often frightens away prospective buyers, using incentives from electric utilities, utility "public purpose" programs, and local, state and federal governments to maximize points of leverage. There are also a growing number of third-party financing sources for energy-efficiency and renewable energy investments in large building projects.
*   Trying to duplicate successful project results for institutional buyers who represent about half of the current market for LEED-registered buildings. This means documenting the full range of green building benefits so that building owners with a long-term ownership perspective can be motivated to find the additional funds to build high-performance buildings.
*   Use good project management and cost management software to show the benefits of various green building measures in real time. Decisions about green building measures are often made quickly, during project meetings that can last all day. Having good information about costs, benefits and ROI can be critical to keeping good green measures under consideration, instead of losing them to strictly cost considerations.

Paul Shahriari is the developer of a leading software for green project cost management, *Ecologic 3*.[7] He developed this project management product because of his experience with advising dozens of green building projects, where cost was the only consideration ever placed on the table. He says,

> We created web-based collaborative software that allows a team to attribute certain cost savings or premiums to each LEED credit sought. They can also attach a cost impact profile to each LEED credit. The tool combines the soft costs of design, consulting and engineering and the hard-cost component (construction) and presents a life cycle benefit structure. So far, for every project that's in the system right now, the average payback period is less than five years for certified projects. Our philosophy is that we want to harness economic value from the environmental performance of a project. The most important thing I discovered is that prior to having an economic framework with which to discuss LEED, I had a lot of projects that never went forward. I've never had a client that's seen the output from the software decide not to build a green project.[8]

BENEFITS THAT BUILD A BUSINESS CASE

The business case for green development is based on a framework of benefits: economic, financial, productivity, risk management, public relations and marketing, and funding.[9] Table 3.1 presents an outline useful for understanding the wide-ranging benefits of green buildings, which are examined in detail in the following section.

Economic benefits

As we will see in Chapter 9, increased economic benefits are the prime driver of change in all new innovations; for green buildings, these benefits take a variety of forms, and their full consideration is vital for promoting any sustainable design.

Reduced operating costs

With the real price of oil likely to stay above $50 per barrel for the next 20 years,[10] natural gas prices at record levels and peak-period (typically summer air-conditioning times) electricity prices rising steadily in many metropolitan areas, energy-efficient buildings make good business sense. Even in triple-net leases (the most common type) in which the tenant pays all operating costs, landlords want to offer tenants the most economical space for their money. For a small additional investment in capital cost, green buildings will save on energy operating costs for years to come. Many green buildings are designed to use 25–40 percent less energy than current codes require; some buildings achieve even higher efficiency levels. Translated to an operating cost of $1.60–2.50 per square foot for electricity (the most common fuel), this energy savings could reduce utility operating costs by $0.40–1.00 per year. Often these savings are achieved for an investment of just $1.00–3.00 per square foot. With building costs reaching $150–300 per square foot, many developers and building

Table 3.1 Business-case benefits of green buildings

1. Utility cost savings for energy and water, typically 30% to 50%, along with reduced "carbon footprint" from energy savings

2. Maintenance cost reductions from commissioning and other measures to improve and assure proper systems integration and performance

3. Increased value from higher net operating income (NOI) and better public relations

4. Tax benefits for specific green building investments

5. More competitive real estate holdings for private sector owners, over the long run

6. Productivity improvements, typically 3%–5%

7. Health benefits, reduced absenteeism, typically 5% or more

8. Risk management, including faster lease-up and sales and lower employee exposure to irritating or toxic chemicals in building materials

9. Marketing benefits, especially for developers and consumer products companies

10. Public relations benefits, especially for developers and public agencies

11. Recruitment and retention of key employees and higher morale

12. Fund-raising for colleges and nonprofits

13. Increased availability of both debt and equity funding for developers

14. Demonstration of commitment to sustainability and environmental stewardship; shared values with key stakeholders

owners are seeing that it is a wise business decision to invest 1–2 percent of capital cost to secure long-term savings, particularly with a payback of less than 3 years. In an 80,000 square foot building, the owner's savings translates into $32,000–80,000 per year, year after year.

Reduced maintenance costs

More than 120 studies have documented that an energy-saving building, properly commissioned shows additional savings of 10–15 percent in energy costs. Commissioned buildings tend to be much easier to operate and maintain.[11] By conducting comprehensive functional testing of all energy-using systems before occupancy, it is often possible to have a smoother-running building for years because potential problems are fixed in advance. A recent review of these studies by Lawrence Berkeley National Laboratory showed that the payback from building commissioning in terms of energy savings alone was about 4 years, while the payback fell to about 1 year when other benefits were considered, such as fewer callbacks to address thermal comfort problems.

Increased building value

Increased annual energy savings also create higher building values. Imagine a building that saves $37,500 per year in energy costs vs. a comparable building built to code (this savings might result from saving only $0.50 per year per square foot for a 75,000 square foot building). At capitalization rates of six to eight percent, typical today in commercial real estate, green building standards would add $468,750 ($6.25 per square foot) to $625,000 ($8.33 per square foot) to the value of the building. For a small upfront investment, an owner can reap benefits that typically offer a payback of three years or less and a rate of return exceeding 20 percent.

Tax benefits

Many states have begun to offer tax benefits for green buildings. Here are three examples, two based on tax credits, the third based on property and sales tax abatements. Oregon offers a state tax credit that varies based on building size and LEED-certification level attained. At the Platinum level, a 100,000 square foot building can expect to receive a net-present-value tax credit of about $2.00 per square foot.[12] This credit can be transferred from public or nonprofit entities to private companies, such as contractors or benefactors, making it even more beneficial than one that only applies to private owners.[13]

New York's state tax credit allows builders who meet energy goals and use environmentally preferable materials to claim up to $3.75 per square foot for interior work and $7.50 per square foot for exterior work against their state tax bill. To qualify for the credit, a building must be certified by a licensed architect or engineer, and must meet specific requirements for energy use, materials selection, indoor air quality, waste disposal and water use. In new buildings, this means energy use cannot exceed 65 percent of the New York State energy code; in rehabilitated buildings, energy use cannot exceed 75 percent.[14]

A Nevada state property tax abatement (changes in 2007 by the Legislature) offers up to 25 percent reduction, for up to 10 years, for private development projects achieving a LEED Silver certification. Assuming the property tax is 1 percent of value, this abatement could be worth up to 2.5 percent of the building's construction cost, typically far more than the actual cost of achieving LEED Silver on a large project. As a result, a large number of Nevada projects are pursuing LEED certification, including the world's largest private development project, the $7 billion and 17 million square feet City Center project in Las Vegas.[15]

The 2005 Federal Energy Policy Act (Table 1.4) offers two major tax incentives for aspects of green buildings: a tax credit of 30 percent on both solar thermal and electric systems and a tax deduction of up to $1.80 per square foot for projects that reduce energy use for lighting, HVAC and water-heating systems by 50 percent compared with a baseline standard.[16] In the case of government

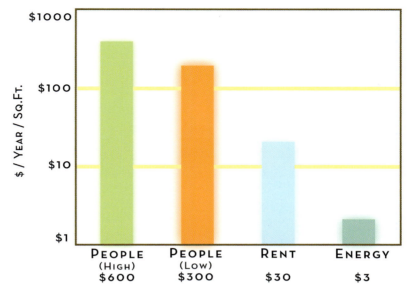

▶ **3.1** People costs far exceed rent and energy costs in a service economy (author's estimates).

projects, the tax deduction may be taken by the design team leader, typically the architect.

Productivity gains

In the service economy, productivity gains for healthier indoor spaces are worth anywhere from 1 to 5 percent of employee costs, or about $3.00–30.00 per square foot of leasable or usable space. This estimate is based on average employee costs of $300–600 per square foot per year (based on $60,000 average annual salary and benefits and 100–200 square feet per person).[17] With energy costs typically less than $3.00 per square foot per year, it appears that productivity gains from green buildings could easily equal or exceed the entire energy cost of operating a building (Figure 3.1).

Here's an example: Median productivity gains from high-performance lighting of 3.2 percent in 11 studies were reported by Carnegie Mellon University in Pittsburgh, or about $1–2 per square foot per year, an amount equal to the cost of energy.[18] This is in addition to a reported average savings of 18 percent on total energy bills from proper lighting. For corporate and institutional owners and occupiers of buildings, that is too much savings to ignore (Figure 3.2).

Look at it this way: If a building owner could get a 10 percent improvement in productivity from a green building, or about $30–60 per square foot increase in output, it would always pay for that company to build a new building and put its employees to work there. In other words, the productivity increase could pay

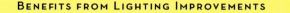

BENEFITS FROM LIGHTING IMPROVEMENTS

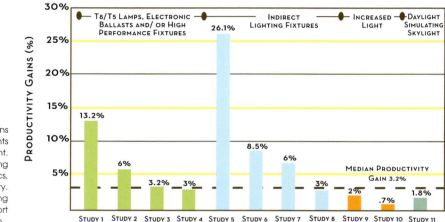

▶ **3.2** Productivity gains from lighting improvements can be quite significant. Courtesy of Center for Building Performance and Diagnostics, Carnegie Mellon University. eBIDS™: Energy Building Investment Decision Support Tool, redrawn with permission.

Table 3.2 Financial benefits of green buildings (per sq.ft.)[20]

Productivity and Health Gains	$36.90–55.30 (70–78% of Total Benefits)
Operation and maintenance savings	$8.50
Energy savings	$5.80
Emissions savings	$1.20 (from energy production emissions)
Water savings	$0.50
Total savings	**$52.90–71.30 (life cycle, net present value)**

for the entire building! Even a 5 percent improvement in productivity would pay for half or more of the rent or cost of the new green building. What, then, you might ask, is the business case for a "brown building," one that doesn't have these benefits? From another ground-breaking study of the costs of green buildings, Table 3.2 shows the 20-year "net present value" of the various categories of green building benefits.[19] Productivity and health gains provide more than two-thirds of the total benefits of green buildings in this analysis.

Risk management

Green building certification may provide some measure of protection against future lawsuits through third-party verification of measures installed to protect indoor air quality, beyond just meeting code-required minimums. With the national focus on mold and its effect on building occupants, developers and building owners are focusing considerable attention on improving and maintaining indoor air quality.

Faster permitting or special permit assistance can also be considered a type of risk mitigation. In Chicago, for example, the city government has created the position of green projects administrator and is allowing green projects to receive priority processing. For large projects, above minimum requirements, the city waives fees for independent code consultants. Projects with high-level green goals are promised a 15-day permit review.[21] In Austin, Texas, the city fast tracked the development reviews for a large big box retailer, so that it was able to open 12 months ahead of schedule; the resulting profit gain of about $3 million reportedly paid for the entire $2.8 million building![22]

Another risk management benefit of green buildings in the private sector is the faster sales and leasing of such buildings, compared to similar projects in the same city. Green buildings tend to be easier to rent and sell, because educated tenants increasingly understand their benefits. In some cases, a building may be fully leased before construction completion, reducing the developer's market risk. Imagine the benefit to a developer from having all the leases signed and deposits in hand before having to pay all the bills for construction.

Green buildings are also seen as less risky by insurers. In September 2006, Fireman's Fund, a major insurance company, announced it would give a 5 percent reduction in insurance premiums for green buildings. The insurer also announced its "Certified Green Building Replacement and Green Upgrade" coverage.[23]

Health improvements

Of course, a key element of productivity is healthy workers. By focusing on measures to improve indoor environmental quality such as increased ventilation, daylighting, views to the outdoors and low-toxicity finishes and furniture, people in green buildings show an average reduction in symptoms of 41.5 percent on an annual basis, as shown in Figure 3.3.

Since most companies are effectively self-insured (i.e., your health insurance costs go up the more claims you have) and most government agencies and large companies are actually self-insured, it makes good economic sense to be concerned about the effect of building design on people's health. In addition, given what is already known about the health effects of various green building measures, a company might be inviting lawsuits if it didn't take all feasible measures to design and construct a healthy building.

Public relations and marketing

Many developers and building owners, both public sector and private companies, are finding considerable marketing and public relations benefits from creating LEED-certified green buildings.

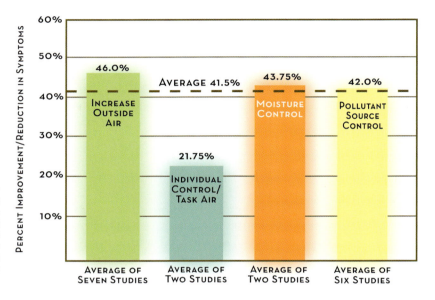

ANNUAL GAINS FROM AIR QUALITY IMPROVEMENTS

▶ **3.3** Health gains from better indoor air quality argue for better building ventilation schemes. Performance and Diagnostics, Carnegie Mellon University. eBIDS™: Energy Building Investment Decision Support Tool, redrawn with permission.

Stakeholder relations and occupant satisfaction

Tenants and employees want to see a demonstrated concern for their well-being and for that of the planet. Savvy developers and building owners are beginning to realize how to market these benefits to a discerning and skeptical client and stakeholder base, using the advantages of green building certifications and other forms of documentation, including support from local utility and industry programs. This is not "greenwashing," it is a positive response to a growing public concern for the long-term health of the environment. A good indication of how corporations have embraced this concept is the explosion in green building projects and associated public relations in 2006 and 2007; if you sign up to receive Google Alerts and put in "green buildings" as a keyword, you will be inundated with 6–12 news stories almost every day from the nation's press, as well as numerous blog entries.

Environmental stewardship

Being a good neighbor is appropriate not just for building users, but for the larger community. Developers, large corporations, universities, schools, local government and building owners have long recognized the marketing and public relations benefits (including branding) of a demonstrated concern for the environment. Green buildings fit right in with this message. As a result, we expect to see major commitments by corporate real estate executives for greening their buildings and facilities. A good example is Adobe Systems, Inc., a major software maker based in San Jose, California. In 2006, Adobe announced that it had received three LEED-EB Platinum awards for its headquarters towers; not only did it reap great publicity, but the firm showed that the investments as a whole had returned a net present value almost 20 times its initial cost.[24]

Many larger public and private organizations have well-articulated sustainability mission statements and are understanding how their real estate choices can both reflect and advance those missions. Developer Jonathan F.P. Rose notes that "having a socially and environmentally motivated mission makes it easier for businesses in the real estate industry to recruit, and retain, top talent. Communities are more likely to support green projects than traditional projects, and it is easier for such projects to qualify for many government contracts, subsidies, grants and tax credits. The real estate industry can prosper by making environmentally responsible decisions."[25]

Green buildings also reinforce a company's brand image. A consumer products company such as Toyota, Starbucks or PNC Bank can improve or maintain their brand image by being associated with green buildings, and so they are moving in this direction.[26] Large corporations, including those that issue sustainability reports every year – and there are more than 1,000 of them – are beginning to see the benefits of building green to demonstrate to their employees, shareholders and other stakeholders that they are "walking the talk."

More competitive product

Speculative commercial and residential developers are realizing that green buildings can be more competitive in certain markets, if built on a conventional budget. Green buildings with lower operating costs and better indoor environmental quality are more attractive to a growing group of corporate, public and individual buyers. *Greenness* will not soon replace known real estate attributes such as price, location and conventional amenities, but green features will increasingly enter into tenants' decisions about leasing space and into buyers' decisions about purchasing properties and homes. We've already seen anecdotes from developers using the pre-certification available from the LEED-CS rating system to attract tenants and financing for high-rise office towers, in such places as Chicago and Atlanta. One such project, 1180 Peachtree in Atlanta, by Hines, was voted green development project of the year in 2006 for NAIOP, the National Association of Industrial and Office Properties.[27] Figure 3.4 shows another large building, a large office tower in Chicago that opened in 2005 and received a LEED-CS Gold rating along with the marketplace benefits

▶ **3.4** 111 South Wacker in downtown Chicago is a 53-story office tower that was the first LEED-CS Gold project. Developed by the John Buck Co. and designed by Goettsch Partners, the building was able to re-use existing caissons and foundation walls. Copyright © James Steinkamp, Steinkamp photography. Courtesy of Goettsch Partners reprinted with permission.

of fast leasing and great tenants. Designed by Goettsch Partners, the 51-story tower contains 1,456,000 square feet (134,000 sqm) of space, including a 370 car parking garage. The building, *111 South Wacker*, is anchored by the professional services firm Deloitte, which leased 451,259 square feet (41,440 sqm), more than 43 percent of the building.

Recruitment and retention

One often overlooked aspect of green buildings is their effect on people's interest in joining or staying with an organization. It costs $50,000–150,000 to lose a good employee, and most organizations experience 10–20 percent turnover per year, some of it from people they didn't want to lose. In some cases, people leave because of poor physical environments (as well as the "boss from hell"). In a workforce of 200 people, turnover at this level would mean 20–40 people leaving per year. What if a green building could reduce turnover by 5 percent, for example, 1–2 people out of 20–40? Taken alone, the value of that would be $50,000 to possibly as much as $300,000, more than enough to justify the costs of certifying a building project. If a professional service firm, say a law firm, lost just one good attorney, typically billing $400,000 per year, with $250,000 gross profit, that would more than pay for the extra cost of a green building or green tenant improvement project that would keep that lawyer at the firm. What about the impact of a healthy work environment on employees' belief that their employer really cares about their well-being?

Table 3.3 confirms the growing shortage of people to serve the needs of the US economy. Owing to an aging labor force, in 2014 there will be 2.6 percent fewer people in the 35–44-year-old age group than in 2005, typically the leadership group in most organizations: managers, executives, experienced employees and senior technical people, typically at the peak of their career. Getting and keeping them will tax the ingenuity and resources of most companies; green buildings can demonstrate that the company or organization and the key employees share the same values. Working in a company that rents or owns green buildings give employees another reason to tell their friends and spouses why they are staying with an organization. See also the discussion in Chapter 11 about how a focus on sustainable design can help a firm deal with these inevitable demographic changes.

Table 3.3   The aging labor force, 2005 vs. 2014, in millions[28]

Age Group	2005	2014 (estimate)	Change in Size
25–34	32.5	36.8	+4.2
35–44	35.9	33.3	−2.6
45–54	34.2	35.5	+1.3
55 and older	24.1	34.3	+10.2

Financing green projects

Whether you are a private developer or a nonprofit school or organization, raising money for projects is always an issue. For private developers, raising both debt and equity capital is their challenge. The rise of socially responsible property investing promises to reward those developers who build green. For example, a large property developer in Portland, Oregon, Gerding Edlen Development, built about $900 million of new projects in 2006. The firm has a strong commitment to building LEED Silver or better buildings in each project.[29]

Investing in green buildings has begun to attract considerable attention as a form of socially responsible investing, a practice which is growing faster than overall investing. One expert, Professor Gary Pivo, puts it this way: "We have yet to see the first real estate investment fund squarely committed to green real estate. But until such funds are created, there are some other options worth considering. One is to acquire shares in companies that commonly own Energy Star-labeled buildings or have been recognized by Energy Star for their conservation efforts."[30]

Corporate Office Properties Trust (COPT) developed 318 Sentinel Drive in the National Business Park in Annapolis Junction, Maryland; this project received the 2005 NAIOP National Green Development Award. A four-story, 125,000 square foot office building, this project was fully leased during construction. The property earned a LEED Gold rating and is one of 12 projects currently under development that COPT intends to certify under the LEED-CS program. A companion project at 304 Sentinel Drive received a LEED-CS Silver rating. Incorporating tenant design and construction guidelines to promote green practices during tenant build-outs, 318 Sentinel Drive effectively promotes LEED-CI projects.

The building had a $2.84 per square foot green construction premium, with an estimated $0.70 per square foot annual energy savings. However, the company's analysis showed a 6-month ROI, once extra green costs were offset by energy savings, waste reduction charges, stormwater management (site development) savings and other green practices.[31]

In 2006, New York-based developer Jonathan Rose created the *Rose Smart Growth Investment Fund* to invest in green building projects. The $100 million limited partnership focuses on acquiring existing properties near mass transit. The fund expects to make green improvements to the properties and hold them as long-term investments.[32] The focus on transit-centric developments takes into account the energy savings from enabling people to use mass transit. The fund's first project is in downtown Seattle, Washington, a renovation of the 1920s-era Joseph Vance and Sterling buildings, a total building area of about 120,000 square feet, with ground-floor retail and office space above.[33]

According to the Fund, it is "re-branding these buildings as the 'greenest and healthiest' historic buildings in the marketplace, to increase market awareness of the buildings, attract and retain tenants."

For nonprofits and for private colleges and universities, representing about 17 percent of all LEED-certified projects through early 2007 (see Table 2.5), the funding issue is vastly different. They are dependent on private donors to fund most of their new buildings. Many nonprofits have successfully used greening their buildings to attract funds for renovation projects. The Ecotrust organization in Portland, Oregon, received a major gift from a single donor to renovate a 100-year-old, two-story brick warehouse into a three-story, 70,000 square foot modern building with two floors of offices above ground-floor retail. The Jean Vollum Natural Capital Center was only the second LEED Gold-certified project in the US when it opened in 2001.[34] In 2003, the Natural Resources Defense Council completed one of the first LEED Platinum-certified projects in the world when it opened the Robert Redford Building in Santa Monica, California.

Over the next few years, there is no doubt that many private colleges and universities will find that their green buildings attract donors. To accelerate this process, since 2003, the Kresge Foundation's *Green Building Initiative* has been giving grants of up to $100,000 to nonprofits that will use an integrated design process to build a green building. Kresge also offered a "bonus grant" challenge program for projects that became LEED certified. By February 2006, the Initiative awarded 64 planning grants totaling $4,146,000, averaging about $70,000 each. One early success was Herman Hipp Hall at Furman University near Greenville, South Carolina, a liberal-arts university with about 2,600 students; Hipp Hall was the first LEED Gold-certified project in higher education in the US.[35]

WHO BENEFITS?

One of the biggest issues in green buildings is that the benefits are unequally distributed between those who pay for the project and those who benefit. For example, the benefits of green schools (see Chapter 5) accrue mostly to the students, but it is the school district that incurs the cost. In speculative commercial development, the tenants receive most of the benefits of reduced operating costs and higher productivity, but the developer must bear the initial cost increase. Table 3.4 shows the distribution of green building benefits; when marketing green buildings, design firms should always consider these distinctions in tailoring their case for green buildings to various stakeholder groups. Public policy for green buildings should take the distribution of benefits into account and create incentives to overcome gaps in the marketplace. For example, faster permit processing for speculative development can have a

Table 3.4 Distribution of green building benefits

Owner Type	Energy Savings	Productivity Gains	Health Benefits	Marketing/PR	Recruitment	Financing
Private, owner occupied	Yes	Yes	Yes	Yes	Yes	Yes
Private, speculative	No	No	No	Yes	No	Yes
Retail	Partial	No	Maybe	Yes	No	Maybe
K-12 public school	Yes	Yes, for staff	Yes, for staff	Yes	Yes, for teachers	No
Private college or K-12 school	Yes	Yes	Yes	Yes	Yes, for faculty	Possibly, new donors
Public university	Yes	Yes	Yes	Yes	Yes	Yes, for private donors
Nonprofit healthcare	Yes	Yes, for staff	Yes	Yes	Yes, for nurses	Typically not
Nonprofit organization	Yes	Yes	Yes	Yes, very important	Not too important	Yes, for donors
Federal government	Yes	Yes	Yes	Not too important	Not too important	No
State government	Yes	Yes	Yes	Not too important	Not too important	No
Local government	Yes	Yes	Yes	Somewhat important	Somewhat important	Not very important

huge impact on project returns and is generally a strong incentive that costs the government relatively little.

NOTES

1   There are buildings that may have green elements, but do not pursue formal certification. My estimate is that these represent less than half the green building market at present and will decline rapidly over the next 3 years as a share of all green buildings. As is often said, "The road to hell is paved with good intentions." The fact is that most people who claim to be doing green design but don't bother to certify the project through an independent third party are practicing self-deception, since without certification as a goal, many of the green elements are cut from most projects for budget reasons.

2   Charles Lockwood, "As Green as the Grass Outside," *Barron's*, December 25, 2006, http://online.barrons.com/article/SB116683352907658186.html?mod=9_0031_b_this_weeks_magazine_main (accessed March 6, 2007).

3   Peter Verwer, CEO of Australian Property Council, presentation to *Green Cities 07* Conference, February 13, 2007, www.gbcaus.org.au.

4   Interview with Jerry Lea, Hines, March 2007.

5   Interview with Richard Cook, Cook+Fox Architects, March 2007.

6   Turner Construction Company [online], www.turnerconstruction.com/ greensurvey 05.pdf (accessed March 6, 2007).

7   GreenMind, Inc. [online], www.ecologic3.com (accessed March 6, 2007).

8   Interview with Paul Shahriari, Green Mind, Inc., March 2007.

9   US Green Building Council, *Making the Business Case for High-Performance Green Buildings* (Washington, DC: US Green Building Council, 2002), www. usgbc.org/resources/usbgc_brochures.asp (accessed March 6, 2007). See also *Environmental Building News*, 14, No. 4 (April 2005), www.buildinggreen. com (accessed March 6, 2007).

10 US Energy Information Administration [online]. For the November 2006 forecast, see www.eia.doe.gov/oiaf/aeo/key.html (accessed March 6, 2007).

11 Lawrence Berkeley National Laboratory, *The Cost-Effectiveness of Commercial-Buildings Commissioning*, 2004 [online], http://eetd.lbl.gov/ emills/PUBS/Cx-Costs-Benefits.html. This research reviewed 124 studies of the benefits of building commissioning and concluded that based on energy savings alone, such investments have a payback within five years.

12 Oregon Department of Energy [online], www.oregon.gov/ENERGY/ CONS/BUS/docs/SustainableAp.doc (accessed March 6, 2007).

13 Oregon Department of Energy [online], www.oregon.gov/ENERGY/ CONS/BUS/BETC.shtml (accessed March 6, 2007).

14 Natural Resources Defense Council [online], www.nrdc.org/cities/building/ nnytax.asp (accessed March 6, 2007).

15 Personal communication, Lynn Simon, Simon & Associates, February 2, 2007. Also see US Department of Energy [online], www.eere.energy.gov/ states/news_detail.cfm/news_id=9149 (accessed March 6, 2007) and http:// www.leg.state.nv.us/22ndSpecial/bills/AB/AB3_EN.pdf (accessed March 6, 2007).

16 US Department of Energy [online], www.energy.gov/taxbreaks.htm (accessed March 6, 2007).

17 Eleven case studies have shown that innovative daylighting systems can pay for themselves in less than 1 year due to energy and productivity benefits. Vivian Loftness et al., *Building Investment Decision Support (BIDS™)* (Pittsburgh: Center for Building Performance and Diagnostics, Carnegie Mellon University, n.d.), http://cbpd.arc.cmu.edu/ebids (accessed March 6, 2007).

18 Carnegie Mellon University, http://cbpd.arc.cmu.edu/ebids/images/group/ cases/lighting.pdf (accessed March 6, 2007).

19 Capital E Consultants [online], www.cap-e.com/ewebeditpro/items/ O59F3303.ppt#2 (accessed March 6, 2007).

20 Gregory Kats, "Financial Costs and Benefits of Green Buildings," [online], www.cap-e.com, study of 33 buildings (accessed March 6, 2007).

21 "Speedy Permitting has Developers Turning Green in Chicago," *Building Design & Construction*, November 2005, p. 28; www.BDCnetwork.com (accessed March 6, 2007).

22 Personal communication, S. Richard Fedrizzi, CEO, US Green Building Council.

23 www.buildingonline.com/news/viewnews.pl?id=5514 (accessed March 6, 2007).

24 US Green Building Council [online], www.usgbc.org/News/PressReleaseDetails.aspx?ID=2783 (accessed March 6, 2007).

25 "The Business Case for Green Building," *Urban Land*, June 2005, p. 71, www.uli.org.

26 For example, PNC Bank has committed to making all of its new branches LEED-certified, at least at the basic level.

27 National Association of Office and Industrial Properties [online], www.naiop.org.

28 Bureau of Labor Statistics, cited in *Investor's Business Daily*, March 6, 2007, p. 1.

29 Gerding Edlen Development, www.gerdingedlen.com; story in the Portland *Daily Journal of Commerce*, February 26, 2007, p. 4.

30 Urban Land Institute [online], www.uli.org/AM/Template.cfm?Section=GreenTech1&Template=/MembersOnly.cfm&ContentID=37654 (accessed December 31, 2006).

31 Corporate Office Properties Trust [online], www.copt.com/?id=62 (accessed March 6, 2007).

32 *New York Times*, January 10, 2007.

33 Jonathan Rose Companies [online], www.rose-network.com/projects/index.html (accessed March 6, 2007).

34 Ecotrust [online], www.ecotrust.org/ncc/index.html (accessed March 6, 2007).

35 Kresge Foundation [online], www.kresge.org/content/displaycontent.aspx?CID=7 (accessed March 6, 2007).

4 COSTS OF GREEN BUILDINGS

Understanding the costs of green building is important, because the single most important factor in the development and construction world is cost. Construction costs are "hard," but benefits such as projected energy savings, water savings and productivity gains are considered "soft" because they are speculative and occur in the future. Therefore, performing a cost–benefit analysis for each project is crucially important, to convince building owners, design teams and developers to proceed with both sustainable-design measures and the LEED certification effort.

The biggest barrier to green buildings is the perception that they cost more. Jim Goldman, an experienced project executive with Turner Construction Company in Seattle says, "There's still a lot of bad information out there with respect to costs. If you want to kill a green project, there's nothing easier than using (the prospect of higher) costs."[1]

Architect Peter Busby, Principal of Busby Perkins+Will in Vancouver, British Columbia, has designed a number of LEED-certified projects. His approach to controlling costs involves several key elements:[2]

- Have a clear green design goal from the outset.
- Make sure the design team is completely integrated.
- Incorporate green elements from the beginning.
- Have centralized management of the green building process.
- Teams should have experience with/knowledge of green building.
- Make sure there's sufficient technical information.
- Provide sufficient upfront time and funding for studies.
- Always insist on life cycle costing of green investments.

We will return to these points in several places in this chapter, since each design team has to address the challenge of identifying green building costs and justifying them to clients. (Chapter 3 presented the business case for green buildings by putting the full range of benefits into perspective, often a necessary prelude to considering whether to bear additional costs.)

High-performance on a budget

A large developer-driven, build-to-suit project in Portland, Oregon, completed in the fourth quarter of 2006, exposed flaws in the notion that higher levels of performance must always lead to significantly higher capital costs. The 400,000 square foot, 16-story, $145 million Center for Health and Healing at Oregon Health & Science University received a LEED Platinum rating early in 2007, the largest project in the world to achieve this highest green building rating. The developer has reported a total cost premium, net of local, state and federal incentives, of one percent.[3] The total costs for the mechanical and electrical systems were about $3.5 million below the initial budget estimates from the general contractor. At the same time, energy and water modeling indicated a 61 percent savings on future energy use and a 56 percent savings in water consumption. In other words, from a performance standpoint, this demonstrates the benefits of an integrated design process, coupled with an experienced developer and design team willing to push the envelope of building design.

The more developers engage experienced green design and construction firms, the more they require their consultants to produce high-performance results (without excuses), the more likely it is that overall project costs will not exceed costs for a conventional project that doesn't have the benefits of a high-level green project.

Many of the green building measures that give a building its greatest long-term value – for example, on-site energy production, on-site stormwater management and water recycling, green roofs, daylighting and natural ventilation – often require a higher capital cost. However, many project teams are finding that these costs can be paid for by avoiding other costs, such as stormwater and sewer connection fees, or by using local utility incentives, state tax breaks and federal tax credits.

While it is often possible to get a LEED-certified (and sometimes LEED Silver) building at no additional cost, as building teams try to make a building truly sustainable, cost increments often accrue. This is especially true when the building owner or developer wants to showcase their green building with more expensive (but visible) measures such as green roofs or photovoltaics for on-site power production, or where there is a strong commitment to green materials such as certified wood.

Cost drivers for green buildings

In Chapter 3, we discussed many business-case benefits of green buildings, but costs are real, occur first and must be justified to various stakeholders. Benefits are generally long term, and costs are immediate, so many people tend to shy away from anything that will add costs, no matter what the potential benefits.

Table 4.1   Cost drivers for green buildings

Cost Driver	Source of Possible Cost Increases
1. Level of LEED certification sought	Zero for LEED certified to 1–2% for LEED Silver, up to 5% for LEED Gold
2. Stage of the project when the decision is made to seek LEED certification	After 50% completion of construction drawings, adding green features get a lot more costly
3. Project type	With certain project types, such as science and technology laboratories, it can be costly to change established models; designs for office buildings are easier to change
4. Experience of the design and construction teams in sustainable design and green buildings	Every organization has a "learning curve" for green buildings; costs decrease as teams learn more about the process
5. Specific green technologies added to a project, without full integration with other components	Photovoltaics and green roofs are going to add costs, no matter what; it is possible to design a LEED Gold building without them
6. Lack of clear priorities for green measures and lack of a strategy for including them	Each design team member considers strategies in isolation, in the absence of clear direction from the owner
7. Geographic location and climate	Climate can make certain levels of LEED certification harder for project types such as laboratories and even office buildings

Table 4.1 shows some of the elements of green building design and construction decisions that may add cost to a project. From this table of "cost drivers," you can see that there is no right answer to the question: "how much does a green building cost?" I often tell audiences that the definitive answer to this question is – it depends!

Overall, costs associated with green design and construction may exceed one percent of construction costs for large buildings and five percent of costs for small buildings, depending on the measures employed.

Higher levels of sustainable building (e.g., LEED Silver, Gold or Platinum standard) may involve some additional capital costs, based on case studies of completed buildings in the US, LEED projects also incur additional soft (non-construction) costs for additional design, analysis, engineering, energy modeling, building commissioning and certification. For some projects, additional professional services, for example – including energy modeling, building commissioning, additional design services and the documentation process – can add 0.5–1.5 percent to a project's cost, depending on its size.

THE 2003 COST STUDY FOR THE STATE OF CALIFORNIA

A 2003 study by Gregory Kats was the first rigorous assessment of the costs and benefits of green buildings.[4] (Chapter 3 presented the benefits assessed by

Table 4.2   Incremental capital costs of 33 LEED-certified projects

Certification Level	Cost Premium (%)	Number of Projects Analyzed
Certified	0.66	8
Silver	2.11	18
Gold	1.82	6
Platinum	6.50	1
Average, all certification levels	**1.84**	**33**

this study.) Drawing on cost data from 33 green building projects nationwide, the report concluded that LEED certifications add an average of 1.84 percent to the construction cost of a project. For Silver-certified office projects, construction cost premiums ranged from 2 to 5 percent over the cost of a conventional building at the same site. Table 4.2 shows the results of this early study of green building costs.

Green building advocates frequently resort to rhetoric ("green is good") when promoting their point of view. However, for owners and developers, justifying additional costs traditionally rests on the economic payback or ROI for energy (and sometimes water) conservation measures. Green building standards such as LEED incorporate requirements beyond energy and water use, including indoor environmental quality, daylighting and views of the outdoors, use of recycled materials, and sustainable-site development, so it is often difficult to justify green building investments on the value of utility savings alone.

Davis Langdon cost studies

As more projects are LEED certified, it is becoming easier to identify LEED-related and green building-related costs, making it easier to budget for such costs in the next project. It is also becoming cheaper to realize green building goals, especially LEED certification, as more building teams and consultants learn how to achieve these goals within conventional building budgets. A 2004 study by the international cost-management firm of Davis Langdon offered evidence, based on 94 different building projects of vastly different types, that the most important determinant of project cost is not the level of LEED certification sought, but rather other more conventional issues such as the building program goals, type of construction and the local construction economy. In this study, the authors concluded that there was no statistically significant evidence that green buildings cost more per square foot than conventional projects, primarily because so many factors influence the cost of any particular type of building.[5] The analysis was updated in late 2006, as shown in Figure 4.1. From these results, we expect more pressure from owners and developers

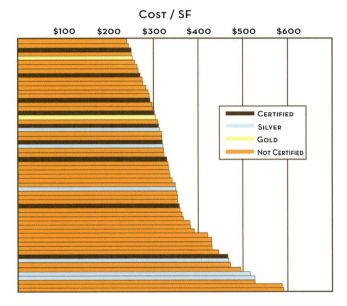

▶ **4.1** Davis Langdon study: costs for academic buildings, green and non-green. Courtesy of Davis Langdon, redrawn with permission.

for design and construction teams to aim for high LEED goals, because these buildings are indeed perceived to offer higher value for the money spent.

The study's authors comment, "From this analysis we conclude that many projects achieve sustainable design within their initial budget, or with very small supplemental funding. This suggests that owners are finding ways to incorporate project goals and values, regardless of budget, by making choices. However, there is no one-size-fits-all answer. Each building project is unique and should be considered as such when addressing the cost and feasibility of LEED. Benchmarking with other comparable projects can be valuable and informative, but not predictive."

Davis Langdon also studied the impact of climate on the costs of a research laboratory. Costs ranged from 2.7 to 6.3 percent premium for a LEED Gold project, and 1.0 to 3.7 percent for a LEED Silver project (the study assumes the same design was constructed in various cities at the same time). A 2006 report by Davis Langdon on 230 projects resulted in these conclusions: Most projects by good design teams have "embedded" 12 LEED points (out of 26 needed for certification) and most could add 18 points to get certified with minimal total cost, through an integrated design approach.[6] Of 60 LEED-seeking projects analyzed, over half received no supplemental budget to support sustainable goals. Of those that received additional funding, the supplement was typically less than 5 percent, and supplemental funding was usually for specific enhancements, most commonly photovoltaics. In other words, any design team should be able to build a LEED-certified building at no additional cost, and a LEED Silver building with only a minor cost increase.

The key cost message to owners and developers (and design and construction teams) is that sustainability needs to be a "program" issue, that is, it needs to be embedded in the goals of the project and not treated as an add-on cost element. This conclusion is not just a matter of semantics; it goes to the very heart of the question, "What is the purpose of this building or project?" If sustainability is not a core purpose, then it is going to cost more; if it is essential to the undertaking, then costs will be in line with nongreen buildings of the same type.

However, recent examples of academic LEED projects built with no additional cost indicate that design and construction teams are learning how to deliver high performance on conventional budgets. Leith Sharp, Director of the Harvard University Green Campus Initiative, says, "We've focused a lot of energy on reducing any cost associated with green building design through effective process management. As a result we've just completed a LEED Platinum project that had no added cost."[7]

THE 2004 GSA COST STUDY

A 2004 study for the GSA of the costs of achieving various levels of LEED certification for government buildings looked at both new construction and remodeling projects. It supports somewhat similar conclusions to the work for the State of California. For example, in the California analysis, a $40 million public building seeking a LEED Gold level of certification might expect to budget about 2 percent, or $800,000, extra to achieve this rating.

Table 4.3 shows the results of the 2004 study that carefully detailed two typical projects, a new federal courthouse (with 262,000 square feet and a construction cost of $220 per gross square feet) and an office building modification (with 307,000 square feet and a construction cost of $130 per gross square feet). At that time, the study estimated the additional capital costs of both types of GSA projects, ranging from negligible for LEED-certified projects, up to 4 percent for Silver level and 8 percent for Gold level.[8]

Soft costs for design and documentation services were also estimated in the GSA LEED Cost Study, and ranged from about $0.40 to $0.80 per square foot

Table 4.3 Incremental costs of LEED certifying two prototypical GSA projects

Level of LEED Certification	Range of Green Cost Premiums – (Percentage of Total Construction Cost)	
Building Type	**New Courthouses**	**Office Modernization**
1. Certified	−0.4–1.0%	1.4–2.1%
2. Silver	−0.0–4.4%	3.1–4.2%
3. Gold	1.4–8.1%	7.8–8.2%

Table 4.4 Soft costs of LEED certification, 2006[9]

Element	Cost Range	Required in LEED?
1. Building commissioning	$0.40–0.75 per sq.ft., $20,000 minimum	Yes
2. Energy modeling	$15,000–30,000	Yes; depends on size and complexity
3. LEED documentation	$25,000–90,000	Yes; depends on complexity of project, team experience and level of certification
4. Eco-charrettes	$5,000–20,000	No
5. Natural ventilation modeling	$7,500–20,000	No
6. Enhanced commissioning services	$3,000–15,000	No
7. Daylighting design modeling	$3,000–10,000	No (some utilities offer this as a free service)

(0.2 to 0.4 percent) for the courthouse and $0.35 to $0.70 per square feet (0.3 to 0.6 percent) for the office building modernization project. One caution: the added percentage of total cost may be higher for smaller projects. Therefore, each building team should look at every cost that a project will incur, from permitting to site development to furniture and fixtures, before deciding that a particular green measure is "too costly." Deciding which costs are going to provide the highest value in a given situation is a primary task of the architect, working in concert with the client, the building owner or developer, and the builder.

SOFT COSTS FOR GREEN BUILDING PROJECTS

One thing is certain: there are costs associated with green building projects that need to be taken into account, especially with those aiming at LEED certification. Many projects do not consider these costs especially onerous, but some do. Table 4.4 shows some of the potential cost increases in soft costs. Some of these costs should be considered essential to good project design and execution, specifically building commissioning and energy modeling, while others are clearly associated with the LEED certification effort. Note that because some of the costs are fixed, smaller projects may incur higher costs per square foot than shown here.

THE GREEN SCHOOLS REPORT

Released in late 2006, the report, "Greening America's Schools" has already become one of the most important documents to justify green buildings for a very large market segment, K-12 schools.[10] In Chapter 5, we profile the benefits of green schools as outlined in that report. In this section, we note that the report studied 30 green school projects in 10 states, completed from 2001 through 2006, and concluded that the average green cost premium was 2 percent, or about $3 per square foot ($33 per sqm). As defined by the report, the "green premium" is the "initial extra cost to build a green building compared to a conventional building. Typically this cost premium is a result of more expensive (and sustainably sourced) materials, more efficient mechanical systems, and better design, modeling and integration, and other high-performance features. Many school architects use a state or school district's predetermined budget as their metric for appropriate school cost. Some green schools are built on the same budget as conventional schools. "[11]

USING INTEGRATED DESIGN TO REDUCE COSTS

Often, the traditional "design-bid-build" process of project delivery works against the development of green buildings. In this process, there is often a sequential "handoff" from the architect to the building engineers to the contractor, so that there is a limited "feedback loop" arising from the engineering aspects of building operating costs and comfort considerations back to basic building design features.

In a standard design process, for example, the mechanical engineer is often left out of the architect's building envelope design considerations, yet those decisions are often critical in determining the size (and cost) of the HVAC plant, which can often consume up to 15 percent or more of a building's cost. Along the way, the standard "value engineering" exercise often involves reducing the value of the HVAC systems by specifying lower-efficiency (cheaper) equipment, possibly reducing the R-value of glazing and insulation, measures that reduce first costs, but require the project to incur higher operating costs for energy for the lifetime of the building. (Lifetime operating costs are typically 80 percent or more of a building's total costs.)

As a result, key design decisions are often made without considering long-term operating costs. Most developers and designers find that a better process for creating green buildings involves an integrated design effort in which all key players work together from the beginning. Developers and owners have discovered cost savings of 1 to 3 percent in building design and construction through the use of integrated design approaches as well as other non-traditional measures, which might include bringing in the general contractor and key subcontractors earlier in the process to help with pricing alternative approaches to achieve required comfort levels in a building.

The essence of an integrated design process is shown in Figure 4.2. Without taking time to bring together all of the relevant parties and to study alternatives before fixing on a final design, a project foregoes opportunities to make single systems do multiple tasks, which is the essence of integrated design. Without an effort to integrate the various design disciplines, often individual subsystems (such as the HVAC system) are optimized, but the entire system less cost effective. In other words, one might pay more for a more efficient chiller for a building, to get more energy savings, but if the same amount of money was spent it on energy conservation, one could have achieved three to 10 times the energy savings of just an efficient-air-conditioning system.

Gail Lindsey is an experienced green architect based in North Carolina. She shares her experience with cost management: "Early questioning is essential. The best thing that I can do is ask questions."[12] This illustrates a key precept of integrated design: asking the right questions at the right time. An integrated

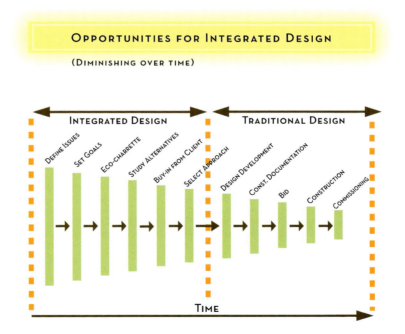

▲ **4.2**   Integrated design process emphasizes more upfront investment.

design process begins with the project team holding goal-setting sessions in which green building measures are introduced. Integrated design follows several basic steps. To start a project, the project team holds an eco-charrette, to get the best ideas out in the open for everyone's consideration. With an experienced facilitator, this process often results in lower overall project costs and much higher building performance.

The integrated design process, particularly for a LEED-registered project, typically covers the following steps:

- Analyzing green building and LEED-related design tasks, with specific assignments given to each design team member.
- Coaching and facilitation by an experienced green building expert, including use of an eco-charrette to bring together the design team and key stakeholders to review site and project information and to explore the environmental and energy impacts of alternative designs.
- Modeling key energy-using systems; this process may include daylighting modeling, and often involves modeling initial and life cycle costs of various alternative methods to achieve building program objectives.
- Materials research for green materials and availability in a given location.
- Preparing green specifications for the construction team.
- Commissioning the building near completion to make sure all energy-using systems are working according to design intent.
- If aiming at LEED certification, someone must document the achievement of specific LEED requirements.

Each of these steps has specific cost and schedule implications, and each need to be thought about from the beginning of the process, if the costs of green buildings are to meet budgets, often established well in advance of anyone thinking about achieving a LEED certification.

A more effective refinement of the eco-charrette process requires spending time on goal-setting sessions with the owner or developer and key stakeholders in the building process. These goal-setting sessions need to happen early on, and sometimes can take a full day to reach consensus. However, they often provide clearer guidance to design teams about preferred sustainability measures for the project and can assist in making budget-driven tradeoffs later in design.

Integrated design requires (considerably) more upfront effort, including dialog, charrettes, studies, timely decision-making and so on, before the traditional start of a project with the schematic design phase. This implies that architects and engineers are going to require additional fees, and owners and developers are going to have to pay them, to get the results each party desires. On small projects, these fees might add 1–2 percent to the total project cost (e.g., 1 percent of a $5 million project is $50,000, a typical amount for a full charrette-based design process with energy and daylight modeling studies), but perhaps pay for themselves in a quicker design process and possibly reduced HVAC system sizing, for example.

Relating her own experience with building teams in Western Pennsylvania, Rebecca Flora of the Pittsburgh-based Green Building Alliance, says: "To help control costs, the first thing we do is to help people understand that green building should not be a LEED point-chasing game. We ask them to focus first on their values and then rethink how to use the LEED system as a tool to help achieve those value and goals."[13]

So for a building team just setting out to build its first green project, green development or green renovation, the most important advice is this – do your homework, visit other projects, talk to several experienced design teams and retain a knowledgeable green building consultant to help you manage the process.

Notes

1   Interview with Jim Goldman, Turner Construction, March 2007.
2   Real Estate Forums [online], www.realestateforums.com/greenestate/pdf/Peter%20Busby%20A2.pdf (accessed April 23, 2007).
3   Personal communication, Dennis Wilde, Gerding Edlen Development, 2006.
4   Gregory Kats et al., *The Costs and Financial Benefits of Green Buildings*, 2003, www.cap-e.com/ewebeditpro/items/O59F3303.ppt#1 (accessed March 6, 2007).
5   Lisa Matthiessen and Peter Morris, "Costing Green: A Comprehensive Database," Davis Langdon, 2004, www.davislangdon.com/USA/research. Further 2006 update information provided to the author by Davis Langdon.
6   US Green Building Council, November 2006, LEED Cost Workshop.
7   Interview with Leith Sharp, Harvard Green Campus Initiative, March 2007.
8   Steven Winter Associates, "GSA LEED Cost Study," downloadable (578 pages) from the *Whole Building Design Guide* web site, www.wbdg.org/ccb/GSAMAN/gsaleed.pdf (accessed March 18, 2007). The authors note: "The construction cost estimates reflect a number of GSA-specific design features and project assumptions; as such, the numbers must be used with caution [and] may not be directly transferable to other project types or building owners" (ibid., p. 2).
9   Based on the author's professional experience.

10   Capital-E [online], "Greening America's Schools, Costs and Benefits," October 2006, www.cap-e.com/ewebeditpro/items/O59F11233.pdf (accessed April 26, 2007).

11   Ibid., p. 5.

12   Gail Lindsey, FAIA, Personal communication, March 2007.

13   Interview with Rebecca Flora, Green Building Alliance, March 2007.

5 VERTICAL MARKETS FOR GREEN BUILDINGS

In this chapter, we address several selected vertical markets for green buildings i.e., markets that are already developed or that are expected to develop rapidly. These include commercial offices, K-12 education, higher education, public facilities, high-rise housing and healthcare (still a developing market). In this terminology, a *vertical* market refers to a particular type of use for a building — office, education, medical, etc., whereas a *horizontal* market applies to green technologies that could be used in a wide variety of building types, for example, solar energy systems can be used in offices, schools, churches, etc. Vertical markets for green buildings exist in every area of the country, so it makes sense to look at how these markets view green buildings at the present time and how marketers are trying to address the needs of particular building types.

Table 5.1 shows the projected growth rates of various vertical markets from 2007 through 2010. Some observers believe that green buildings will experience an "inflection point" in 2007, as a number of factors coincide to give this market an accelerated boost. From Table 5.1, it is easy to see that a design firm should be focused on the fast-growth sectors, including education, commercial offices, government, and institutional projects and healthcare, while waiting for the rest of the market to catch up. Some potentially slower growing green building markets such as high-rise residential, retail and hospitality should still offer good marketing potential for firms already established in them.

It pays to remember two key facts when addressing each of these markets: few architects have designed a LEED-certified building (as of the end of 2006), and few owners have purchased one. Therefore, we are still very much in the early adopter stage of market development. Many building owners now put out requests for proposals that specify that a building project must achieve a LEED rating, but only a few selected government agencies are demanding a higher-level LEED Silver or Gold rating. Some nonprofits are even going so far now as to specify that a new project has to achieve a Platinum rating, but these are still relatively rare occurrences.

Table 5.1 Projected annual growth rates for green buildings by market sector[1]

Market Sector	Projected Growth Rate in Green Construction (%)
Education	65
Government	62
Institutional	54
Office	48
Healthcare	46
Residential	32
Hospitality	22
Retail	20

COMMERCIAL OFFICES

Commercial and office construction represented a $115 billion market (annualized) in 2006, with offices accounting for $45 billion. Examining data on the first 511 LEED-NC-certified projects as of April 2007, 137 (27 percent) appear to be some form of office project.[2] Clearly, the market for LEED projects is still highly concentrated in the easiest market to approach; office buildings. Certification of an office building project is easy and fairly inexpensive, with most projects receiving 20 or more LEED points just from their basic design (out of 26 points needed for basic certification). LEED Silver certification costs might run $100,000–200,000 for a typical 100,000 square foot building, including documentation, energy modeling and building commissioning, or about $1.00–2.00 per square foot. Cost premiums for basic LEED-certified buildings might be even less or nonexistent. As we discussed in Chapter 4, a lot of the cost premium depends on the experience of the design and construction teams.

The National Association of Realtors (NAR) headquarters building in Washington, DC, shown in Figure 5.1, is a good example of a private commercial office built to LEED Gold standards. Construction of the $46 million, 92,000 square foot (8,450 sqm) Class "A" building was begun in October 2002, and the building opened for business two years later. NAR occupies 44,000 square feet (4,100 sqm) on five floors of the 12-story building. By installing efficient HVAC systems and a high-performance glass curtain wall, the project uses 30 percent less energy than a standard building. The NAR also committed to purchase green power to supply 50 percent of the building's energy consumption. Innovative measures taken to extend the LEED requirements included implementing Green Tenant Improvement Guidelines to ensure that the sustainable design intent is carried out in the rented office space; creating a comprehensive green housekeeping plan which requires the use of nontoxic cleaning products, recycled content paper and plastic supplies to be used by cleaning services; and conducting

▲ **5.1** The 92,000 square feet NAR building in Washington, DC is LEED-NC Silver certified. Courtesy of National Association of Realtors.

a public education program to teach the building's visitors about its sustainable features.

The NAR building is a good example of an owner-occupied building, even though the owner in this case is leasing out more than half the premises. Another market that bears watching is the developer driven, corporate build-to-suit market, largely commercial offices.

According to April 2007 USGBC data on LEED-registered projects by building type, 13 percent of these projects were commercial offices and 25 percent were multi-use, a category that includes commercial offices with, for example, ground-floor retail, parking garages or other uses. (The multi-use category may also include housing with retail, and other forms of multiple use that do not include commercial offices.) Given that LEED is most clearly usable as a green building design and rating tool for office buildings, it is no surprise that office buildings would constitute more than 25 percent of the total projects. These LEED-registered buildings include projects for private companies, major corporations, developers, government agencies and nonprofit organizations.

► **5.2** Designed by BNIM/360 and aiming for LEED-NC certification, the IRS Kansas City Service Center provides daylight to 90 percent of the employees. Copyright © 2006 Assassi, design by BNIM/360, reprinted with permission.

About 27 percent of the first 137 commercial office projects certified under LEED were built by or for public agencies, about the same as the 28 percent share of all registered projects belonging to local, state or federal government agencies. Design firms should stay connected to the public agency market, which will likely represent nearly 25 to 30 percent of all commercial offices to be built to LEED standards through 2010. Many public agencies are adopting LEED requirements for their own commercial building projects, which should encourage firms to develop an expertise in delivering these projects on conventional building budgets.

A typical federal government project is the one million square foot (92,000 sqm) Internal Revenue Service (IRS) campus in Kansas City, Missouri, shown in Figure 5.2. In designing the project, the team sought to utilize daylighting and building orientation to optimize solar light and heat, filling the facility with natural light and improving energy efficiency and connection to the outdoors. The project team worked to integrate recycled, reused, low toxicity and local/ regional materials into the campus construction. Completed in the fall of 2006, the $370 million project expects LEED-certification in 2007.[3]

In addition to commercial offices, a considerable number of nonprofits and utilities have certified headquarters or branch offices, as exemplified in a new headquarters building for Mid-state Electric Cooperative in La Pine, Oregon, certified in 2006 at LEED Gold, as shown in Figure 5.3. The building consists of a total of 53,000 square feet (4,867 sqm) of which 13,000 square feet (1,200 sqm) is for office use, the balance for dispatch and shops. A 7-kilowatt solar array supplies

▲ **5.3** The LEED-NC Gold Midstate Electric Cooperative's Administration Building. Architect: Scott Steele, AIA, LEED AP, Steele Associates Architects LLC.

about 12 percent of total estimated annual energy use, or about 10,000 kilowatt hours, with the balance of electricity purchased from wind power installations. A geothermal heat pump helps reduce overall energy use by 40 percent or more, in a cold, dry, high-desert region of central Oregon.[4]

EDUCATIONAL BUILDINGS

The value of educational construction exceeded $50 billion (annualized) in 2005.[5]

Imagine that this market consists of 2,500 to 5,000 buildings valued at $10 million to $20 million each. Now further imagine that eventually 625 to 1,250 of those will be LEED-registered each year, given that LEED aims to address the top 25 percent of the market in each building sector. Therefore, in 2007 and 2008, based on current market data, I estimate that about 12 to 14 percent of all LEED-registered projects will be from the education market segment, or about 180 to 210 projects (based on 1,500 newly LEED-registered projects), representing a 14 to 33 percent penetration of the immediately accessible market for LEED education projects. Using the terminology of diffusion of innovations theory, this market is now clearly in the early adopter phase of this market, with signs of accelerating growth in 2007 and 2008 that will take it into the early majority market (see Chapter 9 discussion of market adoption phases).

K-12 schools

The Turner Construction Company's green building survey for 2005 specifically addressed the K-12 education market.[6] In summer 2005, Turner surveyed about 650 executives involved with schools and colleges. The importance of this market is indicated by the fact that in 2004, $34 billion of new education buildings were completed. School districts are estimated to spend $6 billion per year on energy costs. Clearly, the energy-saving aspects of green buildings are of critical importance. A 2007 McGraw-Hill report confirmed these conclusions.[7]

For K-12 schools, more than 70 percent those surveyed rated green buildings higher on community image, ability to attract and retain teachers, reduced student absenteeism and student performance. The greatest obstacles to green construction are the perceived higher costs (cited by 74 percent of the survey respondents) and lack of awareness of their benefits (67 percent). The main issue with incorporating more green features in educational construction, assuming that they cost more, is the separation of capital from operating budgets and the difficulty of incorporating life-cycle-cost considerations in initial project budgets. This problem leads to short-term thinking, manifested in a desire to keep capital costs as low as possible.

The 2006 green schools report

In late 2006, a landmark study of the costs and benefits of green schools was sponsored by a coalition of agencies and organizations. The benefits of green schools are overwhelming compared with the extra costs (assumed), as shown in Table 5.2. I believe that this report will have a strong effect on the demand for green schools in 2007–2012 period, which should coincide with the peak period expected for school construction to meet the needs of new immigrant

Table 5.2   Financial benefits of green schools[8]

Financial Benefits of Green Schools, $/sq.ft., 20-Year Net Present Value	
Energy	$9
Emissions reduction	$1
Water and wastewater utility bills	$1
Increased lifetime earnings of students	$49
Asthma reduction from better air quality	$3
Cold and flu reduction from better air quality	$5
Teacher retention	$4
Employment impact from higher costs	$2
Total	**$74**
Cost of Greening (2%, assumed)	($3)
Net financial benefits	**$71**

populations and the last cohorts of Baby Boomer children. Marketers should be sharing this report with their K-12 education clients. Anyone who reads it will require little convincing that all schools should be certified green schools!

The report, *Greening America's Schools*, found that building green would save an average school $100,000 each year, net of costs, enough to pay for two additional teachers. The report broke new ground by demonstrating that green schools are extremely cost effective. Total financial benefits from green schools outweigh costs by a factor of 20 to 1. In Table 5.2, you can see the calculated benefits from green school construction and operations, based on a study of 30 green schools built in 10 states between 2001 and 2006.

The bottom line is very simple. School board members, school superintendents and concerned parents should take this evidence to heart and support building green schools in each school district. Even subtracting the potential benefit of higher lifetime earnings resulting from higher test scores, the net benefits of green schools outweigh the costs by eight to one, an 800 percent gain; forgetting about teacher retention and extra jobs generated by the slightly higher costs of green schools, the benefits outweigh the costs by six to one. For a ROI of 600 percent, you'd be wise to go forward. Even counting utility cost savings alone, the benefits outweigh costs by three to one.

Green schools today

The information presented here demonstrates that the education sector is the fastest-growing market for green building and that education construction is the largest construction sector, by value. A 2006 survey of the school market also found that:

- The concern for "improved health and well-being" was the most critical social reason for driving education green building.
- Fiscal advantages of green building, such as energy cost savings, are the major motivation behind the building of green schools and universities.
- Higher first costs are the primary challenge to building green in this sector, though recent studies point to minor first cost increases, which are more than recouped in operational cost savings.
- Operational cost decreases resulting from green building are the most important driving force for faster adoption of green school buildings.

In the study, people identified as green leaders saw factors such as "publicity," "mission statement" and "staff demand" as important green building drivers, indicating their view of increased green building coming from external factors. On the other hand, educational facility planners tended to identify important drivers that affected measurable outcomes of green building such as "increased health and well-being," "energy cost increases" and "productivity benefits."[9]

In early 2007, the Sidwell Friends School in Washington, DC, was awarded the first LEED Platinum rating for a K-12 school in the US. A private middle school, Sidwell Friends achieved a score of 57 in the LEED-NC rating system, well above the 52 points necessary for a Platinum rating.[10] In this project, a 39,000 square foot (3,580 sqm) addition was added to the existing renovated building, more than doubling the useable space. Most materials in the three-level, U-shaped structure were selected for environmental impact. The skin of the building is 50-year-old western red cedar reclaimed from wine barrels. The walkways inside the school lobby are made from pilings retrieved from the Baltimore, Maryland, harbor. Overall, the new middle school expects to use 60 percent less energy than a conventional building of its size, including 92 percent less lighting energy, and consume 93 percent less water. Photovoltaics provide 5 percent of the building's energy use. The centerpiece of the new school is a constructed wetland, the first of its kind in Washington, DC. The wetland takes wastewater coming out of the building, cleans it using biological processes and then channels it back into the building for use in toilets and cooling systems.

A very different type of LEED-certified school was built for the Hopi Tribe in Polacca, Arizona, the First Mesa Elementary School, shown in Figure 5.4. Designed in 2003 and completed in 2004 at a cost of $14 million, the project includes a 75,000 square foot (6,900 sqm) school, bus barn and 22 staff quarters. The project includes rainwater harvesting to irrigate native vegetation at the school site.

These developments follow along behind a number of exemplary schools built to LEED standards, typically by visionary architects and school district superintendents. An early example in the Portland, Oregon, metropolitan area,

▲ **5.4**   Replacing a 50-year-old school, First Mesa Elementary serves 220 children from the Hopi Tribe in Polacca. Designed by Dryon Murphy Architects, a Native American-owned firm, the school is LEED-NC certified. Courtesy of Dyron Murphy Architects, PC.

the LEED Silver-rated Clackamas High School, was completed in the spring of 2002, at a cost of $118 per square foot ($1,285 per sqm), slightly below the average cost of other local high schools at that time.

In all, there are more than 230 additional K-12 schools registered under LEED and in various stages of design, construction and certification, as of the end of March 2007, an estimate based on 6 percent of 3,817 LEED-NC-registered projects for which data are available.

School design tends to be a rather specialized field, and one must depend on architects who already design a lot of schools to lead the way in greening school construction. Some of these architects are leaders in green design, but my experience is that most are still "feeling their way" into this new area of design and construction. Most school districts are still trying to understand the budget and schedule implications of setting LEED goals for their schools. In areas of the South, Southwest and West Coast with rapid student population growth, there is considerable pressure just to build "anything" that will be ready for a September opening in two years and that will fit within a budget that might have been "sold" to the school board and the community several years earlier.

In fact, until recently it has been rare, in my experience, to see a school district in Oregon or Washington (two prime areas for LEED-registered projects) issue a request for qualifications (RFQs) for architects that includes sustainable design experience or expertise among its scoring criteria. As the saying goes, "what gets measured, gets managed," and one might add, "What gets evaluated, gets selected." However, there are signs of change in 2007, and we are beginning to see some RFQs awarding five to ten percent of total evaluation points for design teams with LEED project experience.

It is very likely that school design will begin to include more and more green design measures, such as daylighting, low-VOC materials, higher levels of energy-conservation and water-conservation, and recycled-content materials, before we begin to see a sharp increase in the number of LEED-certified or even LEED-registered school projects. Marketers and design professionals should be spending their time trying to sell the benefits of green design to school boards, administrators and school facilities people. This is to some degree "missionary work," since LEED registration and certification for new projects are still infrequent in this market sector.

Higher education facilities

According to the LEED statistics, higher education projects comprise 7 percent, or slightly more than 250 of the first 3,817 LEED-registered projects, through the end of March 2007. On the list of the first 450 LEED-certified projects, through early 2007, there are 51 higher education projects represented, including a few dorms. Since college housing is now a very large and growing market, with the explosion of college registrations since 2000 expected to last through 2010, one can expect a significant number of LEED projects in higher education will involve student housing. Beyond housing, the main market for higher education projects involves such facilities as:

- Classrooms
- Offices
- Libraries and performing arts
- Laboratories and research buildings
- Recreation centers and college athletics
- Student unions and combinations of these facilities.

Higher education construction is a significant proportion of total school construction. Some of the representative LEED-certified higher education projects from 2006 include:

- University of British Columbia Life Sciences Centre, LEED-NC Gold.
- Haverford College (PA), Integrated Athletics Center, LEED-NC Gold.
- Central College (IA), Residence Hall, LEED-NC Gold.
- Grinnell College (IA), Environmental Research Facility, LEED-NC Gold.
- Carnegie Mellon University (PA), Collaborative Innovation Center, LEED-CS Gold.
- Warren Wilson College (NC), Orr Cottage, LEED-NC Gold.
- University of Victoria (BC), Medical Sciences, LEED-NC Gold.
- Pennsylvania State University, Landscape/Architecture, LEED-NC Gold.
- Oregon State University, Kelly Engineering Building, LEED-NC Gold.
- Yale University (CT), Malone Engineering Center, LEED-NC Gold.
- University of Colorado, Technology Learning Center, LEED-NC Gold.

Assuming there are about 3,000 colleges in the US, and that each institution starts an average of one building project per year, LEED-registered projects are currently less than 5 percent of the college/university market. As of April 2007, there were only 51 certified higher education projects, so market penetration in this sector is just beginning. In the campus environment, at least 50 percent of the LEED projects exist due to strong support from the institution's top leadership.[11]

Table 5.3 shows driving forces and business benefits for green buildings in higher education. Although the facts are very much on the side of green buildings, the dispersed nature of decision-making and the long, drawn-out process of approving and funding higher education projects make it a tough arena for design firms to sell in, with a strong point of view.

Figure 5.5 shows a significant green building project at the University of Victoria in British Columbia. The University of Victoria's new Engineering/Computer

Table 5.3   Driving forces and business benefits for higher education

1. Savings on energy costs and utility infrastructure

2. Reputation enhancement or maintenance; public relations/marketing

3. State-level mandates (public institutions)

4. CEO-level leadership from University or College president (public/private)

5. Responding to student and faculty pressure for green buildings of all types

6. Recruitment of preferred students

7. Recruitment of preferred faculty (this is still speculative)

8. Attracting a new donor pool for campus buildings (this is still speculative)

9. Demonstrates ecological stewardship

▶ **5.5** The ECS Building on the University of Victoria campus operates at 51 percent below Canada's National Energy Code. Courtesy of Busby Perkins+Will.

Science Building (ECS) is a six-story, 89,000 square foot (8,200 sqm) project with extraordinary green ambitions and high levels of water savings. This LEED Gold project has the first green roof at the University of Victoria, is estimated to save over 660,000 gallons (2,500,000 liters) of potable water per year and is estimated to operate at 51 percent below the Canadian Model National Energy Building Code, thus setting a new benchmark for sustainable design.[12]

The important role played by various stakeholders makes the college and university market markedly different from the K-12 education market. In higher education, students and faculty are far more influential, with sustainability a major buzzword on campus. As a result, green buildings are starting to acquire momentum as a force in new construction. These buildings also offer many opportunities to incorporate green buildings into the curriculum, involving multiple departments such as environmental studies, architecture and engineering. There is considerable faculty interest in getting sustainability issues and considerations into coursework and research.[13] Some university administrators are also beginning to see opportunities for green building programs to assist with fundraising and with student and faculty recruitment.[14] Table 5.4 shows colleges and universities with LEED initiatives, as of March 2007.

Higher education survey

In 2004, I conducted a web-based survey of more than 1,000 college and campus planners, architects and facilities directors, which had more than 200 responses. When asked whether projects had sustainability goals, 89 percent of the respondents said "yes". The goals ranged from green goals in the building program, to green purchasing policies, specific LEED goals and tie-ins to campus programs such as composting and recycling. Energy conservation and recycling were key factors in nearly 90 percent of the projects. Half of the respondents had campuses with coursework in sustainability, and nearly half

Table 5.4   Colleges and universities with LEED initiatives[15]

Arizona State University	Omaha Metropolitan Community College
Ball State University (IN)	Pitzer College (CA)
Bowdoin College (ME)	Pomona College (CA)
Brown University	Princeton University
California State University System (various)	Rice University (TX)
Carnegie Mellon University (PA)	Santa Clara University (CA)
Clemson University (SC)	State University of New York (various)
Connecticut College	University of California (system wide)
Dartmouth College	University of Cincinnati
Duke University	University of Florida
Emory University (GA)	University of North Carolina – Chapel Hill
Georgia Institute of Technology	University of Oregon
Harvard University	University of South Carolina
Lewis and Clark College (OR)	University of Vermont
Massachusetts Institute of Technology	University of Washington
Northwestern University	Washington (State) Community Colleges

had specific LEED goals, formal mission statements about sustainability and some type of sustainability committee.

From a marketing point of view, it's important to note that 80 percent of the survey respondents identified the facilities director and department (along with a campus architect who is frequently situated in that area) as instrumental in these programs and goals, with 60 percent identifying top-level administrators, 59 percent students and 54 percent faculty. This survey clearly shows the role of key stakeholders from the faculty, students and staff in influencing decisions to go green at the campus level. Interestingly, 50 percent of respondents said that top-level support was strong or fairly strong for their green building programs. Top-level support was strongest at the smaller public and private institutions, where one might expect the chancellor, president or provost to be more actively involved in all aspects of campus life.

Energy issues – such as daylighting, energy-conservation goals and use of renewable energy – are quite important in these projects, as are recycling construction and demolition debris and using recycled-content materials. LEED certification is a goal for a majority of the projects. In terms of design process, 52 percent reported conducting a design charrette or sustainability forum as part of a green building project.

This group of buyers and owners cited certain barriers to implementation of green design goals, practices and technologies in their building projects. Most respondents (87 percent) cited increased costs, whether real or perceived, as a barrier; 31 percent said the project was not seen as an administration priority; 23 percent cited the lack of experience with green design and 18 percent mentioned the lack of a strong campus constituency. Other barriers cited included high soft costs for LEED documentation and required services, local building codes, project schedules and other time constraints; difficulty of integrating capital and operating budgets to justify the higher initial cost of energy-conservation investments with future savings; and poor timing of introducing green goals or sustainability values into a project.

When asked what would increase their comfort level with green building goals, processes and technologies, 61 percent of the respondents wanted cost information in standard formats such as RSMeans,[16] while 58 percent wanted standardized cost information on specific green building elements, such as green roofs, photovoltaics and energy-efficiency measures. Nearly half (46 percent) cited the need for more of their own experience to feel comfortable, while more than 40 percent wanted to see detailed case studies of university projects and/or local green building projects they could learn from. More than a third wanted specific information on the cost of LEED projects, particularly at various levels of certification.

As a final guide to marketers, the survey respondents were asked to comment on how they would approach sustainability in future projects. Several suggested that they would add sustainability to campus planning as a guiding principle and that they would add sustainable design criteria to the overall design guidance. (In fact, there is increasing use of sustainability task forces and hiring of sustainability directors at many colleges and universities.)[17] The main difficulty cited in their comments about investments in energy efficiency, for example, was the separation between capital and operating budgets and the difficulty of getting additional capital appropriations for improvements that go much beyond code.

College housing

College housing is a large and growing market, with the explosion of college registrations since 2000 expected to last through 2010, so a significant number of LEED projects in higher education may involve student housing. Stephen E. Epler Hall at Portland State University, completed in 2003, is a LEED Silver-certified project with 123 residential units on five floors. The project is 35 percent more energy efficient than local code, recycles 26 percent of its rainwater for flushing toilets in the first-floor public use area and provides extensive daylighting. Projects such as Epler Hall are becoming increasingly common on campuses and suggest that student housing is an emerging market for green building, particularly developer-led projects. They offer a way to attract students and promote the university's commitment to sustainability. There are a number of nonprofit (and for-profit) organizations in the marketplace that may make good teaming partners for developers, since they can operate the project after it is built.

PUBLIC FACILITIES

The market for green buildings for public agencies is perhaps the largest single green market in the US, and it is growing rapidly. Based on the combined office, public safety and recreation segments, the market exceeds $43 billion per year, much of it in smaller buildings. Whether for office buildings, public safety and justice, libraries, cultural or recreational projects, laboratories or public housing, there is a rising demand to meet the increasing array of public policy directives to achieve LEED certification in all new public buildings above a certain size, typically 5,000 square feet (450 sqm) to 10,000 square feet (900 sqm).

Types of public agency projects with LEED-certification goals often include:

- police stations, fire stations and emergency communications centers;
- community centers, pools and recreation centers, and senior centers;
- museums, libraries and visitor centers;
- city halls and county administrative centers;
- convention centers and performing arts centers;

- airport, rail and transit facilities;
- courthouses and jails;
- warehouses and vehicle maintenance facilities;
- public housing.

Federal projects tend to be the largest, followed by state government buildings. The US GSA has been one of the leaders in adopting LEED and pushing it into their projects through the Design Excellence Program. Through March 2007, about 44 major federal projects have received LEED certification. The federal government budgeting process also seems conducive to using green building measures, since the "feds" have the attitude of a long-term owner-operator of buildings and a long-standing commitment to energy conservation in buildings via the Federal Energy Management Program (FEMP).[18]

A good example of a recent public project is the LEED Platinum certified Science & Technology Facility at the US Department of Energy's National Renewable Energy Laboratory (NREL). Shown in Figure 5.6, this project in

▲ **5.6** Designed by SmithGroup, the Science & Technology Facility at the US Department of Energy's NREL is LEED-NC Platinum certified. Photography by Bill Timmerman. Courtesy of SmithGroup.

▶ **5.7** Designed by David Chipperfield Architects, the Des Moines Library is LEED-NC Silver certified. Courtesy David Chipperfield Architects and Des Moines Public Library/ Photographer Farshid Assassi.

Golden, Colorado, was the first federal facility to be Platinum rated. Dedicated in August 2006, this 71,000 gross square foot, multi-story facility houses solar, basic science and hydrogen research.

To conserve energy, the building is properly oriented to the sun, with appropriate placement of windows, including clerestory glazing, providing abundant natural light to the offices and laboratories within. The project implemented additional sun-control elements such as briese-soleil and horizontal shading fins to reduce solar gain and demand for air conditioning. The engineering design specified state-of-the-art mechanical systems, reduced lighting power density, automated lighting controls and underfloor air systems for the office, reducing energy consumption by over 40 percent as compared to similar new federal buildings.[19]

Another public project is the LEED Silver certified Des Moines Pubic Library, shown in Figure 5.7. The library will become a centerpiece for the urban renewal of Des Moines, Iowa in an area that is undergoing extensive redevelopment.

The glass façade consists of triple glazing units with an integrated metal mesh that decreases solar gain up to 80 percent thus significantly reducing the building's cooling load. The elaborate building shape maximizes daylight, which indirectly helps reduce the demand for air conditioning. In addition to rainwater retention, the green roof provides a sense of visual connection to the Western Gateway Park that surrounds the building.

HEALTHCARE AND HOSPITAL FACILITIES

Healthcare is a potentially large market that is still in early stages of development. As of early 2007, less than 3 percent of the LEED-registered projects represented medical or healthcare facilities. The first LEED-certified healthcare project, Boulder, Colorado, Community Foothills Hospital came on line in 2003, rated at LEED Silver. For that project, there were no water-conservation savings and only 30 percent energy savings, but considerable attention to attaining Indoor Environmental Quality and Materials credits. Currently available are the Green Guide for Healthcare (GGHC).[20] The guidelines cover both construction and ongoing operations, similar to the LEED-NC and LEED-EB standards. Even though GGHC version 2.2 was released in 2007, it is not a formal rating system. As a result, more healthcare facilities are embracing LEED certification because it is the most recognizable brand in the marketplace.[21]

However, what is clear is that architects and facility owners (85 percent of healthcare facilities are owned by nonprofits) have a strong stake in creating healthier environments for doctors, staff and patients. Some larger owners of multiple healthcare facilities, such as Kaiser Permanente in California, have already aggressively begun to address green building and green operations issues.[22]

Table 5.5 shows some of the major drivers that are forcing green building considerations into healthcare projects, led by the need to save money on operations.

Therefore, this market bears watching; if your firm is already active in the healthcare market, it would be wise to start paying attention to these guidelines and making them part of your approach to hospitals, clinics and medical offices. Healthcare is a $33 billion annual construction market, more than four times the religious or public safety markets, almost 75 percent the size of

Table 5.5 Drivers for green buildings and operations in healthcare

1. Economic return on energy and water-efficiency investments
2. Protection against future increases in energy prices through peak shaving, thermal energy storage and other demand-reduction measures
3. Consistency with the health and healing mission these institutions
4. Economic gain from faster healing (and quicker discharge) of patients who have views to the outdoors and healing gardens on premises
5. Public relations benefits, considering the many stakeholders in the hospital and healthcare universe
6. Health benefits to the workforce from use of less toxic chemicals in facilities
7. Recruitment and retention of key employees (nurses and skilled practitioners)
8. Evidence-based healthcare should be evidenced in green buildings!

▶ **5.8** In addition to aiming for LEED-NC Silver certification, the Luma building designed by Williams and Dame in conjunction with Gerding Edlen, will be part of an environmentally friendly, high-density, pedestrian-oriented development in Los Angeles' South Park neighborhood. Courtesy of Gerding Edlen.

the office building market, and about nearly half the size of the education market. As a large and growing green building market segment, it deserves careful attention from design firm marketers.

HIGH-RISE HOUSING

As a specialized market segment for green buildings, housing is just starting to develop. Multiple-unit (above three stories) residential LEED registrations are running at about 3.5 percent of the total, or about 175 of the initial 5,000 registrations through February 2007. The first LEED-Gold high-rise apartment project, *The Solaire* in New York City, was certified at the end of 2003. Another New York City high-rise apartment, *The Helena*, was certified at LEED Gold in 2005. In Portland, Oregon, *The Henry*, a 16-story condominium project, was certified at LEED Silver in 2004. A 16-story apartment building in Portland, *The Louisa*, was certified at LEED Gold in 2007.[23] It is ironic that two very dissimilar

▶ **5.9** Unico's Cobb Building in Seattle, built in 1910, demonstrates that sustainable features can be incorporated in a historic renovation project. The building is aiming for LEED-NC certification. Photography by Young Lee Courtesy of Unico.

cities, New York and Portland, Oregon, host the earliest (and most successful) high-rise LEED residential buildings, but many other cities are developing similar projects.

The same Portland developer who built the Louisa and the Henry has now focused on building green high-rise residential projects in Los Angeles, as shown in a five condominium tower complex under construction in 2007 just south of downtown Los Angeles. Shown in Figure 5.8, the South Park development plans to create a new mixed-use urban neighborhood. This development represents the first housing built in downtown Los Angeles in 20 years.[24] All of the buildings in South Park are to be at least LEED certified, some at higher levels. The $320 million development includes 1.5 million square feet (138,000 sqm) of residential and commercial space and nearly 1,500 new urban residences.

Another type of urban housing project comes from building conversions. Seattle developer Unico Properties took a 1910 Historic Register building, the first medical office building in the West, at a prime downtown location and converted it into 91 luxury apartment units. Completed in the summer of 2006 and 85 percent pre-leased, the project expects to receive LEED Silver certification in 2007. Shown in Figure 5.9, the 97-year-old Cobb building includes a number of green and sustainable components included in the 11-story, 93,000 square foot (8,500 sqm) building redesign, including cleaner indoor air, water savings, Energy Star appliances, noise reduction, use of environmentally friendly outdoor gardens and products, recycling programs, and access to a Flexcar car-sharing service and public transportation.[25]

Based on April 2007 data, LEED has certified only 30 private-sector housing projects, including a number of campus residential halls, so this segment of the market is still very early in development, but should grow quite rapidly as the movement back into the urban downtown areas accelerates over the next few years.

NOTES

1   *Education Green Building SmartMarket Report*, McGraw-Hill Construction Research&Analytics,2007,www.construction.com/greensource/resources/smartmarket.asp, reprinted with permission.
2   US Green Building Council [online], www.usgbc.org (accessed April), author's analysis of LEED-certified projects from versions 2.0 and 2.1.
3   Information supplied by BNIM Architects, www.bnim.com.
4   Mid-state Electric Cooperative [online], www.midstateelectric.coop/About/LEEDBuilding/ (accessed April 26, 2007).
5   US Census Bureau, "Monthly Construction Starts," www.census.gov/const/C30/release.pdf (accessed April 26, 2007).
6   Available at: www.turnerconstruction.com/greensurvey.05.pdf.
7   *Education Green Building SmartMarket Report*, McGraw-Hill Construction Research & Analytics, 2007, www.construction.com/greensource/resources/smartmarket.asp (accessed April 26, 2007).
8   Capital E, www.cap-e.com/ewebeditpro/items/O59F11233.pdf (accessed April 3, 2007).
9   US Green Building Council press release, www.usgbc.org/News/PressReleaseDetails.aspx?ID=2899 (accessed April 18, 2007).
10 US Green Building Council, press release, www.usgbc.org/News/PressReleaseDetails.aspx?ID=3018 (accessed April 18, 2007).
11 Higher education green building proprietary survey conducted by the author, March 2004, with nearly 200 respondents.
12 Busby Perkins+Will [online], www.busbyperkinswill.ca/clients/UnivofVictoriaComputerScience/index.htm (accessed April 26, 2007).
13 See, for example, the Association for the Advancement of Sustainability in Higher Education (www.aashe.org) and Engineers for a Sustainable World (www.esustainableworld.org).

14 See, for example, *Campus Sustainability and Green Building*, Environmental Studies Department, Lewis and Clark College, Portland, Oregon, www.lclark.edu/dept/esm/green_building.html.

15 USGBC, "LEED Initiatives in Governments and Schools," March 2007, https://www.usgbc.org/ShowFile.aspx?DocumentID=691 (accessed April 1, 2007).

16 www.rsmeans.com/costdata/index.asp (accessed April 26, 2006).

17 A good example is the Office of Sustainability Initiatives at Arizona State University in Tempe, www.asu.edu/sustainability.

18 Federal Energy Management Program [online], www.eere.energy.gov/femp (accessed April 26, 2006).

19 SmithGroup press release, April 4, 2007. See the National Renewable Energy Laboratory [online], www.nrel.gov/features/07-04_science_tech_facility.html (accessed April 23, 2007).

20 Nancy B. Solomon, "Environmentally-Friendly Building Strategies Slowly Make Their Way into Medical Facilities," *Architectural Record*, August 2004, 179–186.

21 See Gail Vittori, "Green and Healthy Buildings for the Healthcare Industry," 2002 presentation [online], www.cleanmed.org/2002/downloads.html.

22 See Penny Bonda, "Putting the Healthy Back into Healthcare," [online], *Green at Work* magazine, January/February 2004, www.greenatworkmag.com.

23 Scott Lewis, Brightworks Northwest, Personal communication.

24 Gerding Edlen Development [online], ww.gerdingedlen.com/project.php?id=4 (accessed April 26, 2007).

25 Unico Properties [online], www.unicoprop.com/documents/news/2006/MFTJulyAug%2017-18.pdf (accessed April 26, 2007).

6

SPECIALTY MARKETS FOR SUSTAINABLE DESIGN

In the last chapter, we addressed several important vertical markets for green buildings, markets that are already developed or that are expected to develop rapidly or into major segments. These included commercial offices, K-12 education, higher education, public facilities and healthcare. Specialty markets for green buildings exist in most areas of the country, so it makes sense to look at how these markets view green buildings at the present time and how marketers are trying to address the needs of particular building types.

Remember two key facts when addressing each of these markets: at the end of 2006, relatively few architects had designed a LEED-certified building, and relatively few owners had purchased one. Therefore, we are still very much in the innovator or early adopter stage of market development for most project types except commercial offices, government buildings and education. The same is true, even more so for specialty markets. In this chapter we will take a brief look at the marketing opportunities in some of these: commercial interiors, existing building upgrades, urban planning, mixed-use, retail, hotels and resorts, sports facilities, airports and the Canadian market. Some of these markets are of course quite large, but they are lagging behind other sectors in considering green building.

GREEN COMMERCIAL INTERIORS

Green commercial interiors is a field coming into its own. Most of the focus of green design to date has been on new construction and major renovations of typically large buildings. For example, the average size of LEED-certified buildings is about 110,000 square feet (10,000 sqm). Yet most commercial interiors projects are smaller and take place in a shorter time frame, compared with the design and construction of new buildings. Nevertheless, there are important business drivers for green commercial interiors, shown in Table 6.1.

An additional complicating factor is cost, most landlords have fixed allowances for tenant improvements. A tenant exceeding those allowances must pay for them from its own budget. Despite these limitations, the growth of green

Table 6.1   Key business drivers for green commercial interiors

• Saving money in building operations, particularly if sub-metered
• Shows employees that healthy, productive workspaces are important to the company – aids both recruitment and retention
• Public relations and marketing benefits of LEED certification
• Productivity from improved lighting systems and controls

commercial interiors has been robust. Let's look at the LEED standard and consider how an architectural firm might go about marketing these projects.

LEED for Commercial Interiors

The LEED-CI standard version 2.0 has been available for use by project teams since November 2004. Through the first three months of 2007, nearly 600 projects had registered and 110 had been certified, representing a total of more than 30 million square feet (2,750,000 sqm) of tenant improvement projects, or about 52,000 square feet (4,800 sqm) per registered project.[1] In a typical building, this size would represent about two floors of commercial interior remodeling.

LEED-CI may affect both new construction and building remodels for new tenants who want to meet the higher standard. For new construction, the USGBC foresees that developers who certify buildings under the LEED-CS standard will also want to specify or recommend that their tenants meet the LEED-CI standard as well. In retail settings, individual stores may want to use LEED-CI as a rating system to assess and advertise their "greenness."

As with LEED for New Construction, LEED-CI follows the same basic five-category format (plus a category for innovation and design process), but with fewer overall credit categories and fewer total points. For example, LEED-CI has only a maximum of 57 attainable points vs. 69 for LEED-NC. In this rating standard, the focus is more on furniture and furnishings, lighting and occupancy controls, overall power use of office equipment and lighting, and other factors that might fall under the scope of a typical tenant improvement process. Figure 6.1 shows the five LEED-CI core categories and their relative weighting.

In terms of professional services, the beneficiaries of LEED-CI are likely to be architects and interior designers first, then also mechanical and electrical engineers advising them on tenant improvements, as well as the green building consultants who will assess the referenced sustainability measures and then document the project. As with LEED-NC, there are points available for using significant amounts of certified wood, rapidly renewable materials, and recycled or salvaged furniture and furnishings.

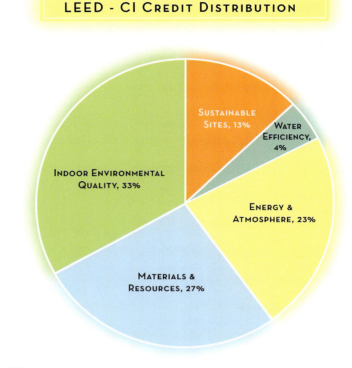

LEED - CI CREDIT DISTRIBUTION

Sustainable Sites, 13%

Water Efficiency, 4%

Indoor Environmental Quality, 33%

Energy & Atmosphere, 23%

Materials & Resources, 27%

▲ **6.1**   LEED-CI credit categories.

In our estimation, LEED-CI is a very workable standard and is likely to see considerable use both in tenant improvements in new Core and Shell buildings and in remodels of existing buildings. The demand is likely to be strong from corporate users who will see an opportunity to pick up some "sustainability" credits and secure the business benefits of productivity and health gains, while not spending a lot more than a traditional tenant improvement project would cost. However, since the individuals at architecture and interiors firms who will have to sell the LEED-CI program tend to be different than those involved in new construction, each interior design firm should have its people accredited under the LEED-CI examination for LEED APs.[2]

Figure 6.2 shows the 29,000 square foot (2,663 sqm) Haworth showroom in Chicago, designed by Perkins + Will as a LEED-CI Gold-certified project.

▲ **6.2**   Designed by Perkins+Will, the 29,000 square feet Haworth Chicago showroom is LEED-CI Gold certified. Photography by Bob Shimer, Hedrich Blessing.

With these criteria and caveats in mind, let's look at some of the typical measures that architects and interior designers might use to bring sustainable design principles to a commercial interiors project:

- Location is important, to give employees options other than auto commuting, as is providing bicycle lockers and showers for those who walk or bike. Of course, selecting a LEED-CS-certified building is the best location decision!
- Water use can be reduced by working with the landlord to change out older water-using fixtures for newer low-flush toilets and water-free urinals.
- Energy use can be reduced through re-lamping, better lighting controls and selecting only Energy Star office equipment and computers. A client can

work with the landlord to install sub-meters and only pay for actual electricity use, instead of a pro-rated share of total use. Occupancy sensors can turn off equipment when no one is around.

- For materials and resources, look at buying high-recycled-content, locally produced materials wherever possible, including any new furniture. Consider using furniture and furnishings made with agricultural fiberboards, cork, bamboo or linoleum. Specify Forest Stewardship Council (FSC) certified lumber or composite wood products when possible.
- Indoor environmental quality can be affected by operable windows, use of low-toxic finishes, choice of low-emitting carpets and cabinetry, careful attention to indoor air quality during construction, supplying individual lighting and ventilation controls where possible, and creating view corridors so that everyone can see outdoors from their workplaces. Plants inside the workspace can help clean the air and lift the spirit.

From this brief rendition, it is clear that many professional disciplines can contribute to a LEED-CI project, including architects, interior designers, mechanical engineers, lighting designers, electrical engineers and even landscape architects. Since most projects happen fast, it is important for a firm to do its homework ahead of time and come equipped with standard approaches and specifications that can meet clients' budget and schedule needs.

EXISTING BUILDING SUSTAINABILITY UPGRADES

Green building advocates realized early on that existing developments represented a major opportunity for achieving energy and water savings and reducing the overall environmental impacts of building operations. After all, in any five-year period, new construction and major renovations deal with only a fraction of the existing building stock. As a result, the USGBC created the LEED-EB, standard, in 2004, as a means to benchmark building operations against a variety of sustainability criteria. By the end of 2006, nearly 250 projects had registered to participate in LEED-EB, and more than 40 had been certified. Compared with the success of the LEED-NC program, this program has had a slow start. Nevertheless, there is considerable evidence that the LEED-EB program is poised to take off, as more organizations track their carbon footprint and attempt to reduce it.

Of course, building owners have long been reducing their buildings' energy use, especially through the federal Energy Star program for commercial buildings. Energy Star benchmarks energy use, in terms of BTUs per year per square foot, for buildings of a similar type within the same climatic region. By the end of 2006, Energy Star awarded ratings to about 3,200 buildings, representing 575 million square feet in all 50 states.[3] An Energy Star designation indicates that a building is in the top 25 percent of all similar buildings for lowest annual energy use per square foot.[4] Overall, Energy Star-rated buildings use about 35 percent less energy than similar buildings.

At the national government level, the FEMP has been in place since 1973. At present, federal agencies are tasked to reduce their energy use by 35 percent by 2010 compared to 1985 levels.[5] Many state and local governments have had similar programs for many years. Reducing energy use is a clear payoff for most government agencies and many private businesses, because the ROI is very high, especially at the beginning, when programs can capture the easiest retrofits. In recent years, there has been a strong effort to reduce lighting energy use and associated cooling demands, by replacing incandescent with fluorescent bulbs, especially compact fluorescents. And, of course, many people are familiar with the demand–reduction programs of most electric utilities, which offer incentive payments and technical assistance to both businesses and consumers.

The commercial office building industry spends approximately $24 billion annually on energy and contributes 18 percent of US carbon dioxide emissions. Energy represents the single largest operating expense for office buildings, typically a third of variable expenses.[6] In 2006, recognizing the need to assist building owners and managers to reduce energy use, Building Owners and Managers Association (BOMA) International, the trade group representing 16,500 members from this sector launched the BOMA Energy Efficiency Program (BEEP), to provide education for its members to learn about energy-efficiency upgrades. According to BOMA International, if only 2,000 buildings adopt BEEP's no- and low-cost best practices over the next three years, energy consumption and carbon emissions will be reduced by 10 percent, resulting in $400 million in energy savings and 6.6 billion pounds less carbon dioxide released into the atmosphere.[7]

For energy-efficiency upgrades in commercial buildings, there is a federal tax deduction of $1.80 per square foot for energy-efficiency measures in new or existing buildings that save at least 50 percent of heating and cooling energy, using a 2001 performance standard referenced in the 2005 Energy Policy Act. Separate partial credits of $0.60 per square foot are available for measures affecting only one of three systems: lighting, HVAC and building envelope (insulation and glazing) upgrades. For public agency buildings, the law allows the design team to take the deduction, since governments don't pay taxes.[8] (This is a unique example of a situation in which a design or engineering firm could do well for a client that is a government agency, and not have to charge any fees, except as a bridge to the future tax deduction.) In the commercial sector, for example, energy-saving renovations in a 500,000 square foot commercial structure that met the requirements of the law could create a $900,000 tax deduction for the building owner. At a 30 percent marginal tax rate, that amount could be worth $270,000, or about $0.54 per square foot.

LEED for Existing Buildings

But energy savings alone don't make for green operations. The LEED-EB standard encourages facility managers and building owners to broaden their horizons to include other issues:

- Increased health of building occupants, through better indoor air quality.
- Lower water use, with savings on utility bills.
- Greater recycling efforts, with reduced waste disposal costs.
- Reduction in the use of toxic materials, both inside and outside buildings, to improve worker health and productivity.
- Lower overall operations and maintenance costs.

Figure 6.3 shows the relative weightings of the LEED-EB credit categories. From this chart, one can see the large importance of energy-efficiency and related measures (nearly 30 percent of the total). There are a large number of actions that any facility, office or factory can take to create a healthier and more

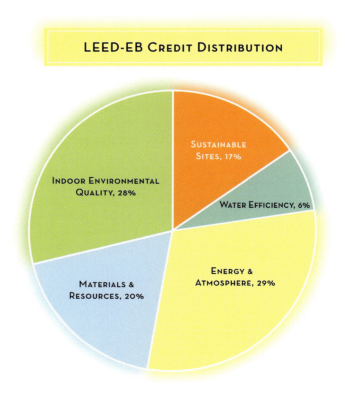

LEED-EB CREDIT DISTRIBUTION

SUSTAINABLE SITES, 17%

WATER EFFICIENCY, 6%

ENERGY & ATMOSPHERE, 29%

MATERIALS & RESOURCES, 20%

INDOOR ENVIRONMENTAL QUALITY, 28%

▲ **6.3**   LEED-EB credit categories.

resource-efficient place to work. LEED-EB can be used as a benchmarking and rating system to assess both current performance and annual improvements. The most difficult part of the journey is just getting started, because most of these changes cut across departmental lines and require coordination among many levels of the organization.

A successful LEED-EB project

A good private sector example of the benefits from using the LEED-EB program is the Platinum certification of three buildings at the headquarters of Adobe Systems, a software maker in San Jose, California. To demonstrate its commitment to environmental stewardship, an important public issue in the Bay Area of California, Adobe decided to invest $1.1 million over five years to turn its three existing office towers – ranging in age from 3 to 10 years and totaling almost one million square feet of offices and nearly the same amount of garage space – into an environmentally friendly campus and chose the LEED-EB program to do it.

From 2001 to 2006, Adobe reduced electricity use by 35 percent, natural gas use by 41 percent, building water use by 22 percent and irrigation water use by 75 percent. Through saving energy and buying green power, Adobe reduced pollutant emissions by 26 percent. By the company's own reckoning, the projects resulted in an overall 114 percent ROI. Retrofit and upgrade projects include reduced lighting energy use; the addition of motion sensors to turn off lights and HVAC equipment when spaces are unoccupied; installation of variable-speed drives on pumps and fans to match supply to demand; real-time metering to reduce electricity bills by avoiding power use during peak periods; upgraded building automation and control systems; and recommissioning of major energy-using systems.[9] While these measures all involve energy and water use, much of the project leadership could have come from an integrated A/E team and should provide a model for firms seeking to market LEED-EB projects to corporate and institutional clients.

From the example of Adobe Systems and other successful LEED-EB projects, we can draw some ideas about the key business drivers for sustainable operations and maintenance programs, as shown in Table 6.2.

Table 6.2 Key business drivers for sustainable operations programs and LEED-EB

• Operations savings for energy and water stemming from the recommissioning program required by LEED-EB
• Reduced costs from less use of chemicals in building maintenance and less waste generation
• Public relations and marketing benefits
• Increased productivity and health of employees
• Demonstrated evidence of corporate sustainability commitment
• Benchmarking sustainability efforts, including reducing carbon footprint

Higher education offers considerable opportunities to apply LEED-EB to an entire campus as part of a long-term facilities planning effort. For example, in December 2006, the University of California, Santa Barbara campus, agreed to use LEED-EB to assess 25 buildings over the next five years.[10] Marketers should become familiar with this particular commitment and use it to approach other educational and public sector clients with proposals for similar long-term LEED-EB projects.

Barriers to greener building operations

Many LEED-EB case studies demonstrate substantial savings and other benefits from a comprehensive evaluation and retrofit program at large facilities. So, what's holding everyone back? The most significant reason is that it is always hard to get money for operations and maintenance in most companies and institutions. In public agencies, the split between capital and operating budgets means that facility managers and building operators need to argue their case every year for enough money to operate their buildings, making it even more difficult to get new investments in longer-term savings programs.

Private building ownership is also fractured, with a split many times between ownership and operations. Specialized building operations and maintenance firms typically get a percentage of rents to operate buildings. Any other investments need to be sought from the owners. According to BOMA, 41 percent of all building owners operate fewer than six buildings, making discretionary investments more difficult. Only 17 percent of all properties are owned by firms with more than 50 holdings; but these firms are more likely to have access to capital and to see the broader benefits of green upgrades and operations. For a design firm they should be the first marketing prospects.[11]

One major barrier to existing building sustainability beyond energy-efficiency measures is that, without a comprehensive corporate or institutional commitment to sustainability, it is difficult for the facility manager or sustainability director, someone lower on the corporate "food chain," to get the funds required for a good LEED-EB certification effort. In commercial real estate, the often-divided responsibilities between owners and tenants make it difficult to have the dialog necessary for a LEED-EB upgrade. Wherever there is a long-term lease with a single tenant, design firms often can lead the effort for a LEED-EB project, making it easier for the property owner to see the returns from a certification effort.

URBAN PLANNING AND DESIGN

Urban planning is a new frontier for sustainable design. The design of subdivisions, neighborhoods, urban districts and entire new cities offers major new opportunities for architects, planners and civil engineers engaged in urban planning, transit-oriented development, new urbanism, town planning and similar activities. More than 25 years of development of such concepts as new urbanism and transit-oriented development provide a strong foundation for assessing sustainability of these new planning and design approaches. Mastery of new assessment methods, rating systems and planning tools will allow architects, planners and engineers to successfully market these services to an emerging client base of municipalities and private clients. As one example, the new LEED for Neighborhood Development (LEED-ND) rating system offers opportunities for those who master it and can persuade clients to apply the program to their developments.

LEED for Neighborhood Development

Along with the Congress for the New Urbanism and the Natural Resources Defense Council, the USGBC launched the LEED-ND pilot program in 2007. LEED-ND integrates the principles of green buildings, smart growth and new urbanism into the first national US rating system for neighborhood design. Enrolling about 240 projects in the pilot program, LEED-ND will assess, rate and certify the elements constituting green development on a broader scale than just one building. USGBC expects to release version 2.0 of LEED-ND in November of 2008, so it is not too early to begin preparing for that marketing opportunity.

LEED-ND can be applied to mixed-use developments, urban infill housing and commercial projects, new urban villages on remediated brownfield sites, corporate campuses and to residential projects with densities of greater than eight housing units per buildable acre (20 units per buildable hectare) and walkable distances to commercial centers.

The LEED-ND system focuses on best practices in four key areas affecting residential, commercial and mixed-use development:

1. Smart site selection, including links to transportation systems.
2. Environmental preservation and restoration of selected sites.
3. Design of compact, complete, walkable and connected neighborhoods.
4. Specifying and installing high-performance green technologies and buildings.

The goal of LEED-ND is to develop and redevelop cities and communities that are healthier, use far less energy and water and have a much lower impact on natural habitats. By 2012, we expect version 2.0 of LEED-ND to be used worldwide to define and create the first generation of zero-net-energy communities. Look for this trend to become a small wave by 2012 and a much larger flood by 2015. Table 6.3 presents some potential business benefits of a LEED-ND certification.

Table 6.3   Potential business benefits of LEED-ND certification

1. Public relations for new developments
2. Marketing benefits to prospective office tenants and residents
3. Use of local government green building incentives
4. Attract financing to the development, both debt and equity
5. Faster lease-up and/or sale of properties
6. Reduced fees for infrastructure investments
7. Possible reduction in sizing (and cost) of heating and cooling systems from combining residential and commercial uses
8. Creation of demand for on-site power systems, including cogeneration

Because of the extended duration of most large developments, architects, planners and engineers should begin promoting the LEED-ND system now to clients, so that enough projects can be completed and certified in 2010–2012 time frame, to give the design and planning firm a competitive advantage as the sustainability wave both broadens and deepens its effects.

Sustainable master planning

Sustainable master plans for college campuses and urban districts are just beginning to appear. They deal with most of the LEED-ND issues but in a practical framework, including the realities of campus budgeting and the economics of real estate development. Their goal is to chart a path from today's world toward a more sustainable future. Much of the time, these projects grow out of initial green building efforts, with a goal toward knitting together planning for such diverse themes as:

- transportation;
- land use and stormwater management;
- energy supply, reuse of waste heat and renewable energy development;
- water supply and wastewater treatment/reuse;
- housing and commercial development;
- habitat preservation and restoration.

Sustainable urban planning is an emerging discipline that knits together the activities of architects, planners, engineers, energy specialists, economists, financiers, city government or campus leadership, and futurists to define a sustainable future and a workable pathway toward it. In this way, sustainable master planning blends the activities of new urbanists with those of ecological planners. Campus master planning looks at such areas as new green buildings; building remodels and renovations; chemical use in maintenance and operations; sustainable housing and retail services; water supply; waste management; energy supply; recycling, environmentally preferable purchasing; and food service and transportation, to arrive at a more sustainable future, with lower total cost of operations.[12]

Some good examples of sustainable urban master planning have been completed since 2000: Southeast False Creek series of studies in Vancouver, British Columbia;[13] Resource Guide for Sustainable Development, for the South Lake Union Planning Study in Seattle; and the Lloyd District Sustainable Urban Design Plan in Portland, Oregon.[14] Each of these studies builds on prior work with the Portland plan serving now as a model for future planning. In the Lloyd District plan, the goal was to define a pathway to 2050, so that the ecological impacts of urban settlement would be no greater than those of 1850, roughly corresponding to "pre-development conditions." The study looked at such impacts as carbon dioxide generation similar to a native forest, habitat vitality, water supply solely from natural rainfall, energy supply solely from sun and wind, and waste management at 100 percent recycling levels, all in the context of an economically viable community. The result of the Lloyd Crossing plan was that there was a feasible pathway, both technically and financially, to the desired sustainability goal, but one that would require both long-term political commitment by the city and creation of some new organizational structures for financing the conservation and on-site energy systems. For various reasons the study results have not yet been implemented in Portland.

Each of these studies requires advance planning and often selling of the idea of a study to public decision-makers, well in advance of an actual request for proposal. By utilizing the results of previous studies to show what's possible, planning, design and development firms can often excite interest among public agencies and master developers in financing or cost-sharing such a study. This can then lead the way to future work in infrastructure planning and building design.

MIXED-USE DEVELOPMENT

Mixed-use projects encompass real estate developments with planned integration of some combination of retail, office, residential, hotel, recreation or other functions. A 2006 survey sponsored by four real estate development organizations found that more than 25 percent of members' business was already in mixed-use projects, with 35 percent saying that it accounted for more than half their business.[15] Clearly, multiple-use projects are an important component of today's business environment. For developers, mixed-use development almost always emphasizes pedestrian-oriented designs, combines elements of a live-work–play environment and maximizes space utilization. It often features such amenities as parks and other forms of open space, has significant architectural expression and reduces traffic congestion.

Most architects, city planners and developers expect mixed-use projects to grow in importance in the next five years, primarily because cities are encouraging such development by helping private developers with planning and zoning decisions, incentive programs and, in some cases, assembling land. Rising urban land prices and many urbanites' growing desire to integrate home, work and play also play a key role. One major downside to mixed-use development is the extended time it may take to put all the pieces together and the greater financial risk of a phased development of disparate project elements.

Another type of green mixed-use urban development is rising in Las Vegas, Nevada. The MGM CityCenter project is a huge, 76-acre, city within a city on the Las Vegas Strip. CityCenter anticipates opening in 2009 with a 60-story, 4,000-room hotel and casino along with two 400-room boutique hotels and 500,000 square feet of retail, along with 2,800 residential units. As the largest new mixed-use development in the US, with some 18 million square feet of space and an investment valued at $7 billion, CityCenter is a major undertaking.[16] All buildings except the casino are expected to receive at least LEED Silver certification, owing in large measure to some generous state property tax abatements.[17]

The Noisette Community: a green mixed-use project

In the face of these uncertainties, there are more green mixed-use projects in cities than one might suspect. As an example, consider the Noisette Community. The dream of one man, developer John Knott,[18] the Noisette Community in North Charleston, South Carolina, shown in Figure 6.4 is transforming 3,000 acres into a "city within a city." In the late 1990s, the city and the developer agreed on a public–private partnership to transform 400 acres of an abandoned naval base (closed in 1996) into a vibrant mixed-use community, using an unprecedented master planning effort.

After a five-year planning effort, in 2004 the city gave the developer the green light to begin transforming the military facility into a community. The Noisette plan encourages increased density, walking-distance access between neighborhoods and public and commercial resources, improved and integrated transit options, reduced and slower traffic flow, expanded open space and recreational options, and reestablishment of community links to major environmental assets like the adjacent Cooper River. The state's first LEED-certified elementary school is part of the redevelopment effort. Noisette is directly responsible for developing about 3,000 new housing units and 2 million square feet of new commercial space.[19]

GREENING THE RETAIL SECTOR

Each element of green mixed-use design needs to come together to create the full picture. Two elements that have been lagging are the retail and hospitality

▲ **6.4** A 3,000 acre city within a city located in Charleston, South Carolina, Noisette is modeled on the belief that cities must be equally responsive to social needs, environmental responsibility and economic vitality. Rendering courtesy of Burt Hill.

industries, yet even there, we can see some promising trends and exemplary developments. As of March 2007, about 75 retail projects were registered for LEED certification including a number of grocery stores. Starbucks has LEED-certified its first retail store. Figure 6.5 shows the details of this green proto-type store of the future.

In December of 2006, Forest City Commercial Group opened Northfield Stapleton, a 1.2 million square foot open-air town center in Denver, Colorado, as part of the redevelopment of the former Denver Airport. According to the developer, the center is the first "Main Street" style property to receive the LEED-CS Silver certification. [20]

Abercorn Common in Savannah, Georgia, is a green retail development that boasts the nation's first LEED-certified McDonald's. In 2006, the project became the first retail LEED-CS-certified project in the country, achieving the Silver level of performance.[21] The retail space reduces energy consumption about 30 percent, with such measures as solar water heating and a green roof. Harvested rainwater provides 5.5 million gallons a year of irrigation water, the project's entire requirement.[22]

There are many other examples of retail projects pursuing LEED certifica-tion, either as LEED-NC stand-alone projects, or as LEED-CI projects inside of a larger building. In the Mid-Atlantic region, PNC Bank has already certified

▲ **6.5** Certified at the LEED-NC Gold level, this Starbuck's store in Hillsboro, Oregon is a prototype for future volume-build for future stores. Sustainable measures include:
1. Cabinetry made from 90 percent post-industrial material, with no added formaldehyde.
2. Efficient lights that use less energy.
3. Paints with lower amounts of volatile organic compounds.
4. Eco-Terr® flooring tiles made from 70 percent post-consumer recycled content, 10 percent post-industrial content.
5. Store designed to capture available natural daylight.
Courtesy of Starbucks.

nearly 40 branch bank offices and has committed to LEED certification for all future branches.[23] Gary Saulson, Director of Corporate Real Estate at PNC Financial Services, has led PNC's efforts to green its branch locations across the country, and developed a prototype program for bulk LEED certifications that he hopes will result in more than 100 LEED bank branches by 2007.[24]

To facilitate retail project certification, the USGBC has developed its "volume-build" program that allows a retailer to have one review for all aspects of a prototype building that won't ever change (materials, indoor environment, water use and some energy use) and then only submit and document credits for specific site and energy issues. This approach cuts the cost of LEED certification and provides certainty of outcome, essential elements of any retail project.

Showing what is possible for big box retailers; Lowe's built a large-format retail store in south Austin, Texas, receiving a LEED Gold rating in 2006. The store's green design and construction practices resulted in indoor water savings of 47 percent; energy savings greater than 50 percent; a rainwater collection system that eliminates the use of potable water for landscape irrigation and reduces the use of potable water in the garden center; more than 90 percent of construction waste diverted from the landfill and a commitment to purchase green power (energy produced by renewable sources) for half of the store's utility needs.[25]

GREEN HOTELS AND RESORTS

Green hotels are beginning to be accredited under the LEED standard. As of March 2007, 22 hotels were registered under the LEED-NC system for future certification.[26] The first LEED-certified hotel was the University of Maryland University College (UMUC) Inn & Conference Center, operated by Marriott International, which received its designation in 2005. A 226-room Hilton Hotel in Vancouver, Washington, owned by the city, received a LEED Silver designation in 2006. In this case, the cost premium was less than $1,000 per room, easily recouped in the first year on energy savings. According to the hotel, the free publicity was worth 10 times the initial cost premium.[27] The Orchard Garden Hotel received LEED certification for a San Francisco property that opened in late 2006. Design firms with hospitality industry clients should be actively bringing these examples to them, as the interest in green hotels is growing rapidly.

Both retail and hospitality projects can derive substantial business benefits from greening their new properties as well as their existing operations, as shown in Table 6.4.

Shown in Figure 6.6, the Loreto Bay resort community in desert of the Baja California peninsula is a master-planned green resort, based on principles of new urbanism and green building. The intention is to create a model community

Table 6.4   Business drivers for green retail and hospitality projects

• Save money in operations; cut energy costs, especially in peak periods
• Public relations benefits for the customer base
• Marketing benefits for the firm; for hotels, benefits of increased occupancy at the particular property
• For developers, taking advantage of local green building incentives and other state and federal tax benefits for green buildings
• Recruitment and retention of key employees
• For public companies, a better story to tell to Wall Street
• For developers, greater access to equity capital from socially responsible property investing funds

that will demonstrate how human habitation can not only preserve but also improve the surrounding natural environment and contribute to the reversal of global warming present trends. The 8,400-acre (3,500 hectare) site is located in the Sonoran Desert, 210 miles (350 kilometers) north of La Paz, Baja California Sur, Mexico.[28]

► **6.6** A seaside resort community set in the desert of the Baja California peninsula, Loreto Bay aims to demonstrate how human habitation can not only preserve but also improve the surrounding natural environment. Photography by Russ Heinl.

As part of Loreto Bay's commitment to creating a sustainable environment, building construction also incorporates the following mandates:

- Domestic hot water and swimming pool heating will be solar enhanced.
- Low-energy appliances and water-smart fixtures will be installed in all homes and commercial buildings.
- Paints and finishes will contain low- or no VOC levels. Wood coatings are primarily oil stain, shellac and wax.
- Signature buildings such as the Beach Club in the Founder's Village Center will be designed to LEED Platinum. Loreto Bay will also apply for certification with LEED-H and LEED-ND as these programs mature.

Marketing programs aimed at eco-resorts should find receptive clients. Such developments are now being built all over the world. They typically need to provide creative solutions to energy supply, water supply and waste-water management issues found in most resort locations. Green hotels and resorts are becoming increasingly popular with people interested in eco-tourism.[29]

Large public facilities: transportation and sports

Large public facilities such as stadiums and airports are beginning to look at sustainable design as part of the public process for gaining approvals for these very large, multi-year projects. For example, the Washington Nationals new $600 million baseball stadium in the District of Columbia is expected to be a LEED-certified project when it opens in 2008. In Minneapolis, developers of a new stadium for the University of Minnesota and the Minnesota Twins propose to achieve LEED certification for the project when it opens in the fall of 2008.[30] In 2007, SmithGroup published a design for a "sustainable arena of the future," shown in Figure 6.7, powered by renewable energy, using concrete-duct cooled air for comfort, collecting rainwater for all toilet flushing and nonpotable uses, and accessible without the use of a car. This type of sustainable project marketing will become increasingly used to feed the media interest in all things green.[31]

Airport terminals also represent an opportunity for applying green building concepts on a large scale. Resembling hotels without overnight guests, but with a constant flow of traffic, food, water, waste and energy, airport terminals suck up enormous resources and should be converted to fully sustainable facilities. With the continuing growth of air travel, many airport terminals will be built and renovated. Marketers should be on the lookout for sustainable design opportunities, such as the recent LEED-certified terminal at Boston's Logan Airport, for Delta Airlines, shown in Figure 6.8.

Certified in 2006 and the first new airline terminal to be built in the US in five years, the terminal and a satellite concourse comprise more than 700,000

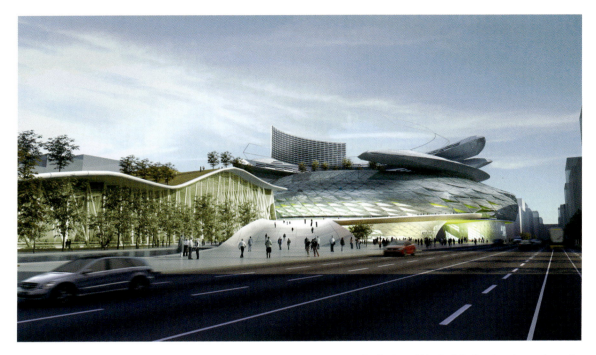

▲ **6.7**   A concept for a sustainable sports complex that would be build in the downtown of a major US city designed by the SmithGroup. Courtesy of SmithGroup.

▶ **6.8**   Featuring public transportation access; heat island mitigation; daylighting; water efficiency, recycled, low VOC materials; and construction waste management, the Delta Air Lines Terminal at Boston's Logan International Airport designed by HOK is LEED-NC certified. Photography by Assassi Productions. Courtesy of HOK.

square feet (64,000 sqm) of space. To combat the accelerated heat island effect and stormwater runoff issues typically caused by impervious surfaces on runways, parking lots and large roofs areas, the terminal features a roofing membrane and paving designed to reflect heat from the building and special stormwater filtration devices to remove suspended solids and total phosphorous. Designed by HOK and built by Skanska, some of the $400 million project's sustainable strategies include: water-efficient plumbing and irrigation; extensive daylighting and high-insulation glass; energy-efficient lighting; high levels of construction waste recycling; and the use of recycled-content, locally manufactured materials.[32]

INTERNATIONAL MARKETS

No discussion of green markets for design firms would be complete without mentioning the growing green building interest exhibited in the international arena, including Canada, China, India, Australia and the United Arab Emirates (UAE). Of course, China, India and UAE host a considerable amount of the world's construction at the moment, with values many times that of the US. Green Building Councils (GBCs) exist in all these countries, each affiliated with the World Green Building Council.[33]

Of course, China does have a small number of LEED-CS and LEED-NC projects certified to US standards and represents project design opportunities for US firms willing to take the risks and spend the time and money to establish a presence in China. The Chinese Government has made a major commitment to green buildings, hosting large annual national green building conferences, beginning in 2005. For the Chinese, the benefits of green buildings are largely found in energy conservation, particularly electricity savings.

Australia also has a robust, but much smaller construction industry, since the country has only about 20 million people. With a green building rating system similar to LEED, Australia has some quite innovative projects.[34] One example is 30 The Bond in Sydney, a project rated at Five Green Stars by the Green Building Council Australia, equivalent to LEED Gold.[35] Shown in Figure 6.9, this project is the Sydney headquarters for Lend Lease, an international development firm. At $112 million (Australian) and nine stories, this project expects to reduce energy use by 30 percent.[36] It features a rooftop garden, natural ventilation, passive chilled-beam cooling, fully operable shading on the façades and a four-story sandstone rock face as thermal mass to cool the atrium.

Canadian market

US firms interested in the Canadian market should consider opening offices in Ontario or British Columbia, the two liveliest markets for green buildings in Canada.[37] Canada also has its own version of LEED, licensed from the

Photo by John Gollings

▶ **6.9** Awarded a 5-star Green Star rating by the Green Building Council of Australia, 30 The Bond has 30 percent lower carbon dioxide emissions than a typical office and uses between 30 and 40 percent less power than today's best-practice buildings. Photography by John Gollings. Courtesy of the Green Building Council of Australia.

USGBC and administered by the Canada Green Building Council, and US firms need to be able to deliver projects that will meet specific Canadian standards; do not assume that the Canadians are willing to accept US LEED certification criteria.

To obtain an understanding of the green building market for US companies in Canada, I managed a survey of 25 organizations in the summer of 2006. We interviewed 10 respondents who were prospective clients or project partners of US companies, including: governments, larger institutional clients such as universities and hospitals, one private developer and other firms that have sought collaborative partners internationally.[38] The consensus among survey respondents are remarks such as "Canada has some talented green building firms," "there are local firms with long-track records and innovative approaches" and, typically, on a project, "local expertise is required in order to have familiarity with institutional culture, as well as laws and regulations specific to the local milieus." Also, Canadian public and private sectors are interested in building green building capacity nationally.

However, not all expertise can be obtained locally, regionally or even nationally in Canada, and US firms have the opportunity to be engaged in partnerships and (less frequently) in sole-source arrangements. Many agencies we interviewed stated that a typical involvement by US firms would be via collaborations rather than as stand-alone providers. However, some agencies expressed a willingness to employ US companies directly. These included: the Greater Vancouver (British Columbia) Regional District, the University of Saskatchewan and the province of New Brunswick.

According to our research, Canadians will collaborate on large-scale projects with firms from the US or other nations, more often than on medium- or small-scale projects, due to the increased expenses and complexities of international collaboration. One private sector respondent stated that his company would "need a significant project to source outside of the country; $20 to $40 million projects at least; such that the client can support travel costs and other reimbursements."

To create an opportunity in a market that is, after all, equal to 10 percent of the US market, a firm must first commit to opening an office in Canada, preferably with a Canadian national at the helm. In addition, the firm must be conversant with cold-weather design; many Canadians we interviewed were deeply skeptical that US designers and engineers were sufficiently interested in energy conservation and knowledgable about HVAC, glazing and building envelope systems that were economically viable in Canada, to be successful project participants. Therefore, the onus is on any firm wanting to work in Canada to demonstrate their capabilities with similar projects in similar climates. This would give the edge to firms working in the Pacific Northwest (for British Columbia projects), the Upper Midwest (for projects in Alberta, Manitoba, Saskatchewan and Western Ontario), and upper New York state and New England (for Eastern Ontario, Quebec and the Maritimes).

NOTES

1   US Green Building Council data furnished to the author, April 2007.
2   US Green Building Council [online] has information on taking the exam to become a LEED AP at www.usgbc.org/DisplayPage.aspx?CMSPageID =1562& (accessed April 23, 2007).
3   Energy Star Program [online], www.energystar.gov/index.cfm?c=business. bus_bldgs (accessed March 29, 2007).

4   Energy Star Program [online], www.energystar.gov (accessed March 29, 2007).

5   Federal Energy Management Program [online], www1.eere.energy.gov/femp/about/index.html (accessed March 29, 2007).

6   Building Owners and Managers Association [online], www.boma.org/AboutBOMA/TheGREEN (accessed March 30, 2007).

7   Building Owners and Managers Association [online], www.boma.org/TrainingAndEducation/BEEP (accessed March 30, 2007).

8   Energy Star Program [online], www.energystar.gov/index.cfm?c=products.pr_tax_credits (accessed March 30, 2007).

9   Adobe Systems [online], www.adobe.com/aboutadobe/pressroom/pressreleases/200607/070306LEED.html (accessed March 29, 2007).

10 University of California, Santa Barbara [online], www.ia.ucsb.edu/pa/display.aspx?pkey=1529 (accessed April 1, 2007).

11 Personal communication, Matthew Fleming, Research Director, BOMA, January 2007.

12 Yudelson Associates [online], "The GIST of Campus Sustainability Planning: Gain Impact. Save Time," prepared for first national conference of the Association for the Advancement of Sustainability in Higher Education, Tempe, Arizona, October 2006, downloadable from http://greenbuildconsult.com/images/uploads/GIST.pdf (accessed April 23, 2007).

13 City of Vancouver, British Columbia [online], www.city.vancouver.bc.ca/commsvcs/southeast/documents/index.htm (accessed April 23, 2007).

14 Mithun [online], www.mithun.com/mithun.htm (accessed April 23, 2007).

15 Personal communication, Sheila Vertino, National Association of Industrial and Office Properties, www.naiop.org, based on a survey commissioned by NAIOP, the International Council of Shopping Centers, the National Multi-Family Housing Council, and the Building Owners and Managers Association, and reported in November 2006.

16 Las Vegas City Center project [online], www.vegasverticals.com/citycenter.html (accessed April 1, 2007).

17 Treehugger Blog [online], www.treehugger.com/files/2007/01/the_huge_cityce.php (accessed April 1, 2007).

18 Noisette Community [online], www.noisettesc.com (accessed March 31, 2007).

19 Noisette Community [online], www.noisettesc.com/press_projectover.html (accessed March 31, 2007).

20 Forest City Enterprises, http://www.forestcity.net/PROPERTIES/northfield-at-stapleton.asp (accessed July 1, 2007).

21 Abercorn Commons [online], www.abercorncommons.com/index.php?option=com_content&task=view&id=20 (accessed March 31, 2007).

22 www.prleap.com/pr/67257 (accessed March 31, 2007).

23 US Green Building Council, LEED certified project listings [online], www. usgbc.org (accessed April 23, 2007).

24 US Green Building Council [online], http://www.usgbc.org/News/ PressReleaseDetails.aspx?ID=2747 (accessed April 23, 2007).

25 PR Newswire [online], http://gbcode.tdctrade.com/gb/tpwebapp.tdctrade. com/prnews/info.asp?catid=13&id=1128655 (accessed April 23, 2007).

26 US Green Building Council [online], https://www.usgbc.org/ShowFile. aspx?DocumentID=2313 (accessed March 31, 2007).

27 Green Lodging News [online], www.greenlodgingnews.com/Content. aspx?id=753 (accessed March 31, 2007).

28 Information furnished by Peter Clark, Sustainability Director for Loreto Bay, April 23, 2007.

29 See, for example, *Travel and Leisure Magazine*, August 2006, www. travelandleisure.com/articles/the-ultimate-green-hotel-august-2006 (accessed April 23, 2007).

30 Green Buildings NYC blog [online], http://www.greenbuildingsnyc.com/? p=125 (accessed April 23, 2007).

31 *Sports Illustrated*, March 12, 2007, pp. 44–45.

32 HOK [online], www.hok.com/news/PressReleases/current/63507125-1422- 77e3-d28c-0edb8ff99c93.htm (accessed April 23, 2007). Skanska press release [online], www.ewire.com/display.cfm/Wire_ID/3239 (accessed April 23, 2007).

33 World Green Building Council [online], www.worldgbc.org.

34 Australia Green Building Council [online], www.gbcaus.org.

35 Green Building Council Australia, "The Dollars and Sense of Green Buildings 2006: Building the Business Case for Green Commercial Buildings in Australia," 2006, Sydney: Green Building Council Australia, p. 20.

36 Architecture Week [online], www.architectureweek.com/2004/0714/ design_1-2.html (accessed April 28, 2007).

37 Canada Green Building Council [online] statistics, www.cagbc.org (accessed March 31, 2007).

38 Survey conducted by Sonja Persram, Sustainable Alternatives Consulting, Toronto [online], www.sustainablealternatives.ca (accessed March 31, 2007).

7 GREEN BUILDING TECHNOLOGIES

This chapter deals with the technology of green buildings in brief. Marketers need to know what types of products, systems and approaches are used in LEED-certified projects, to assist their efforts to differentiate their own services from those of others. For example, as we will discuss later in this chapter, why not make every building "PV ready" (i.e., with a roof that can easily accommodate PV panels) with wiring from the electrical room to the roof and with space in the electrical room for an inverter, to convert the DC-generated power to AC? Why not also design the building's electrical service so that the PV-generated electricity can serve specific daytime loads? Architects and electrical engineers can collaborate on this measure, which could very well have marketing benefits for both.

GREEN ROOFS

Green roofs are becoming increasingly popular, even at costs of $10 to $20 per square foot ($100 to $200 per sqm). On a 10-story building, of course, the effective cost is only $1 to $2 per square foot, or about a 1 percent premium. At that level, a green roof can become a significant building amenity, even divorced from its green building roots. More than 3 million square feet (275,000 sqm) of green roofs were installed in the US and Canada in 2006, a 25 percent growth over 2005.[1] Green roofs can also earn up to eight LEED points for a project team savvy enough to use it for open space and stormwater management. Figure 7.1 shows a green roof project at Evergreen State College in Olympia, Washington. Since 2004, green roofs have been showing up on top of green buildings in cold climates (Chicago, which purportedly has 200 such projects) and hot climates (Phoenix) and everywhere in between.[2] Green building marketers should pay attention to the many public benefits of green roofs and try to get them included in every project's budget.

DEMAND FOR SPECIFIC GREEN BUILDING MEASURES IN LEED-NC CERTIFIED PROJECTS

Using statistics from the USGBC, we can profile specific green building measures that are used by the green building market. The current split of LEED-NC

▶ **7.1** The Evergreen State College campus expansion project features a green roof on the LEED-NC Gold-certified project. Courtesy of DPR Construction.

version 2.1 certified projects is about 41 percent certified, 32 percent Silver, 23 percent Gold and 3 percent Platinum. Higher levels of certification demand more use of specific green building measures. The analysis in Table 7.1 considers only the points gained by LEED-NC version 2.1 Silver projects, just to give a taste of what a building team is likely to do in that situation.

Use of green building measures in LEED-NC-certified projects

Tables 7.1 and 7.2 help a marketer understand not only how to achieve LEED points, but which measures are likely to be used in green building projects. The use of specific green building products and green design measures generally falls into three distinct categories. As the market for higher levels of LEED certification grows, we can expect that certain products in the "somewhat likely" category will be used in more than 67 percent of projects, such as CO_2 monitors, and that certain products such as PV (even though the cost/benefit ratio is high) and FSC certified wood will move into the "somewhat likely" category, because they are more visible signs of commitments to sustainable building measures than others.

Based on the data in Tables 7.1 and 7.2, I estimate in Table 7.3 the market size for various green building measures for a typical year in which 2,000 projects register for LEED certification. This may occur as early as 2008, based on trends emerging in 2007. When creating a high-performance building, with

Table 7.1 Green measures used in LEED-NC version 2.1 Silver-certified projects[3]

Highly likely to be used (67% or more of projects)
Low-VOC paints, coatings, adhesives, sealants
Low-VOC carpeting
20% or more recycled-content materials
20% or more local/regional materials
Proper site selection, avoiding environmentally sensitive areas
Three innovation credits: public education, 95% construction waste recycling and 40% water conservation
Somewhat likely to be used (33–66% of projects)
Daylighting 75% of spaces and views to the outdoors from 90% of spaces
Construction period indoor air quality maintenance
Permanent temperature and humidity monitoring systems
Purchased green power for at least 2 years
30% improvement in fresh air ventilation; underfloor air systems
Two-week building flushout prior to occupancy
Carbon-dioxide monitors to improve ventilation effectiveness
Bioswales, detention/retention ponds and/or rainwater reclamation systems
Green roofs or Energy Star roofs
Reduce urban heat island effect with site shading, reflective hardscape
Site restoration with native plants
Cutoff light fixtures and lower outdoor ambient lighting levels
30% water conservation through low-water-use fixtures and water-free urinals
35–40% energy use reduction over ASHRAE 90.1-1999 modeled levels
Additional building commissioning: peer review of design-phase documents
No added urea-formaldehyde (UF) in composite wood or agrifiber products
Less often used (less than 33% of projects)
Alternative fuel vehicles (hybrids, natural gas, electric)
Measurement and verification systems, using US Department of Energy Protocols
Solar PV
Use of FSC-certified wood products
Operable windows and individual control of lighting and ventilation
Use of rapidly renewable materials, such as cork, bamboo, agrifiber boards, linoleum

high levels of energy efficiency without sacrificing indoor air quality or thermal comfort, architects and engineers will use many new green building products, systems and design approaches. Two of the most important emerging green technologies are green roofs and solar power, dealt with specifically in this chapter.

Table 7.2 Specific LEED-NC version 2.1 points used by Silver-certified projects[4]

LEED Credit Category	Percentage of Certified Projects	Typical Measures Used to Meet Point Requirements
SS 4.3 – Alternative fuels	29	Electric vehicle charging; hybrids; low-emission cars
SS 5.2 – Site restoration	56	Preserve habitat; use native vegetation
SS 6.1 – Stormwater management	40	Bioswales; detention ponds; rainwater capture and recycling
SS 7.2 – Urban heat island effect	63	Green (vegetated) roofs; Energy Star roofs with high emissivity
SS 8 – Light pollution reduction	44	Cutoff fixtures; lower nighttime ambient lighting
WE 3.2 – 30% water use reduction	62	Low-use fixtures; water-free urinals
EA 1.2 – Average project achieved 35–40% reduction in energy use	50	High-performance glazing; reduced ambient lighting levels; better building envelope
EA 2.2 – 10% renewables for electricity use	5	PV; on-site renewables
EA 3 – Additional commissioning	50	Third-party commissioning
EA 5 – Measurement/verification	23	Additional energy monitoring
EA 6 – Purchased green power	45	Buy green power for 2 years
MR 4.2 – 10% recycled content materials	73	Specify recycled-content materials
MR 6 – Rapidly renewable materials	4	Cork; linoleum; agrifiber MDF board
MR 7 – 50% use of certified wood	19	FSC-certified lumber
EQ 1 – Carbon dioxide monitors	59	CO_2 monitors
EQ 2 – High-efficiency ventilation	35	Underfloor air systems
EQ 3.1 – Construction IAQ	55	Best practices/MERV-13 filters
EQ 3.2 – Air quality at occupancy	55	Two-week flush-out before occupancy
EQ 4.1/4.2 – Low-VOC coatings	79	Specify low-VOC materials
EQ 4.3 – Low-emission carpeting	90	Specify low-VOC carpeting
EQ 4.4 – No UF in composite wood	46	No added urea-formaldehyde in composites
EQ 6.1 – Thermal comfort (perimeter)	23	Operable windows
EQ 6.2 – Thermal comfort (interior)	15	Underfloor air systems
EQ 7.2 – Temperature/humidity monitoring	67	Humidification/dehumidification
EQ 8.1 – Daylighting factor of 75%	41	Light shelves; skylights
EQ 8.2 – Views to outdoors for 90% of spaces	59	Space layout; larger windows
ID 1.2 – Two innovation points	83	Public education; 30% recycled content
ID 1.4 – Four innovation points	45	40% water conservation, solar power

This book does not deal directly with marketing green products in commercial building markets, but there are many products that assist in meeting requirements for points in such LEED-NC credit categories as water efficiency, green roofs, low- or no-VOC materials, high-recycled-content materials, Energy Star roofs, certified wood products and materials made from rapidly renewable

Table 7.3 Estimated *minimum* annual market for green building measures in LEED-registered projects at 2,000 annual LEED-NC registrations[5]

Green Building Measures	Percentage of Projects Using Measure[5a]	Percentage of Total Materials Cost	Estimated Market Value in 2005 or 2006
Recycled content	71	10[5b]	$960 million
Rapidly renewable materials	7	5	$48 million
Certified wood	25	1[5c]	$67 million[5d]
Low-VOC paints, sealants, adhesives, etc.	83	0.5[5e]	$55 million
Low-VOC carpet	93	N/A	$360 million[5f]
Solar power systems	10	N/A[5g]	$192 million[5h]
Green roofs	10	N/A	$36 million[5i]
Underfloor air systems	20	N/A	$288 million[5j]
Water-free urinals	40[5k]	N/A	$5 million

materials such as cork, bamboo and agrifiber products. Many of the other measures that receive LEED-NC points, as listed in Tables 7.1 and 7.2, involve design and construction decisions that are made at various stages of the integrated design and building process and do not require specific marketing measures by outside firms. They are more likely to be influenced by the project's LEED goals, by the use of an integrated design process and by the relative green design skills of the firms involved.

If design firms want to become known for something special, then they should pay attention to specific green measures that afford good opportunities for joint marketing efforts with product and equipment vendors, as well as those products and systems that capture media attention. Nothing beats publicity like having your project, with its green roof, PV system and LEED Gold plaque highlighted as a lead story on the six o'clock or ten o'clock network news station in your city. You'll get on camera, and dozens, possibly hundreds of clients, prospective employees and others in your industry will see it, almost guaranteed. This type of "endorsement marketing" is worth tens of thousands of dollars of free advertising.

Even in this brief assessment, we can see that identifiable green building measures in LEED-registered buildings may account for nearly $2,000 million (US $2 billion) in new market value, beginning in 2007 or 2008. Considering that LEED-registered projects do not represent the entire market for green building measures, and adding in the large expenditures for energy-efficiency measures with relatively fast paybacks, it is easy to conclude that there may be tens of billions of additional dollars spent on green materials and systems, much of it replacing expenditures on "less green" items, stemming from projects' decisions to increase their level of efficiency and sustainability.

The next two sections of this chapter deal with marketing energy-efficiency technologies in high-performance buildings and with marketing green buildings with solar power systems. Green building marketers need to understand how to leverage their marketing efforts with specific systems and approaches, so that prospective clients (and employees) are more likely to hear about the projects and want to hire (or join) the firm.

ENERGY-EFFICIENT TECHNOLOGIES

Owners and developers of commercial buildings are discovering that it is often possible to build high-performance, energy-efficient buildings on conventional budgets. For the past 10 years, and particularly in the past five years, in ever increasing numbers, we have begun to see development of commercial and institutional structures, for both build-to-suit and speculative purposes, using green building techniques and technologies.

Delivering high-performance buildings

Along with other green building rating and evaluation systems LEED encourages an integrated design process, in which the building engineers (mechanical, electrical, structural and lighting) are brought into the design process with the architectural, civil and structural team at an early stage, often during programming and conceptual design. Integrated design explores, for example, building orientation, massing and materials choices as critical issues in energy use and indoor air quality, and it attempts to influence these decisions before the basic architectural design is fully developed.

Earlier in this decade, when the integrated design process for green buildings was in its infancy, I developed a system of 365 questions to guide such a design process. As a resource for the integrated design process, the questions are organized by design phase, to ensure that good choices are not precluded, simply because no one thought to ask them at the right time during the fast-track design process of most contemporary projects.[6]

Marketing high-performance buildings

It is indeed possible to market smaller LEED building projects to owners and developers. There are many examples of small office projects that have achieved a LEED-certified rating on a conventional budget, ranging from an owner-occupied, 15,000 square foot, three-story office building in Lake Oswego, Oregon, built in 2000 for $130 per square foot,[7] to a speculative small office park, Ecoworks (about 350,000 square feet in six buildings) in Lexana, Kansas, built in 2002 for under $90.[8] In each of these cases, building developers were convinced that they would be better off long term with a fully documented and certified project. In the Oregon project, the owner had a personal commitment to the environment and wanted to demonstrate it with this project. In the Kansas project, the owner anticipated that the LEED certification publicity would help him find tenants who had similar environmental concerns, and he was right. From a developer's perspective, in a highly competitive market for office space, particularly in suburban areas, often a slight edge will translate into a market decision for one building over another. Therefore, the smart developer will work with a design firm that can deliver this competitive advantage in the form of an energy-efficient, certified green building.

In the case of government buildings, there has been substantial acceptance of LEED as a standard for both developing better buildings as well as demonstrating public commitment to higher levels of environmental responsibility. For example, the city of San Jose, California, adopted a policy in 2007 that all new public buildings over 10,000 square feet would have to be LEED Silver certified.[9] States are trying "performance-based" LEED contracting, as they strive to meet their real estate needs without putting out the upfront capital. In these situations, the agencies are asking for guarantees of specific LEED achievement levels from private developers, typically LEED Silver, and often employing a design/build project delivery method. Such projects offer significant marketing opportunities for design/build teams which really understand the LEED system and the costs of attaining various levels of certification.

Given the resistance of many owners and developers to undertaking the costs and uncertainties of LEED certification for commercial and institutional buildings, it is important for marketers to have another design approach that can be put into place immediately, either in conjunction with LEED or as a stand-alone integrated design tool, to deliver best in class high-performance buildings with the design professionals you are comfortable in using for your projects. As one such tool, the E-Benchmark guidelines for new construction, provides detailed design guidance for the 15 major climatic regions of the US, from dry to humid and hot to cold.[10] In this sense it is more detailed and "prescriptive" than the LEED performance-based standard, but probably easier to approach for most mechanical engineers and architects, in that it tells you what to do in most cases to achieve a given result. The LEED system awards one credit in the energy section for following these guidelines.

Another available resource is "The Advanced Energy Design Guide for Small Office Buildings," for buildings under 20,000 square feet (1,836 sqm), available from ASHRAE.[11] The LEED system awards four energy points for meeting all of the prescriptive requirements of this guide. For smaller projects, in which energy modeling alone can add $1 to $2 per square foot, this guide provides a good alternative to incurring additional costs.

From a marketer's standpoint, we want to sell "the sizzle, not the steak." So we really need to understand how owners and developers see the benefits of these buildings. Often, we need to sell the benefits of a truly integrated design process (see discussion in Chapter 4).

The conventional "design-bid-build" process of project delivery often works against the development of energy efficient and green buildings. In this process, there is often a sequential handoff between the architect and the building engineers, then to the contractors, so there is no feedback loop arising from the engineering design, to building operating costs and comfort considerations, then back to basic building design features such as glazing, envelope, orientation, structural materials and mass.

In a more conventional design process, for example, the mechanical engineer is often isolated from the architect's building envelope design considerations, yet that set of decisions is often critical in determining the size (and cost) of the HVAC plant, which can often consume 10 percent or more of a building's cost. As a result, key design decisions are often made without considering long-term operating costs or the benefits of a life cycle cost analysis. These decisions often result in higher costs and lower operating efficiencies for building owners, well into the future. Often adding cost to the building envelope, through improved glazing and other solar control measures, can reduce the HVAC system costs by far more, thus freeing up funds for further improvements, in what can be described as a "virtuous cycle."

Using an integrated design process

As we said earlier, most developers and designers find that the process for creating green buildings requires an integrated design effort in which all key players work together from the beginning. (See Figure 4.2 for an understanding of the "front-end loading" that occurs in an integrated design process.) Developers and owners have discovered cost savings of 1 to 3 percent (of initial budgeted capital costs) in building design and construction through the use of integrated design approaches. There can also be time savings as well: considering all design elements upfront often prevents costly and time-consuming redesign after value engineering has jettisoned the first design in an effort to meet changes in costs, budgets or project requirements. In my experience, government agencies, universities and nonprofits are more willing to pay for the costs of eco-charrettes than the private sector; perhaps the public and institutional sector is more comfortable with this deliberative approach to project delivery.

Marketing green buildings to owners and developers involves having a good grasp of the costs and benefits associated with the integrated design approach, since very few clients have had the experience of a completely finished green building project at this time, using this new design approach. Such an approach often requires greater design fees for which the owner hopes to make up in lower construction costs. From a marketing standpoint, firms might want to take a risk-sharing approach, in which a portion of the design fees are performance based, and are paid upon achieving specified modeled levels of energy efficiency. This puts the onus particularly on the architect and mechanical engineer to work closely together to integrate decisions involving the building envelope with those involving lighting, daylighting, comfort and the HVAC system.

Marketing integrated design needs to begin when the team is being interviewed for the project assignment. During the interview process, each team is often asked to be specific about their approach to the forthcoming project. For green buildings, the integrated design approach often includes holding eco-charrettes or sustainability forums with key nontechnical stakeholders during programming or conceptual design, as well as an eco-charrette with key design team members at the outset of schematic design. (Typically, the actual occupants of the building are usually missing from these charrettes, an oversight that is often hard to correct, but which can have potentially deleterious consequences for more experimental types of green buildings.) These charrettes are often an economical and fast way to explore design options as a group and all at once, before settling on a preferred direction. In the charrettes, everyone gets to provide input on building design before design direction is set in stone. The owner or developer often gets to hear competing approaches to providing the green measures required and can be a more informed participant in the design process. Often these charrettes and design exercises are facilitated by an outside, well-credentialed third party, and therefore provide a marketing opportunity for additional professional services.[12]

However, integrated design approaches often involve greater upfront costs and time allocations than conventional building programs. In negotiating fees for its work, the architect often needs to re-educate the client about the value of this approach, and to get money (and schedule time) to carry it out. This negotiation is critical to the final outcome of a green building project and needs to be thought about as a continuation of the marketing effort.

Considering the effect of design process on project cost, the first definitive analysis of green project costs, by the international cost management firm Davis Langdon, stated:

> *"We found successful projects – ones that achieve a high LEED score and stay within their original budgets – are ones where the design team sits down with the owner right at the beginning to talk about sustainable design and clarify goals. [That way] everyone on the team has some input. The most successful projects*

have a very integrated process. The projects where it's not working as well is where some member of the design team takes on [the LEED elements], but is doing it separately from the rest of the team."[13]

MARKETING CERTIFIED WOOD PRODUCTS FOR GREEN BUILDING PROJECTS

Certified wood products represent a special case for marketing green products, since wood is not typically a large percentage of the total costs of a commercial or institutional building. The certified wood credit (Materials and Resources credit 7) requires that 50 percent of the value of all new wood-based materials used in a project pass through an FSC-certified chain of custody (COC). For nonprofits, universities and other green building clients, the use of sustainably harvested wood could be an important selling point for a LEED project.

In 2007, there were more than 800 COC certificates in North America (generally in both US and Canada), including 156 issued directly to managed forest owners.[14] There were about 70 million acres (28,160,000 hectares) of FSC-certified forests in North America, indicating there are many providers of FSC-certified lumber and many forest sources. Canada alone represents 22 percent of the global total of FSC-certified wood. For many cities in the US, this marketplace is very healthy and very cost-competitive, especially for dimensional lumber ("2 × 4's"). For design firms in major cities who want to encourage clients to support the use of certified wood in their projects, there should be plenty of supply, especially since this is an item which can be bought and stockpiled ahead of use. However, a 2006 survey of design professionals found that only 54 percent of those wanting to use certified wood were able to, primarily owing to cost and availability considerations, as well as a lack of education about this product type. Another survey found that some regions of the country such as the Pacific Northwest have much higher rates of certified wood use in LEED projects, as much as 15 percent above the national average.[15]

Looking at various LEED-certified projects, we often see very different results in terms of certified wood use. The lesson for marketers of certified wood products is to know an architect's and owner's project goals intimately and be prepared to argue that the public relations benefit is worth the extra money that would be spent on certified lumber for rough carpentry or finish items. In many cases, the cost premium for dimensional lumber is not significant; however, its use is probably not enough to meet the requirement for certified wood to represent 50 percent of the value of total wood products. In this case, add some combination of dimensional lumber and cabinetry, and the total cost for buying this lumber as certified will be enough to meet the 50 percent test of total value for all wood-based materials.

Even though much of the green building to date has been commercial construction, project teams are still using FSC-certified framing lumber on more than 25 percent of the successful projects. As expected, interior products such as doors, interior finishes and plywood/paneling were the next most included certified products after framing lumber.[16]

Case study: Marketing certified wood in the Northwest

For this case study, we interviewed Lee Jimerson, manager of manufacturing accounts and Wade Mosby, Senior Vice President for the Collins Companies, one of the more experienced growers of certified forests in the US. Collins is a relatively small (over $200 million revenues in 2007), but sophisticated marketer of certified wood products headquartered in Portland, Oregon (www.collinswood.com). Collins has 300,000 acres of certified forests in Oregon, California and Pennsylvania. The 152-year-old company sells FSC-certified hardwood and softwood lumber, veneer logs and particleboard known as CollinsWood®. Collins also sells a product called TruWood® Siding and Trim, but only in the West (Figure 7.2).

Collins' brand identity is tied up with the claim that it is "the first privately owned forest products company to be independently certified by the FSC" and the "first forest products company to adopt the principles of The Natural

► **7.2** CollinsWood FSC-certified lumber was used in the LEED-NC Platinum certified Oregon Health & Science University's Center for Health and Healing. Courtesy of Collins Company.

Step"[17] for its corporate and manufacturing practices. Collins manufactures engineered wood products such as particleboard, using 100 percent recycled fiber from post-industrial sources, and TruWood Siding and Trim using a minimum of 50 percent recycled and recovered waste.

Clearly, while Collins' brand and key point of differentiation is heavily tied to its sales of certified lumber and sustainable forestry practices, as a practical matter, it must also sell products into regular lumber channels and must compete with noncertified forest products on price, terms, customer service and quality for a good part of its sales. Selling close to the point of production is also important, since distribution costs can often be important factors in making or losing a sale. Having a good supply chain is therefore a key factor in being able to meet demand, in competition with local and regional lumber chains.

At present, institutional projects are driving demand for certified wood, since nearly 50 percent of the LEED-registered projects are with institutional users: government agencies, schools and colleges, and nonprofit organizations, for whom environmental commitment and responsible stewardship are key principles to demonstrate in new buildings. Certified wood is also benefiting from the rapid growth in LEED-CI projects, which gain valuable points for their LEED rating goals by using not only certified wood in cabinetry, but also in furniture and furnishings.

A big issue for the green building industry is the existence of two major competing certification programs for certified wood: the FSC program, supported by most major environmental organizations, and the Sustainable Forestry Initiative (SFI) program which had been industry-dominated until about 2004. At this time, only FSC-certified wood is allowed to claim a credit in the LEED system. In the Green Globes system and in most residential certification programs from local home builder associations, certified lumber from both systems can receive credits toward certification.

What has Collins gained from its early adoption of environmental responsibility? According to Jimerson, *certification has delivered market share and customer loyalty*; it has helped develop strong partnerships and relationships with manufacturers and assemblers of wood products, including veneers and furniture. In my view, the company's commitment also demonstrates vision and integrity, both internally and externally, that makes it a valued business partner and supplier. However, there are still issues with how LEED standards are written, as they impact the company's products. For example, a ban on using products with urea-formaldehyde (UF) resins works against using the company's particleboard in furniture, even though it is sealed and never off-gasses. In this case, a LEED measure to protect indoor air quality works against using sustainable and recycled wood products!

As an indication of customer loyalty, Collins was able to have its certified wood specified and used in the world's largest LEED Platinum building, the Center for Health and Healing in Portland, Oregon, a project completed in 2006 by a developer who is a long-time user of the Collins products.

From a marketing standpoint for LEED projects, the devil is still in the details. It is important for Collins to get into a project early, so that product specifications don't inadvertently specify types of lumber not available in certified form or not in the regional supply chain. In Jimerson's opinion, the ground-breaking work that Collins has done with architectural specifiers has paid off, but there are still issues with familiarizing contractors with how to procure the specified product. In the end, if the ultimate buyer does not value certification (i.e., is not willing to pay extra for the certified product), Collins can elect not to maintain the COC certification of the wood and just sell it as regular lumber.

MARKETING SOLAR ENERGY SYSTEMS

Market transformation for solar energy systems is gaining increasing importance as we move through the second decade of green building practice (using the formation of the USGBC in 1993 as a starting point). Recent project experience illustrates the opportunities and challenges facing marketers for solar energy products and systems in commercial and institutional projects. The US Navy in San Diego installed one of the largest systems for a commercial or institutional setting, with a nearly 1-megawatt (peak rating) system, as shown in Figure 7.3. The PV system also serves as the canopy for a carport, used for long-term parking of vehicles.

▶ **7.3** The 924-kilowatt PV system installed by PowerLight on the carport at the US Naval Base in Coronado, California generates enough energy during the day to power over 935 homes. Courtesy of SunPower Corporation.

Survey of solar power use

In May of 2004, I conducted a proprietary survey of nearly 1,000 building industry professionals in my professional database, using a web-based survey tool and a 20-question survey instrument. I eventually received 223 responses or about 22 percent of the total surveyed population. Survey participants came from a range of disciplines and occupations, including 47 percent architects, and 22 percent other design team members (typically engineers) and contractors. So, about two-thirds of survey respondents were directly involved in building design and construction. At that time, 18 percent had already completed a LEED-certified project, and 25 percent were designing or building a LEED-registered project. Another 31 percent were doing projects with sustainability goals (but not LEED registered).

Survey results

When asked if they had considered using solar energy in any of their projects, 84 percent said "yes," with 73 percent considering PV (including 51 percent with building-integrated PV), 57 percent solar water heating and 19 percent solar pool heating. Of these respondents, 59 percent currently had a project in design, 28 percent had at least one project in construction and 26 percent had an operational project. This indicates that firms designing for PV or solar thermal applications tend to do more than one project, as their design, construction and operational experience grows. Only 16 percent of those who considered a PV or solar thermal project ultimately decided not to go ahead with it. (This means that once solar gets "on the table," a project is likely to use it.)

Survey participants who decided not to go ahead with a solar project overwhelmingly (55 percent) said cost was too high and (52 percent) the payback period was too long. The plain fact is that most solar applications (even in the sunny Southwest) cannot compete with other building energy-efficiency measures that have a much higher economic return. Less than 10 percent said that they didn't have proper solar exposure or that there were design considerations that prevented the use of solar. Since a 100-kilowatt solar system costing $600,000 or so to install (without considering tax incentives or rebates) will produce less than 200,000 kilowatt hour of electricity per year in most US locations (valued at $12,000–30,000 in most utility service areas), it is not surprising that cost is the major barrier to more widespread solar adoption.

To reduce barriers, survey respondents wanted mostly independent, reliable cost information and good performance data, and gave less weight to case studies and visible local projects. In their comments under "other" reasons, many of our survey respondents focused on the need for financial incentives (to cut initial cost), a receptive client insistent on using PV or solar thermal (perhaps because it is so visible and most people would recognize a solar power system without being told) and perhaps dramatic increases in local electric utility rates (an unlikely repeat of the contrived electric power "crisis" in the summer of 2000 and 2001). While the return on investment (ROI) for solar projects may be fairly good for private owners in some states, the intangible PR benefits of a visible green building measure are also significant.

At this time, LEED has gained 10 percent or more of the institutional market for new buildings but scarcely 3 to 5 percent of the corporate market. So, for the private-sector market, the clients can be described as innovators and for the public buildings market and the client base is more likely of the early adopter category. Even in the public-buildings client base, many project managers who supervise large projects could be characterized as early to late majority. They require strong mandates from upper management to promote sustainable design projects or expensive solar systems, especially since most building projects have constrained budgets.

Anecdotal evidence of overall benefits favors solar power, but it has not filtered yet into the general marketplace enough to overcome perceived cost hurdles. Since most green building markets are project based, it may take some time for perceived benefits to find appropriate projects, for a fuller implementation. Oftentimes, adoption of innovation is incomplete. For example, when a technology is desired (in the way of desired outcomes such as LEED certification or PV use) but not deployed into general use; this phenomenon has been called the "acquisition gap" and has been found in a number of technology diffusion studies. In one study, the authors claim that "knowledge barriers impede deployment."[18] Therefore, green building marketers interested in promoting solar in their projects would do well to spend time educating the client on the multiple benefits of such systems, preferably early in the design process.

The importance of cost data and project experience

In the light of the current state of the solar power market, the survey respondents' desires for more independent cost and performance evaluations of solar power systems are critical for gaining credibility and overcoming perceived barriers. In my own professional experience, the expectation of real benefits has to exceed the likelihood of increased costs by 25 percent or more (I call this immodestly, "Yudelson's Law of New Technology Adoption") to change most decisions in favor of new technologies or methods. As a technology or approach such as LEED moves into the mainstream, it is more likely to meet with this type of resistance. Many studies of the psychology of decision-making have shown that consumers and clients are likely to resist change unless they perceive the "downside" risk to be heavily outweighed by a well perceived "upside" benefit (see Introduction).

The current market for solar PV in buildings

The installation of solar PV in grid-connected commercial and industrial applications in 2003 was about 32,000 kilowatts (32 megawatts), valued at about $256 million (at $8,000 per installed kilowatt) and representing nearly 50 percent of the total US installed solar power that year. Installed solar PV applications in distributed grid-connected applications have grown nearly 600 percent since 2000 and exceeded 60,000 kilowatts (60 megawatts) in 2005, possibly reaching 80 megawatts.[19] In 2006, solar installations increased 33 percent, to a total of about 140 megawatts in the US.[20] In 2007, installations are expected to increase another 20 percent, according to the leading solar industry association.[21] Leading PV incentive programs in 2007 were found in the states of Oregon, Washington, Nevada, California, New Jersey, Florida, New York, North Carolina and New Mexico.

This rapid growth augurs well for PV applications in commercial, institutional and industrial buildings, as costs are coming down and experience with designing and specifying the technology is growing. Table 7.4 shows the many reasons to install solar power in buildings, beyond just the economic benefits, profiled in the following section.

The economics of solar power in buildings

To be honest, there is no compelling economic case for including solar energy systems in commercial and institutional projects, such as there is for energy-efficiency measures, daylighting, passive solar design and similar measures. However, as shown in Table 7.5, there are a number of economic and financial incentives for private-sector owners that could tip the balance in favor of solar power systems.

Let's take a look at the economics of solar power, for projects that will be built in the US in 2007 and 2008, using the analysis in Table 7.6. One could conclude that right now, in Oregon, California, New York and other states with generous PV incentives, *there is reasonable economic case for private-sector projects* to consider using solar electric technology, if one thinks of it as equivalent to an inflation-protected 20-year bond. Note that the ROI is based on current power prices; the actual economic benefits might be greater if peak power prices are much higher, if base power prices are higher than $0.10 per kilowatt hour, and might be much less if annual maintenance costs are significant!

Mainstreaming solar technology

If solar building technology is to enter the mainstream represented by the early majority, it must begin to take note of the problems of marketing new technology well illustrated in the classic "Crossing the Chasm," in which Geoffrey

Table 7.4   PV system benefits (Non-economic)

PV Feature	Benefit to User or Owner
PV systems are visible on buildings	It is immediately recognizable to the public that your green building uses solar energy
PV output can be measured and displayed easily	PV can be incorporated into public education about green buildings, specifically in school and college settings, as well as public buildings
Building-integrated PV systems can contribute to the architectural design of a project	BIPVs can substitute for costly exterior cladding materials or placed on top of external shading, reducing their net cost to the project
Larger PV systems are still newsworthy in most locations	Because they are visible and don't pollute, PV systems may be perceived as attractive and thus gain media attention to publicize the project
Rooftop PV systems can be physically separated from the underlying building and owned by different entities	PVs can be part of a "micro-utility" that can be owned and operated by a private company, even for public projects, qualifying them for full tax benefits. PV systems may also qualify for accelerated depreciation
To the public, PV systems represent a commitment to using renewable energy	PVs can be part of the branding of an office park or commercial building
PV systems have esthetic appeal	Architects are beginning to work with the deep blue color and other esthetic features of PV panels
PVs can be separately financed from the rest of the building	Some public and university projects may find it useful to "sell" PVs to their public stakeholders via partnerships, rather than financing them out of the base building budget
PVs can help get additional LEED project credits for energy efficiency and renewable energy, especially under LEED version 2.2, which lowered the threshold for PV system output	For example, the value of moving from a basic LEED-certified project to a LEED Silver level may be significant where there are tax credits, or where there is an owner or public policy requirement for LEED Silver

Table 7.5   Economic and financial PV incentives

Economic and financial incentives for PV system owners (private sector)
• Federal and state accelerated depreciation (for stand-alone systems)
• Federal tax credits (30% for commercial PV systems put in place in 2007 and 2008) – deadlines may be extended by Congress in 2007or 2008
• State tax credits (e.g., Oregon tax credit is valued at about 25% of initial cost)
• State and local subsidies ($2.50 per watt in some places like California)
• Utility credits and payments for power produced ($0.15 per kwh or more)
• Peak period power savings, in areas where power demand is monitored "real time" (though solar power tends to only partially overlap peak-power periods)
• Greenhouse gas emission reduction credits (not much real effect yet)

Moore demonstrates how difficult it is to go beyond the early adopters to the more general marketplace, using the same marketing mechanisms and communications tools as for the smaller, more specialized and less-risk-averse group of innovators.[22] In other words, the mainstream market and the "gearhead" market

Table 7.6 Economics of solar electricity in buildings

Basic cost of the system	$6,000 per peak kW (can be less for larger systems)
Power output	1,500 kwh per year per kW of rated power (average for a good part of the US, lower in the Pacific Northwest and maritime Northeast)
Value of energy produced	@ $0.10 per kwh, $150 annually per kW (peak); @ $0.20 per kwh, $300 annually per kW (peak) (assuming all power produced can be sold back to the local utility at full retail rates)
Return before incentives	$150/$6000=2.5% (excluding annual maintenance costs), or 5% at the higher rate of $0.20/kwh
Potential incentives	30% federal tax credit (in place through end of 2008), state support in California at $2.40 per watt; other incentives may vary. Federal depreciation credits may also apply for profit-making entities. Oregon has Business Energy Tax Credit valued at about 25% of initial cost and utility payment of $0.15 per kwh produced, from the Oregon Energy Trust
Tax-paying (Oregon) entity, Return on Investment	7.5%, assuming $0.15 per kwh value of power, net federal depreciation present value of 25% of cost; Business Energy Tax Credit, net present value @ 25%. *Note*: State tax credit reduces federal tax deductions for state taxes paid, by the amount of the effective tax rate
Tax-paying (California) entity, Return on Investment	9.4%, assuming $2.40 per watt state grant (40% of cost), net federal depreciation present value of 25%, 30% federal tax credit, no state tax credits and power valued at $0.10 per kwh ($150 value for power, $1,600 net system cost)

require totally different marketing approaches and communications channels. For solar power systems, we would argue that they need to be packaged in standard modules, not requiring any advanced design engineering, representing more of a "plug and play" solution. For commercial systems, this might include putting inverters and all other electronics on the roof of a building, with simple connections to the building's electric power system or even directly running DC lamps and other related equipment from the PV system (to reduce efficiency losses through inverters converting DC power output to AC power).

The emotional appeal of widespread solar energy adoption in American homes and businesses might be an unexpected consequence of the current war in Iraq and the resurgence of oil prices to $60 per barrel in 2007, if the American public finally wakes up to the true costs of the current energy dependence on oil imports and determines for the first time in 25 years to do something about it. (Witness the considerable consumer demand for hybrid autos, beginning in 2003.) Solar power solutions are well positioned to take advantage of these trends.

Past experience with marketing solar energy systems

As a state official, lobbyist and marketer, I watched and participated in the diffusion of residential solar water heating technology in California from the period of 1977 through 1985. In spite of awesome tax and energy saving advantages and a relatively simple technology, *it was not until major sales organizations became involved that technology adoption accelerated.* In other words, most people were not picking up the phone and trying to buy a solar water heater; they were waiting to be sold. Imagine the automobile industry succeeding without sales-oriented local dealerships. The difference is critical: in most surveys I've seen and conducted, building owners are waiting for someone else to take the lead in green buildings.

Recommendations for marketing solar power for green buildings

It was not until in 2003 that architects began to recognize that building-integrated PV systems, for example, can be part of a significant architectural statement, with projects such as Colorado Court, in the Los Angeles area, a $4.2 million, 30,000 square foot (2,750 sqm) low-income apartment project, which won a National Architectural Award for a five-story high wall of 200 PV panels.[23] Designed by the firm of Pugh+Scarpa, the south wall of the building uses PV for both energy production and visual appeal, as shown in Figure 7.4.

In the marketplace for solar PV systems, marketers need to push their companies to prepare the following information:

• Case study data, with solid cost information, including initial cost increases. This means widely publicized data, by region, based on actual project costs.

▶ **7.4** Designed Pugh+ Scarpa Architects, the LEED Gold-certified Colorado Court provides affordable housing for low-income residents in Santa Monica. Courtesy of Pugh+Scarpa Architects.

- Comparative cost information within and across building types, as to the full costs of solar power applications, the resulting benefits and ancillary features such as public education. Solid, measured performance data, in the field, will also be as necessary as cost data, to encourage trial by early adopters.
- Demonstrable information on the benefits of solar power systems beyond well-documented operating cost savings from energy conservation. Such benefits might include better public relations, more newspaper and media articles (yes, large PV systems are still novel in most areas) and more responsiveness to stakeholders (such as "walking the talk" for a firm committed to sustainable practices).
- Personal stories, by both practitioners and building owners, about the costs and barriers to completing projects with solar energy systems/applications. While most of the people in our survey were satisfied with their solar applications, 15 percent said the PV systems were not performing up to expectations, and 27 percent didn't know.
- Stronger use of multimedia approaches and other modern sales tools, to increase the emotional bonding with solar goals and methods on the part of stakeholders and final decision-makers. One of the tactics I have explored with several clients is to sell the PV panels, one by one, in the manner of theater seats, to local stakeholders. This might work especially well for schools and nonprofits, which often seek ways to bond the community to their projects. For example, a local utility (electric or water) could charge $5 per month for 5 years ($300 total), enough for a family to buy a PV panel for a school or public project.

Strategic marketing considerations

Green building marketers wanting to include solar power in their repertoire need to understand how their marketing approaches must evolve:

- They must pick a strategy that incorporates either high levels of differentiation or low cost, with explicit focus on particular market segments receptive to solar power.
- This strategy must be reinforced to become recognizable as a brand identity of the firm and its specific products or services. Internal reinforcement includes training, certification and reputation as solar experts; external reinforcement includes speaking, publishing and getting publicity for successful solar projects.
- Companies should consider developing their own proprietary tools, as part of a branding approach. Firms should also develop methods to execute solar projects with modest additional design fees and to utilize all available state, federal and utility incentives for solar power applications.

- Architects and engineers must form closer working alliances with contractors and other project professionals to ensure that their solar power designs can actually get built within prevailing project budget, time, technology, expertise and resource constraints.
- Designers should look for opportunities to level the playing field for solar power by incorporating building-integrated PV (BIPV) into the next project they design; BIPV systems substantially change the economics of solar power by offsetting some of the building's expensive "skin" costs ($60 to $100 per square foot) with solar panels costing $50 to $100 per square foot. They also offer a wide range of colors and esthetic possibilities in building design that would make the energy production a bonus feature instead of an essential requirement. In this approach, payback, in terms of energy savings, may become relatively unimportant, but widespread tax and other financial incentives may become more important.

NOTES

1 Green Roofs for Healthy Cities [online], press release, http://phoenix. bizjournals.com/phoenix/prnewswire/press_releases/Arizona/2007/04/12/ DCTH043 (accessed April 26, 2007). For the Phoenix, Arizona, project; see the Optima condominiums web site, www.optimaweb.com/MediaCenter/ news_article.html?community=biltmore&article=arizona_republic_ 062304.html&site= (accessed April 26, 2007).

2 Chicago Green Roofs [online], www.artic.edu/webspaces/greeninitiatives/ greenroofs/main.htm (accessed April 26, 2007).

3 First 450 projects through April 2007 based on USGBC web site statistics and available LEED scorecards for certified projects.

4 *Note*: SS, sustainable sites; WE, water efficiency; EA, energy and atmosphere; MR, materials and resources and EQ, indoor environmental quality. *Source*: USGBC web site data, April 2007, analysis of scorecards from the first 450 LEED-NC 2.0/2.1 certified projects.

5 Table assumptions: 2,000 LEED registrations, average project size 100,000 square feet (9183 sqm), project construction cost @ $150 per square foot ($1,634 per sqm), materials cost at 45 percent of construction cost (default value in the LEED calculator), giving an estimate of total materials cost at $13,500 million for LEED projects.

5a See Table 7.2.

5b Recycled content at 10 percent of total materials cost achieves two LEED points in materials and resources.

5c For certified wood, assume 4 percent of total materials cost is wood and certified wood is 50 percent of total.

5d The total market for recycled wood products is much larger, probably exceeding $400 million per year, according to industry insiders, most of it sold in home improvement centers.

5e   At this point, a guess.

5f   Based on carpeting at $1.50 per square foot, 100,000 square feet per project, 2,000 projects. Total market for low-VOC carpet is probably much greater.

5g   Not included in total project materials cost; same for green roofs and underfloor air systems.

5h   Estimated at 10 megawatts total, $8 million per megawatt installed price (total US commercial/industrial installations in 2005 likely exceeded 60 megawatts. *Source*: Paul Maycock, Publisher, PV News, Personal communication.

5i   Estimated at 10,000 square feet per system (20,000 square feet average floor plate), $15 per square feet incremental cost, or $150,000 per installation. Based on 53 percent of projects choosing a green roof at 50 percent coverage, or an Energy Star/high-emissivity roof at 75 percent coverage, and green roofs representing about 20 percent of the total.

5j   Estimated at 200 projects, 100,000 square feet per project, $6 per square feet premium cost for flooring system and diffusers; does not include carpet tile or other approaches to underfloor air systems.

5k   Estimated based on 53 percent of projects achieving 30 percent water use reduction inside the building and about 80 percent of those using 10 water-free urinals per building at a cost of $5,000.

6   Yudelson, Jerry. 2003. *365 Questions for Your Next Green Building Project*. Portland, OR: Interface Engineering (privately published, 40 pp.). Also available in an expanded 2004 edition from the Corporate Realty Design and Management Institute, www.squarefootage.net.

7   Viridian Place was the first LEED-certified building in Oregon.

8   Buildings magazine [online], www.buildings.com/Articles/detail.asp?ArticleID=2197 (accessed April 26, 2007).

9   City of San Jose, California [online], www.sanjoseca.gov/clerk/Agenda/112106/112106_9.1att.pdf (accessed April 25, 2007).

10   New Buildings Institute, www.poweryourdesign.com/benchmark.htm (accessed April 25, 2007).

11   American Society of Heating, Refrigeration and Air-Conditioning Engineers [online], www.ashrae.org, bookstore (accessed April 25, 2007).

12   For further discussion of *Sustainable Services Forums: A Green Design Tool and "Eco-Charrettes,"* see the author's interview at: www.betterbricks.com.

13   Lisa Matthiessen and Peter Morris (2004), *Costing Green: A Comprehensive Database* [online], available for download at www.davislangdon.us/USA/Research/ResearchFinder/2004-Costing-Green-A-Comprehensive-Cost-Database-and-Budgeting-Methodology (accessed April 25, 2007).

14   Forest Stewardship Council, FSC News, March 2007 issue, www.fscus.org/certified_companies/index.php?num=20&start=21 (accessed April 17, 2007).

15   Personal communication, Shawn Kallio, EcoTimber, April 2007.

16   Forest Stewardship Council, US, http://www.fscus.org/images/documents/ Green_Building_Market_Report_2006.pdf (accessed April 25, 2007).

17   www.naturalstep.org (accessed July 5, 2007).

18   Fichman, R.G. and Kemerer, C.F. 1999. The illusory diffusion of innovation: an examination of assimilation gaps. *Information Systems Research*, 10(3), 255–275.

19   Paul Maycock, editor, *PV News*, Personal communication, October 2004, www.pvenergy.com.

20   The Energy Blog [online], http://thefraserdomain.typepad.com/energy/ 2007/03/solar_installat.html (accessed April 25, 2007).

21   Solar Energy Industries Association [online], www.seia.org/Year_in_Solar_ 2006.pdf (accessed April 25, 2007).

22   Moore, G. (1999) *Crossing the Chasm: Marketing and Selling High-Tech Products to Mainstream Customers*. 1999 Revised edition. New York, HarperBusiness.

23   www.californiasolarcenter.org/solareclips/2001.12/20011204-8.html   and Fairley, P. 2004. "In the US, architects are ramping up the design power of photovoltaics." *Architectural Record*, March, 161–164.

8 Experiences of Green Building Marketing

There are many opinions about green building marketing and most firms find out what works for them only through experience with various approaches. Craig Park is Chief Marketing Officer for Leo A Daly, an Omaha, Nebraska based architecture and engineering (A/E) firm. Consistently ranked among the top 10 largest A/E firms and the top 10 interior design firms, today Leo A Daly has 1,200 professionals in 22 offices in 16 cities worldwide.[1] Based on 2005 revenues, Leo A Daly was ranked ninth among A/E firms nationally.[2] Park said of his firm's efforts:

Sustainable design is incorporated into our long-range corporate strategic plan so every office – both our architecture and engineering offices – has a commitment to the "2010 Imperative" and the "2030 Challenge," which are the two mandates to reduce the impacts of buildings on the environment.

Twenty-five percent of our technical staff is LEED accredited, and we have LEED accreditation study groups and testing going on throughout the firm to get that to at least 50% within the next few years. Whenever we go to collegiate recruitment fairs, it seems that sustainability is a mandate for the new generation of young architects and engineers.

We also have a corporate director of sustainable design. He coordinates a forum of similarly-minded architects and engineers, throughout our organization who advise on many of our projects. As we began formally promoting the firm's history and approach to green buildings, he stepped forward. He said that cared strongly about this in the community and in his work and that he wanted to lead the firm's effort in developing sustainable ideas and solutions for our clients. So we created the role of sustainability director. We think that sets an example for the rest of the firm and for our clients [about our priorities].[3]

Figure 8.1 shows one of Leo A Daly's green projects, the 68,000 square foot (6244 sqm) Carl T. Curtis Midwest Regional Headquarters for the National Park Service, in Omaha, Nebraska, certified at the LEED-NC Gold level.

▲ **8.1** Developed under the GSA Design Excellence program, the National Park Service's Carl T. Curtis Midwest Regional Headquarters Building was designed by Leo A Daly to LEED-NC Gold-certification level. Photography by Tom Kessler. Courtesy of Leo A Daly.

SURVEYS OF GREEN BUILDING MARKETING

To find out what it will take to accelerate green building adoption, it helps to examine leading surveys of marketplace of green practitioners for guidance. In 2006, *Building Design & Construction* (BD&C), a leading building industry trade magazine, published a survey of 872 building industry participants, including those with both commercial and residential experience.[4] Of the respondents, 59 percent were design professionals (architects, consultants and engineers), while the balance consisted of contractors, government agencies, facility managers, product manufacturers and building owners.

In terms of measurable experience, 59 percent of survey respondents characterized themselves as "very experienced" or "somewhat experienced"

Table 8.1   Response to the emerging market for sustainable design services

	2006 Survey, Percentage of Total	2003 Survey, Percentage of Total
Encouraged staff members to obtain expertise in sustainable design	64	57
Made an effort to LEED certify at least one project	59	46
Created new marketing materials	18	16
Recruited professionals with green building experience	15	9
Hired outside experts	23	19
Created a new division/profit center	8	5

in sustainable design, compared with 42 percent in BD&C's first survey in 2003.

Participants were asked to characterize how their firm has responded to the green building market opportunity. The survey found that 36 percent had completed at least one green building project, while 45 percent had attempted a green building project. Responding to the LEED rating system, 24 percent had sought to acquire certification for at least one project, while 20 percent had actually achieved certification. The percentage of respondents who were LEED APs had not increased from 2004, but the number of firms with LEED APs had increased from 25 percent of respondents in 2003 to 37 percent in 2006, indicating the gradual acceptance of this designation in the marketplace.

Table 8.1 shows what firms have done to respond to the market for sustainable design. Most of the totals have increased from 2003, indicating that companies see that they have to respond and are actively taking steps to acquire expertise, green their projects to LEED or other standards and hire outside experts. Most firms have not created separate profit centers for sustainable design, rightly thinking that sustainability thinking has to permeate all of the firm's projects, a subject covered more fully in Chapter 11.

Firms that were more committed to sustainable design had a tendency to try to LEED certify at least one project and encourage staff members to acquire the necessary expertise, typically through taking LEED training workshops and passing the examination to become a LEED AP. Less experienced or committed firms were more likely to engage primarily in staff training and to work with existing clients on LEED-related projects.

Table 8.2   Most effective means for marketing sustainable design services

Means for Marketing Services	Percentage of Total
Successful projects with LEED certification	37
Networking or speaking	18
Direct selling to interested prospects	12
Successful projects without LEED certification goal	9
Public relations	8
Writing articles	6

Most effective methods for marketing sustainable design services

In a proprietary survey I conducted in 2003, nearly 500 respondents chose the most effective methods for marketing green building services. The results are shown in Table 8.2, and reinforce the tendency of firms to aim at successful green projects.

The most effective marketing tool reflects the strong desire of building design professionals to let successful projects represent their preferred marketing approach, which also reinforces the effect of networking, speaking and writing articles. This strong preference for completed projects is also shared by clients, who want to see evidence of costs and features in green buildings.

Business benefits of sustainable design focus

Of BD&C survey respondents, 39 percent said that they had been able to attract new clients or projects based on their expertise, with 11 percent of the total survey saying this focus had resulted in a significant amount of new business. This result points out the importance of developing expertise, project experience and a recognizable name in the early stages of an emerging market. In addition, 42 percent of survey respondents felt that this expertise had *helped them retain existing clients*, and 39 percent reported that sustainable design expertise and reputation had *helped them differentiate their firm and capabilities in the marketplace*.

Of survey respondents, 66 percent in 2006 reported having attempted to sell clients and/or those in their organization on the virtues of using LEED on a particular project vs. only 42 percent in the 2003 BD&C survey. This points out the important role that developing internal expertise plays in convincing building professionals to "stick their necks out" and become advocates. It also shows that firms are getting more insistent with clients that they take a look at green design and project certification.

In the survey, of those who attempted to persuade clients to carry out a LEED project, more than one-third (35 percent) are working on a LEED-registered

Table 8.3   Perceived barriers to incorporating sustainable design into projects

Barriers	Percentage of 2006 BD&C Results	Percentage of 2003 BD&C Results
Adds significant first costs	56	44
Hard to justify, costs or otherwise	57	44
Market/clients not comfortable with new ideas/technologies	30	19
Too complicated, too much paperwork	36	16

project vs. only 21 percent who had actually completed such a project. Again, if a firm asks for an opportunity to do something new and is trusted by the client, the firm is far more likely to get that opportunity. However, of the one-third who had not made the attempt, the reasons were many: the client didn't require it, there was a lack of interest by the client (or by their own firm), they weren't sure of the payoff, and there was insufficient budget and staff to add sustainable design to the project goals. These excuses point out the need for marketers who believe in the benefits of sustainable design to make sure that their staffs know how to present sustainable design in a persuasive way, have the data they need to justify such an approach and understand the budgetary and staff implications before the project begins.

Barriers to incorporating sustainable design and LEED into projects

In responding to this question about perceived barriers, Table 8.3 shows that BD&C survey respondents gave the most weight to first-cost increases, found LEED projects harder to justify because of costs and found that the market was not willing to pay a premium for sustainable design. Only 14 percent thought that there were no significant barriers to incorporate sustainable design into their projects.

Even though respondents experienced in green design and aggressive in promoting it still find it hard to justify to clients. Somehow they are unable to connect their own personal or professional interests with the policy and project goals of their clients, or that they find the market too uncomfortable with new ideas/technologies. This suggests that incorporating sustainability and integrated design into the basic practice of a firm ("if you hire us, you get the following green measures, no discussion, no argument" approach) might be more effective than trying to persuade clients on each project. This approach will also help firms to differentiate themselves in the marketplace. An architect friend in Seattle calls his approach "stealth sustainability," just doing sustainable design within the context of project goals and budgets and not making a big deal about it.

What can be done to more effectively promote sustainable design?

In responding to this question about more effective promotion, my 2003 survey respondents gave significant weight to independent cost information and less weight to case studies and more training. These survey respondents, perhaps confident of their own abilities to sell projects, wanted to see more of their own project experience and more successful local projects that could be shown to clients. BD&C's 2006 survey respondents mostly wanted better information on life cycle assessment (LCA) for product selection and better overall green building marketing materials. BD&C survey respondents especially want to see sustainability standards incorporated into state and local building codes, reflecting the experience of design professionals that many clients will just not pay for project elements that exceed code requirements.

Sales vs. marketing to get sustainable design into the mainstream.

At some point in the evolution of sustainable design, marketing considerations have to be supplemented with strong sales activities. Unfortunately, most design professionals are opposed to ever marketing their services. (The appropriate euphemism in the design and construction industry is "business development.") A number of my 2003 survey respondents indicated that they would never sell professional services – their idea of selling is to do a good job and hope someone notices. They are not very good at sales, in my experience, so this lack of presentation and persuasive skills presents a real barrier to more widespread adoption of sustainable design. There is of course a major cadre of sales professionals for manufacturers who somewhat make up for this gap, by selling specific hardware solutions, but they seldom influence the decision for or against general green building approaches.

ONE FIRM'S APPROACH: BRUNER/COTT ARCHITECTS

Bruner/Cott Architects of Cambridge, Massachusetts, has just certified its first LEED Platinum project. Principal Leland Cott spoke about what his firm had done to establish a reputation as a green firm.

What has worked so far is that we have had results. Our first LEED Platinum project just received certification. It was the highest-scoring building renovation in the country. We had a wonderful client partner on that project who wanted to go all the way to Platinum, and as a result there is proof to other potential clients that we can provide effective service to anyone wanting to push the limits of sustainable design. Giving conference presentations on our Platinum project has been a big help, along with winning a sustainable design award this year and being featured in publications.

Each firm that achieves success in sustainable design knows it can't rest on its laurels, that dozens of local firms are actively building their own capabilities and project experience in sustainable design. So what does a firm do? Cott says,

> We have to continue to push ourselves. We can't simply respond to LEED guidelines. That is what everyone is doing now. We have to go beyond what is currently on the market. Partnering with our clients to take sustainable design further has been and will continue to be the key to keeping our reputation as a cutting-edge design firm. Bringing sustainable design to projects not conventionally thought of as green has been and continues to be another way to distinguish ourselves. We did this on our Platinum project and on a smaller historic adaptive reuse project recently.[5]

CASE STUDY: SERA ARCHITECTS, INC.

John Echlin is design principal at SERA Architects in Portland, Oregon.[6] Echlin joined the firm in 1997 as director of design, and brought with him a strong sustainability focus. He spoke of the firm's marketing transition as the push for sustainable design gets ready to enter its second decade:

> We're really transitioning from short-term, turnaround speculative projects and clients to long-term owners. The majority of our clients have legacy ownership interest, whether public or private. There's a high-return value proposition [in sustainability that] just makes sense. The ones who have gone out to the bleeding edge and experimented with it have realized the value of these investments. They are investing for the future and the energy and operational paybacks are real. It's really about buildings that have lasting value – we're not building temporary structures, we're building buildings that last 50 to 100 years. When you do that you've really got to build in efficiency measures and all of the beneficial attributes in terms of materials and healthy indoor air quality.

With close to 90 employees, SERA is a fairly typical well-established architecture firm, with studios for public and private architectural projects, as well as a planning studio. Echlin comments, "Within the education sector, sustainability is now no longer a differentiator – it's really the baseline whether you're doing classroom buildings, residence halls or campus planning."

As to the marketing benefits, Echlin alluded to the 1980s movie, *Field of Dreams*, when he said,

> Our focus on sustainability has helped our business. Because we've really made a strong effort to be at the leading edge, we've brought people on board with the knowledge, passion and interest to provide those services. Because this is a new business paradigm, as well as an ethical and aesthetic shift, you have to get people on board who are passionate about it and who also understand it. The clients are strongly interested as well. It's true that "if you build it they will come." The clients

we make connections with come to us because of the people we have on our team and the [green design] services that we provide.

What really made a difference at SERA Architects was to look internally first, to their own office practices, using the lens of an environmental assessment framework called The Natural Step.[7] Echlin talks about how they got started. "We asked ourselves: 'How do we become a more sustainable business practice?' That attracted a lot of interest because it sent the message to our employees that we're not just doing this for a niche market, but we're really doing this because we're serious about it and it's a value that we share. We went through a two-year exercise of redesigning our office operations around a sustainable paradigm." SERA then took its own experience and shared it with other design firms in Portland, thereby widening its circle of influence.

In addition, in 2002 the firm became an 100% employee-owned ESOP (Employee Stock Ownership) company and moved its offices to accommodate growth. In 2003 SERA Architects received a LEED-CI Gold certification for its office remodel in an older building, a former hotel in Portland's Old Town district. In 2006, a remodel of a second floor of the same building was done to LEED-CI Platinum standards, and the firm expects certification in 2007.

RECOMMENDATIONS FOR MARKETERS AND PRACTITIONERS

The following recommendations for green building practitioners and those organizations marketing sustainable design, while not surprising, follow from both industry surveys and from the well-established theory of innovation diffusion (described further in subsequent chapters). The marketplace wants and needs:

- Case study data, with solid cost information, including initial cost increments.
- Comparative cost information within and across building types, as to the full costs of LEED certification, including documentation.
- Demonstrable information on the benefits of green buildings beyond well-documented operating cost savings from energy and water conservation.
- Anecdotal stories, by both practitioners and building owners, about the costs and barriers to completing LEED-certified projects.

Practitioners need to understand how their marketing must evolve in order to compete effectively in the rapidly growing sustainable design market:

- They must pick a strategy that incorporates either high levels of differentiation or low cost, with explicit focus on particular market segments (see Chapter 9).
- This strategy must be reinforced internally and externally so that it becomes recognizable as a brand identity of the firm. Internal reinforcement includes

training and certification of employees as LEED APs, for example. External reinforcement includes activities to increase the visibility of the firm and its key professionals, including speaking, lecturing, networking, publicity for successful projects and similar measures.

- Larger companies should consider developing their own proprietary tools for measuring the costs and benefits of sustainability for their clients, as part of a branding approach. Along with these tools, firms should develop methods to successfully execute LEED projects without additional design fees.
- Architects and engineers must form closer working alliances with contractors and other project professionals to ensure that their designs will actually get built within prevailing budget, time, technology options and resource constraints.

CASE STUDY: THOMAS HACKER ARCHITECTS, INC.[8]

Thomas Hacker Architects, Inc. of Portland, Oregon is widely recognized for the design of libraries, museums, theaters, higher education buildings, and urban design. Since the firm's founding in 1983, Thomas Hacker's designs have received 40 national, regional and local design awards. Jonah Cohen is the firm's President and says that "sustainability has been part of our core values for a long time. Even before there was LEED, we approached design by trying to make sure our projects were appropriate to their settings and oriented in ways to take advantage of natural forces at work on the site."

From a marketing standpoint, sustainability is a core value of the 40-person firm, and that's what gets communicated to clients. One way the firm demonstrates this commitment is that for most projects, Cohen claims, "we will do a sustainability charrette whether or not the project is aiming for LEED certification. We do it regardless of whether the owner wants to participate because we're interested in pushing the boundaries [of sustainable design with each project]."

Thomas Hacker was the first architectural firm to have its own office LEED Silver certified. This was a valuable learning experience, according to Cohen. "It was interesting because it really tested our values; we had to spend a little more money that we had anticipated. Sustainability is definitely part of values, and from a marketing standpoint it has been important to us."

Cohen says, "I often give tours of the building; during one particular tour there was someone who later became a client. He became very interested in our firm because he saw us talking about our own work environment." So a strong marketing recommendation to any design firm is to first take care to green your own workplace, using one of the LEED rating tools, then use your own experience as one of the marketing tools for clients. In other words, you have to first "walk the talk," before clients will accept your commitment to sustainability at face value.

Thomas Hacker often enters design competitions in many parts of the country. Cohen notes that, "Often one of the questions [in a RFQ is: What is your experience in sustainable design? So we are able to directly answer the question with our own experience," offering some insights into how a client can manage a green project. "[For example], we just finished a LEED Gold project at Lewis and Clark College, and they specifically wanted the students to be actively involved with the sustainable aspects of the project. The building is designed as laboratory and has a lot of transparent walls and floors that show some of the measures that add to the sustainable design. For instance, some of the floor panels are glass without any carpet so you can see into the displacement ventilation system." For Thomas Hacker, then, client education is an ongoing part of their green building marketing.

Marketing is more subtle at Thomas Hacker. Like most professional service firms, it prefers to let the work speak for itself. Cohen's approach is to not to say, "You should hire us because we're great sustainable architects." Rather, the firm prefers to maintain that it is more "interested in a balance between everything that it takes to make great projects, with sustainability as just one component of how we present ourselves. While some firms really feature that aspect as their strongest point, we're trying to do it in the context that we're also doing buildings that are very well designed, very responsive to the programmatic needs and are on budget." In other words, sustainability is a program element, but Cohen's firm recognizes that all other program elements and budgetary constraints also need to be respected.

In terms of cost, Cohen says that "at a LEED Silver level, the [increased] construction costs used to be 5–6 percent, now it's nearly a wash. It's easy to get LEED Silver in Oregon without too much effort. The costs are definitely going down for institutional projects, city projects and government agencies – it seems like it's becoming the norm."

There is a trend underway called "LEED Lite," something that "tastes great, but is less filling," and that is the tendency of clients to take LEED for granted. Cohen observes that "a lot of institutional clients will go through a LEED-certification process once or maybe twice and they'll prove that they can do it and beyond that they don't feel the need to keep proving it over and over again. So they tell the designers that they'd like to use LEED guidelines and the LEED point system but not go through the formal certification process …. There's so much budgetary pressure on these projects that it's one more line item where they can reduce costs. It's a slippery slope because you sort of get back to where we were before LEED in that you just have to trust us [to do the right thing]."

A FUNDAMENTAL MARKETING PROBLEM

Turner Construction Company surveyed more than 719 building owners, developers, architects, engineers and consultants during the summer of 2004.[9] The survey reported "executives at firms involved with more green buildings were far more likely to report that ongoing costs of green buildings were much lower than those not involved with green buildings." The main obstacles to widespread adoption of green buildings were found to be the following three, more or less in order of importance:

1. Perceived higher construction costs (at 14 to 20 percent premium!).
2. Lack of awareness about the benefits of green buildings.
3. Short-term budget horizons for building owners and developers.

Looking at these issues from a marketer's perspective, we can say that green building marketers are trying to sell a product or an approach that:

- costs more;
- does not demonstrate significant benefits to balance the costs;
- must be sold to people heavily concerned about initial cost increases.

This is really hard work, as anyone experienced at all in sales and marketing can tell you! The solutions then become fourfold:

1. Work aggressively to lower the costs of building green, through project experience and a focus on integrated design.
2. Rely heavily on case studies, testimonials from CEOs (and other believable business people) and make good use of the available academic research that demonstrates the benefits of green buildings.
3. Find ways to finance green building improvements to reduce or eliminate the "first-cost penalty" that often frightens away prospective buyers, using utility, state and federal incentives to maximize financial leverage.
4. Become more creative and assertive in documenting the full range of green building benefits, so that building owners with a long-term ownership perspective will be motivated to find the funds for greening their projects.

The Turner survey showed that most executives and practitioners believe green buildings are healthier (86 percent), create higher building value (79 percent) and higher worker productivity (76 percent). They were more skeptical about such issues as higher ROI (only 63 percent believed that), attracting higher rents (62 percent believed that to be the case for green buildings) and higher occupancy rates (only 52 percent), and while only 40 percent of the respondents believed that greening retail stores could bring about higher sales. The results of the survey are skewed even more when the relative experience of the respondents with green buildings is factored in; for example, 75 percent of experienced green building professionals believed that these buildings created a greater ROI vs. only 47 percent of professionals not experienced with green buildings.

One can draw the conclusion that the more marketing and production experience a firm has with green buildings, the more the firm is able to build a case, first in the firm's own mind, then in a client's mind, that this is the right way to go, and then to have the skills to execute one's intention to create high-performance buildings. At this point, the early adopters among the clients are ready for this strong advocacy — they are inherently more sold on the benefits of green buildings, less skeptical about their ability to achieve the desired results, and more willing to work with design and construction teams to solve the problems that usually arise in trying new technologies and new approaches to building design.

CASE STUDY: TURNER CONSTRUCTION COMPANY

Turner Construction is the largest commercial construction firm in the US, with annual revenues of more than $7 billion in 2005.[10] In 2004, Turner's then-CEO Thomas Leppert announced a formal commitment ("Turner Green") to sustainable construction and business practices, as a means to continue strengthening Turner's leadership position.[11] Leppert asserted that Turner's plan to be the leading responsible builder is good for the environment, and also for building owners, developers and occupants. Equally important, he stated that these practices are good for the bottom line and serve as an example to the entire construction industry. As the largest firm in the industry, Turner has effectively thrown down the gauntlet for other major construction firms wanting to compete with it. This was an extremely important development for the growth of the green building industry, since most building owners and developers rely heavily on the advice of their contractors in deciding to adopt green building design for their projects.

By early 2007, Turner had made great progress in LEED projects. The company reported that it had completed 34 LEED-certified projects and had completed or is currently working on more than 65 additional LEED-registered projects. In addition, Turner has completed or has under contract more than 195 projects with green building elements.[12]

As announced, the "Turner Green" program consisted of:

- Construction site recycling on all Turner projects, not just green design projects. Recycling efforts will be phased in until Turner reaches 100 percent. Turner estimates that it will recycle 75,000 tons of construction waste in 2007 alone.

- Ensuring that over time, all Turner field offices will incorporate field waste-recycling programs, energy-efficient lighting, operable windows for natural ventilation and water-efficient fixtures.
- Instituting a major green training program for Turner employees. Turner's online tool, *Turner Knowledge Network*, helps employees learn about the LEED standard, adds to their knowledge of green field operations guidelines. (In our view, this internal training role is critical to the marketing of the green capability and is often overlooked, especially in the construction field. Without internal training, it is difficult if not impossible for a company to "walk the talk." We discuss this issue at greater length in Chapter 10, as "Internal Marketing".)
- Increasing the number of Turner's LEED APs (at April 2007, the number stood at about 260).
- Creating an advisory council of outside industry experts to provide objective advice on sustainable design best practices and to drive their adoption with the company and its clients.
- Naming a Senior Vice President to lead Turner's *Center of Excellence*, to link Turner's local and national green information.

"From now on, whenever businesses consider undertaking a new building project they should first think green, and then think of Turner because we have the resources, the experience and the knowledge to do green right," Leppert said.

One of the projects Turner completed in 2003, The Genzyme Center in Cambridge, Massachusetts, was the first large LEED Platinum-rated building. Within Genzyme's budget, Turner was able to incorporate innovative features including sun-tracking mirrors to direct daylight into the building, natural ventilation using the atrium, and a double-skin exterior wall and extensive indoor gardens for the enjoyment of occupants and to improve indoor air quality. During procurement, Turner helped Genzyme and the design team to ensure that the contract documents incorporated the green elements desired by Genzyme and that subcontract bidders used cost-effective products and methods to achieve the LEED Platinum rating within the budget constraints.

Also in 2003, Turner was able to partner with Toyota Motor Sales, USA to develop a LEED Gold-certified building in Torrance, California, that cost no more than a traditionally constructed building. The Toyota Motor Sales – South Campus building consists of 636,000 square feet (58,000 sqm) on a 38 acre (16 hectare) site. Used as administrative offices, it features 53,000 square feet (4867 sqm) of rooftop PV panels that can generate 550 kilowatts of electricity – or about 20 percent of its total energy usage. Its first cost was competitive with the cost of similar, conventional office buildings.

NOTES

1 Data taken from the firm's web site, www.leoadaly.com (accessed April 25, 2007).

2 "Giants 300," *Building Design & Construction*, July 2006, p. 59.

3 Interview with Craig Park, Chief Marketing Officer, Leo A Daly, April 2007.

4 "Green Buildings and the Bottom Line," *Building Design & Construction Magazine*, November 2006, Special Supplement, www.bdcnetwork.com. All survey data reprinted with special permission from *Building Design + Construction*. Copyright 2006 Reed Business Information. All rights reserved.

5 Interview with Leland Cott, Bruner/Cott Architects, April 2007.

6 All material in this section comes from an interview with John Echlin, design principal with SERA Architects, Portland, Oregon, www.serapdx.com. See also Oregon Natural Step Network [online], www.serapdx.com/resource/publ/SERA_NSCS.pdf for a case study of SERA Architects sustainability activities through the end of 2004 (accessed April 25, 2007).

7 Oregon Natural Step Network [online], www.ortns.org.

8 All material in this section comes from an interview with Jonah Cohen, President of Thomas Hacker Architects, Inc., April 2007, www.thomashacker.com.

9 Turner Construction Company [online], 2004 Market Barometer Survey, www.turnerconstruction.com/corporate/files_corporate/Green_Survey.pdf (accessed April 25, 2007).

10 "Giants 300" Survey, op. cit.

11 Turner Construction Company [online], www.turnerconstruction.com/corporate/content.asp?d=3793 (accessed April 25, 2007).

12 Turner Construction Company [online], www.turnerconstruction.com/greenbuildings/content.asp?d=2199 (accessed April 25, 2007).

PART

2

Marketing Sustainable Design Services

9 CONTEMPORARY MARKETING THEORY AND PRACTICE

Having considered green buildings and green technologies in depth, it is now time to turn our attention to marketing theory and practice. How does a design firm put in place a comprehensive marketing strategy and devise a set of tactics that will give it competitive advantage in the green building marketplace? First of all, it is important to understand green building as an innovation in an established marketplace and to realize how to tailor marketing approaches to the level of adoption of green building approaches in various market segments.

Second, we consider the rudiments of competitive strategy and look at three primary strategic thrusts a firm can choose: differentiation, low cost and focus. Third, we show how differentiation results from market segmentation, appropriate targeting and positioning statements that a firm reinforces with its marketing communications and tactical marketing plan. We present several examples of successful marketing communications programs, focused around high-level sustainable design projects.

UNDERSTANDING THE "DIFFUSION OF INNOVATIONS"

To approach the green building market, it is useful to think of it in terms of technological innovation. In classical marketing theory, people have found that innovations take time to get into the marketplace. Typically, the time for more than 90 percent of the market to adopt an innovation is 15–25 years (i.e., a generation). In order to be adopted, an innovation typically has to have a major cost or business advantage over existing methods. In my experience, this advantage has to be greater than 25 percent, if cost alone is the criterion. This "cost-effectiveness barrier" exists because of the costs of learning new methods, the economic risk of investing capital in new things and the business risk inherently involved with trying something new. In the building industry, there has been historic resistance to discontinuous innovation, so that in many ways, buildings are built much the same as 20 years ago, relying on incremental innovations to improve performance.

Figure 9.1 illustrates how innovation enters the marketplace. Initially, a group of innovators with strong technical expertise and a tolerance for risk tries

ADOPTION RATE AS PERCENTAGE OF TOTAL POTENTIAL MARKET

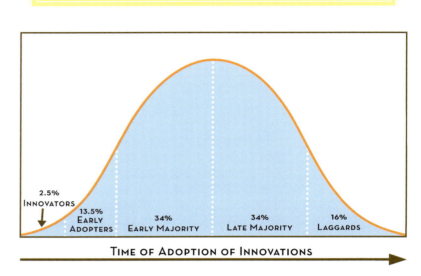

2.5%
INNOVATORS

13.5%
EARLY
ADOPTERS

34%
EARLY MAJORITY

34%
LATE MAJORITY

16%
LAGGARDS

TIME OF ADOPTION OF INNOVATIONS

▶ **9.1a** Diffusion of innovation showing progressive stages of adoption over time.

something new. When the size of this group reaches about 2.5 percent of the total potential market, then a group of early adopters begins to find out about what the innovators are doing, observes successful field trials and then begins to incorporate the innovation into their own work. This group of early adopters has less tolerance for risk, but is attracted to the benefits of the innovation. When the size of the group adopting the innovation reaches about 16 percent of the potential market, then a new group, the early majority, begins to use the innovation and begins the process of "mainstreaming" it. Finally, at about half the potential market size, a group of late adopters signs on, not wanting to be left out forever. Near the end of the adoption process, a large group of laggards reluctantly adopts the innovation, and some people, of course, never adopt. (Think of the Amish in Pennsylvania, still driving a horse and buggy 100 years after the automobile was introduced.)

Of course, many technical and technological innovations never achieve mainstream status, owing often to cost or complexity. The process of mainstreaming is never smooth, and according to author Geoffrey Moore, it can be compared to "crossing a chasm." Many technological innovations never have appealed to more than the early majority, either because something better comes along, or because they have high switching costs, offer few comparative economic benefits or are just too complex for the average user. One can think for example,

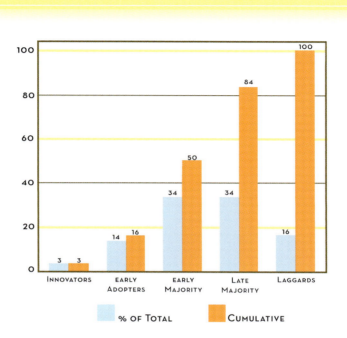

CUMULATIVE ADOPTION BY PHSYCHOGRAPHIC TYPE

▶ **9.1b** Diffusion of innovation showing total adoption rates by psychographic type.

Table 9.1   Categories of responses to new technological innovations

Name of Category	Percentage of Total	Characteristics
Innovators	2.5	Venturesome
Early adopters	13.5	Respectable
Early majority	34.0	Deliberative
Late majority	34.0	Skeptical
Laggards (or "nevers")	16.0	Traditional

of all the PDA products developed in the 1990s before the Palm Pilot finally came along and captured the imagination of the mainstream business market.

Classical diffusion theory, now more than 50 years old, was popularized by Everett Rogers[1] and is widely known among marketers of new technologies. Basically, it posits a group of five distinct personality types who adopt innovations in different ways and at different times. Table 9.1 shows these distinctions. This theory also posits a normal distribution of innovation adoption, with an average time to reach 50 percent of the potentially available market of typically 10 years or more.

As may be expected, the major issues in determining the rate of adoption of innovation include:

- Relative economic or social advantage (still being debated for green buildings, but generally considered a positive factor).
- Compatibility with existing methods (generally this is the case for sustainable design).
- Ease of trial at relatively low cost (not the case for new building technologies).
- Observability by those who would try it (this is definitely the case for green buildings).
- Simplicity of use (which LEED and sustainable design are not, at this time).

Of these five factors, relative economic advantage is the major driver of response to innovation. According to Rogers, there are four overall key factors in determining the rate at which an innovation will spread from the relatively small innovator segment that welcomes new things, to broader segments that are far more risk averse and intolerant of ambiguity.

- The nature of the innovation itself, including its relative advantages.
- Communications channels used by subsequent market segments.
- Time required for the decision to innovate, the process of adoption to occur and additional adopters to learn about it (the time dimension for completing new buildings, typically 2–3 years, is short-circuited by the sharing of information from multiple similar projects, in this case).
- Social system in which the innovation is imbedded, particularly the barriers to innovation.

At this time, LEED has gained perhaps 10 percent of the institutional market for new buildings but scarcely 3 to 5 percent of the corporate market. (See the discussion in the earlier chapters about the state of market adoption of LEED in 2007.) So, for the private-sector market, the client base can be described as more likely to be innovators and, for the public buildings market, the client base is more likely of the early adopter mind-set. Even in the public buildings client base, many project managers who supervise large projects could properly be characterized as late adopters, and will need strong mandates from upper management to pursue sustainable design projects.

The relative economic advantage of green buildings and LEED has yet to be shown in either of these markets, given the demonstrably higher capital costs and certainly higher certification costs, compared with conventional practice. (See discussion of costs of green buildings in Chapter 4.) Certain benefits, such as energy savings, are already a standard part of conventional project payback analysis and are often a positive factor in promoting green buildings. Benefits appear greater for long-term owner occupants of buildings, but many of the reported and putative benefits are harder-to-measure "soft costs" such as employee productivity, improved morale, reduced absenteeism and illness. From our experience, these benefits have relatively little acceptance at this time among building owners and project financiers.

Anecdotal evidence of the business-case benefits (see Chapter 3) is strongly in favor of green buildings, but it has not filtered yet into the general marketplace enough to overcome perceived cost hurdles. Since the green building market is project based, it may take sometime for perceived benefits to find appropriate projects, for a fuller implementation. Oftentimes, adoption of innovation is incomplete, for example, when a technology is acquired (in the way of desired outcomes such as LEED certification) but not deployed into general use; this phenomenon has been called the "acquisition gap" and has been found in a number of technology diffusion studies, which observe that "knowledge barriers impede deployment."[2] This is happening with LEED: 45,000 people have taken the LEED training course, more than 35,000 have passed the LEED AP examination, yet relatively few are actively pursuing LEED registration for their design projects, primarily because of their own limited knowledge and fear of client rejection.

In the light of the current state of the market, building owners' and developers' requirements for more independent cost and performance evaluations of green buildings are critical for building credibility and overcoming perceived barriers. According to "Yudelson's Law," (cited in Chapter 8) the *expectation of real benefits has to exceed the likelihood of increased costs by 25 percent or more* to change most decisions in favor of new technologies or methods.

Green buildings as an innovative product

To the degree that green buildings are simply higher performing buildings, one can argue that there's not much new here, that designing and building better buildings can readily be accomplished by the existing industry. However, if one considers the innovation to be rating and certifying buildings against various energy and environmental design criteria, as in the LEED green building rating system, then we can apply the classical theory of diffusion of innovation to forecast market demand. This theory encompasses the substitution of new ways of doing things for old ways, in a predictable pattern. (See Chapter 13 for specific market forecasts.)

In addition, if we look at particular green building features that are becoming popular, then we could also apply this theory to forecast their adoption rates.

In particular, one could look at the following technologies and forecast their likely individual market adoption rates, but that is beyond the scope of this book. We should note that certain products still have a lot of market skepticism, owing to concerns about longevity, maintenance costs and possible unintended consequences; such building technologies as green roofs, agrifiber MDF (medium density fiberboard), water-free urinals and on-site sewage treatment may fall into this category:

- Photovoltaics (PV, both stand-alone and building-integrated).
- Green roofs, for both esthetics and stormwater management purposes.
- Rainwater recovery and reuse systems, along with innovative stormwater management systems.
- On-site energy production, including microturbines and cogeneration systems.
- Water-conservation products, including water-free urinals, ultra-low-flush toilets, etc.
- LEED-compliant roofs, including Energy Star roofs that have high emissivity.
- Low-VOC paints, sealants, coatings and adhesives.

Cumulative adoption rates will follow some version of Figure 9.1a, depending on how economically beneficial the innovation turns out to be. Each of the innovations listed above faces challenges to its adoption based on conventional economics, technical performance in the field, relative ease of specification, use by established competitors in the building industry, government and business mandates for change, and financial incentives from the government and utility sectors. These variables are shown in Table 9.2.

In Figure 9.2, the effect of a critical mass on the rate of adoption is shown graphically. According to Rogers:[3]

> The critical mass occurs at the point at which enough individuals have adopted an innovation so that the innovation's further rate of adoption becomes self-sustaining…. An interactive innovation is of little use to an adopting individual unless the individuals with whom the adopter wishes to communicate also adopt. Thus a critical mass of individuals must adopt an [interactive communication] technology before it has utility for the average individual in the system.

While this example deals explicitly with communications technologies such as telephones, faxes, PDAs, teleconferencing and the like, it has clear relevance for green buildings. Given the large numbers of people trained in the LEED system as of early 2007, one can argue that LEED has all the hallmarks of a self-sustaining innovation. Therefore, its adoption rate can be predicted by utilizing this classical theory of innovation diffusion.

Table 9.2   Variables determining rate of innovation adoption

1. Perceived attributes of innovation	Examples: Relative (economic) advantage; compatibility with existing systems; complexity; trial-ability at reasonable cost; observable to others who might try it out
2. Type of decision required	Examples: Optional; group or committee decision; made by authority figure
3. Communications channels available	Examples: Mass media; word-of-mouth web sites
4. Nature of the social system	Examples: Openness to innovation; network inter-connectedness to communicate results; changing norms favoring sustainability
5. Change agents' promotional efforts	Examples: Writings; speeches; personal appeals

Source: After Rogers (1995).

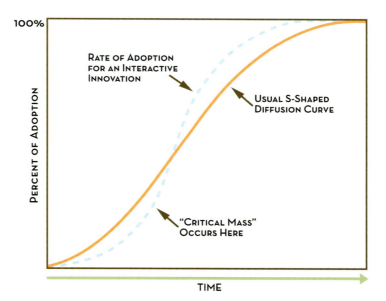

CUMULATIVE ADOPTION RATES

(PERCENTAGE OF TOTAL POTENTIAL MARKET)

► **9.2**   Rate of adoption with critical mass.

According to Rogers, the critical mass occurs at the point at which enough people have adopted an innovation so that its further adoption is self-sustaining. Green buildings may represent a similar phenomenon, given the vast inter-connected industry of designers, specifiers, builders, product suppliers and equipment vendors. For example, the supply chain for certain products such as certified wood may be underdeveloped in various regions of the country, hindering the desire of architects to specify it into their building projects, because of a lack of a critical mass of suppliers and contractors familiar with buying it.

TWO OTHER WAYS TO UNDERSTAND INNOVATION DIFFUSION

Classical studies of innovation diffusion have been updated in recent years to take into account the speed of Internet communications and the reduced difficulties of spreading new technologies beyond innovators and early adopters. With green buildings reaching the threshold of the early majority, these more recent studies assume greater importance for marketers.

Crossing the chasm[4]

If green building is to enter the mainstream, it must begin to take note of the problems of marketing new technology to the early majority, according to Technology Marketing Guru Geoffrey Moore. Many technology companies have experienced difficulty going beyond innovators and early adopters to reach the early majority. Often they try to use the same marketing mechanisms and communications tools for the larger audience that worked for the smaller, more specialized and risk-tolerant group of innovators and early adopters. To extend the reach of LEED beyond the innovator and early adopter market, the argument clearly indicates a need to simplify the LEED tool, make it cheaper and easier to use for each project type, minimize annual changes and feature updates, and address the risk aversion of the early majority. A good example is the update for Microsoft Windows products, which now appears on a longer timetable, to avoid upsetting the marketplace.

Think for a moment how Apple Computer manages to mainstream innovations with regularity. When the iPod was introduced, many thought it was overpriced, with a limited market. At the end of 2006, Apple had sold more than 70 million iPods. What worked? In a word: design. In a phrase: understanding the customer. When green buildings begin to incorporate great design as well as sustainability features, when architects and engineers begin to understand the multiple and varied business-case benefits that appeal to different project and client types, then green buildings will be able to "cross the chasm" into mainstream acceptability and utilization.

The Tipping Point[5]

The study of how epidemics and fads spread is a topic of great relevance to the diffusion of innovation, especially in the areas of understanding the roles of communications channels and social networks. Gladwell posits that innovations spread fastest through the work of a relatively few people who have well developed social networks; when they are "sticky" in terms of the emotional effect of memory and metaphor; and when they are disseminated within a powerful context (almost a tribal setting) among people who know, trust and like each other.

In Gladwell's terminology, green building will spread most rapidly when knowledge about this approach is spread by well-connected individuals (typically senior partners at design and construction firms and leading authorities in the field); through people who widely and openly share their knowledge with others through publishing and speaking (i.e., experts whose judgment is acknowledged and trusted) and through "persuaders" who have the ability to tell compelling stories to others about the benefits of sustainable design. In other words, *innovations finally spread when good communicators ("salespeople") get involved.* Green buildings have the first two categories in abundance, but the third in scarcity.

Can professional services marketers learn how to make the green building story "sticky," in terms of emotional appeal? An architect friend of mine who designs great schools, with lots of daylighting and views to the outdoors, often takes skeptical school superintendents and others on the building committee to nearby schools with such features. The emotional appeal of daylight and views is readily apparent and the benefits so obvious, that the clients sell themselves on green schools. As green building moves into the mainstream, the number of skeptical clients will likely increase, so that the ability to tell or demonstrate a convincing green building story will increase in importance.

Architects and other professionals should practice telling the green building story in engaging ways so clients can appreciate that a LEED certification is not an architectural whim or some existential fad, but an essential element of creating a high-performance building and a quality assurance method for the end-product.

UNDERSTANDING SEGMENTATION, TARGETING, POSITIONING AND DIFFERENTIATION

A marketer's job is always fraught with difficulty. How to make a "purple cow" (something remarkable) out of a "pink sow" (something ordinary) seems to be the perpetual task of the marketing arm of the firm. (In today's marketing environment, a firm must be remarkable just to get some attention, hence the "purple cow" analogy.)[6] The chapter introduces some of the basic concepts of modern marketing and applies them to marketing green buildings, including design services, construction services, technologies and products. *Segmentation, targeting* and *positioning* are often referred to as the "STP" formula and form the essence of strategic marketing planning, as inputs to marketing differentiation. Figure 9.3 shows how these four activities are interrelated.

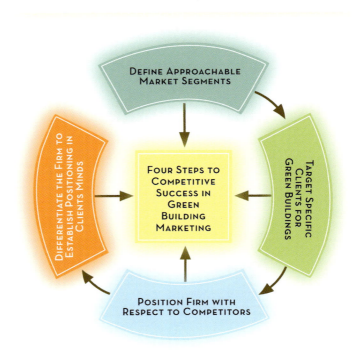

DEFINE APPROACHABLE MARKET SEGMENTS

TARGET SPECIFIC CLIENTS FOR GREEN BUILDINGS

FOUR STEPS TO COMPETITIVE SUCCESS IN GREEN BUILDING MARKETING

DIFFERENTIATE THE FIRM TO ESTABLISH POSITIONING IN CLIENTS MINDS

POSITION FIRM WITH RESPECT TO COMPETITORS

► **9.3** Segmentation, targeting, positioning and differentiation.

Segmentation

Marketers are always trying to understand and segment markets to focus on the most profitable or available segments. Segmentation variables can include considerations of demographics, geographics, firmographics, psychographics and similar issues. In *demographics*, the focus is on the social and economic characteristics of buyers (age, income, race/ethnicity, income, etc.); so far there is little evidence that this approach to segmentation is useful for marketing green buildings. (However, one could argue that those states that are more liberal politically are likely to contain a higher number of "change agents" who would be in favor of green buildings, so that in fact socioeconomic characteristics of buyers and decision-makers may be relevant; however they are contained already in the geographic category.)

In *geographic* segmentation, the focus is on where people are locating and building; as we saw earlier, there is plenty of evidence that green building activity is still concentrated in relatively few places in the US at this time, such as the West Coast, Mid-Atlantic and Northeast states, with other nodes in the large

Table 9.3 LEED registrations (all systems) per state (selected), as of April 1, 2007[7]

State	2007 LEED Registrations	2006 Population (Millions)	LEED Registrations per Million
Oregon	217	4.6	47
Washington	296	6.4	46
Massachusetts	184	6.4	29
Maryland	131	5.6	23
Pennsylvania	285	12.4	23
California	813	36.5	22
Colorado	104	4.8	22
Michigan	193	10.1	19
Arizona	114	6.2	18
Illinois	230	12.8	18
AVERAGE	**5,300**	**300**	**17.7**
New York	338	19.3	17
New Jersey	149	8.7	17
Georgia	135	9.4	14
Texas	203	22.1	8

cities of the South and Southwest, as well as the Upper Midwest. The number of LEED project registrations by state, measured against the population of the state would be the first place to look. On this basis, considering 14 representative states with at least 100 LEED-registered projects (roughly the average number of registrations per state at this time), examine the results shown in Table 9.3. The average number of LEED project registrations (for all systems) was about 17.7 per million (300 million people and 5,300 project registrations), as of April 2007. The 36 states not shown in the table would each average about 50 LEED-registered projects, as of April 2007.

Therefore, geographic location is certainly a prime variable to consider in deciding where green building services can be successfully marketed.

Firmographics is a newer term, coined for business-to-business marketing. The essential elements in firmographics are such variables as the size of the firm or organization (in terms of revenues, number of locations, number of employees, etc.) to which one is marketing; private, public or nonprofit entity; industry type (higher education, commercial offices) and similar characteristics. Data from Chapter 2 show that LEED registrations are prevalent among public entities (31 percent of the total project area), institutions (schools and colleges, hospitals, etc.) and nonprofit groups (17 percent), taken together about equal with the 48 percent of total area of corporate project registrations.

Psychographics refers to segmenting by lifestyle, propensity to take risk or willingness to tolerate ambiguity in potential outcomes. In this classification, a marketer would look for someone with a risk-taking personality, people considered as industry leaders, innovators (in the "diffusion of innovation" sense), as surrogates for early stage segments.

Targeting

Targeting is the essential task whereby marketers decide to focus on one or a few segments. In the case of architecture firms, most specialize in one or a handful of client types (public, private, nonprofit) project size and market segments (e.g., K-12 education, museums, libraries, urban offices, historic preservation and adaptive reuse, healthcare, etc.), so the choice of targets is necessarily limited by the firm's prior experience. Many firms aim to take greater market share in a given industry or else extend the geographic reach of their success in tackling a certain type of client, but most firms focus on current relationships. The more design-oriented the client, the easier it is in general for a smaller "high-design" firm to extend geographic reach. Many small design firms successfully work on national and even international levels, typically by teaming with a larger local architecture or engineering firm that will provide construction documents and construction supervision. For green buildings, architects and builders who have built an early reputation and history of successful projects are often invited to compete for projects far from home, and they are often successful in doing so.

Prime targets for green building marketing at this time share these characteristics: they are early adopters of new technology; they may be potentially significant *users of a* new approach (i.e., they control multiple properties); they may be influencers or opinion leaders (able and willing to sway others, both inside the organization and in a larger community of peers) and they can be reached at low cost (e.g., already clients of a firm or customers for a product).

Positioning

Positioning is the third activity of the STP (Segmentation/Targeting/Positioning) formula. It takes segmentation and targeting analyses and turns them into messages that go out to clients and prospects. A textbook definition of positioning is "the act of designing the firm's marketing offering and image so that they occupy a meaningful and distinct competitive position in the target customers' minds."[8] In other words, positioning is a communications activity that aims at changing the view of a firm in the mind of a target prospect, in such a way as to create a "difference that makes a difference, to someone who makes a difference (to you)." These differences have several important characteristics. They need to be:

- *important* (in terms of benefit delivered);
- *distinctive* (something that not every competitor can claim);
- *superior* (to other ways to get the same benefit);
- *communicable* (and somehow visible to prospective clients or buyers);
- *pre-emptive* (not easily copied by competitors);
- *affordable* (there is little price difference to get this superior benefit);
- *profitable* (the company finds it profitable to be in this market segment).

Firms that have positioned themselves successfully as green building experts (through publicizing individual efforts as well as project successes) have found that it is possible to maintain their positioning even as more firms try to emulate them.

Examples would be firms with certified LEED Gold or Platinum projects or those making the annual Top 10 list of the AIA Committee on the Environment.[9] Positioning, then, is what a firm does to take real facts and position them in the minds of the targeted prospect; positioning deals with creating and managing perception. In marketing green buildings, positioning is an essential component of a firm's communications strategy and needs to reinforce a single powerful message. Because it is a new industry, green buildings offer the positioning strategy of grabbing a new unoccupied position that is valued by clients and prospects. For example, a firm could claim "the most LEED-registered projects" in a given industry or location, or "the most LEED APs," or "the most LEED Gold projects with a certain product or technology" but then would also have to explain why this is a benefit to a client.

Table 9.4 shows some types of positioning strategies with examples of firms that use them. This list of potential positioning strategies makes it quite clear that most firms in the design and construction industry have no clear positioning. Therefore they have to compete on their experience with particular building types and their fees. As a result, most design firms have trouble making sufficient profits to grow and to attract major talent from the outside. Many construction firms, especially those in "hard bid" public-sector environments, have similar issues.

Figure 9.4 shows hypothetical positioning situations that might exist for various firms in the green building industry. While the chart refers to design firms, product manufacturers and construction firms also need to construct effective positioning maps, in terms of how they want clients to perceive their product

Table 9.4   Strategic positioning for design firms[10]

Strategic Positions	Representative Firms
The best	Saks Fifth Avenue, Accenture Consulting
The best value	Hyundai, Schwab (as a discount broker)
Lowest cost	Southwest Airlines, Jet Blue
Innovation, pioneer	Boeing, Bank of America, Schwab, Frank Gehry, Thom Mayne and OMA (architects)
Product focus	Aamco (transmissions)
Target-specific segment	Gerber (baby food)
Product categories	Gatorade, Oracle
Product attributes	Volvo and Michelin (safety), Crest (whitens)
Product line scope (has everything)	Amazon.com; Barnes & Noble
Organizational intangibles	H-P, Kaiser Permanente (healthcare)
Emotional benefits	MTV, Hallmark Cards
Self-expressive benefits	GAP, Mercedes
Experience of buying/using the product	Nike, Nordstrom
Personality of the brand	Harley-Davidson, Tiffany
Vs. competitors	AVIS (vs. Hertz), Ford (vs. GM)

and service offerings, using attributes that make a difference in target-market decision-making. Unless positioning is a conscious effort, it will be imposed on a firm by default.

Differentiation

Differentiation is an approach to marketing strategy that takes the STP variables and focuses them on particular markets. The differentiation approach to marketing strategy was first popularized in the 1980s by Harvard Business School Professor Michael Porter and must be coupled with a specific market, geographic or other focus.[11] In the architecture, engineering and construction professional service industries, the main differentiators for sustainable design are highly qualified people, satisfied clients, high levels of LEED attainment, specific industry and project experience, and the ability to deliver green building projects on conventional budgets. A firm usually needs to show high levels of attainment on the key variables to win major new projects in typical highly competitive situations. Case in point: in 2004, a small ($5 million) green public works project north of Seattle, Washington, attracted 24 serious proposals!

A highly acclaimed and seminal work from the 1990s, *The Discipline of Market Leaders*, points out that every firm needs to excel in one of three key areas

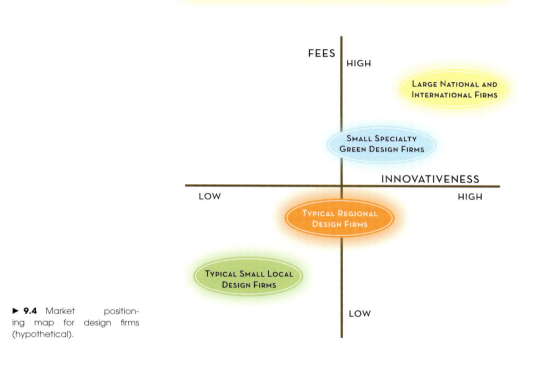

MARKET POSITIONING MAP FOR DESIGN FIRMS

▶ **9.4** Market positioning map for design firms (hypothetical).

of differentiation: customer intimacy, product differentiation and operational excellence, while providing at least good service in the other two areas.[12]

1. In the area of professional services, clients most expect *intimacy* in the form of established and continuing relationships between clients, architects and builders. Green building marketers therefore need to focus considerable attention on relationship management and the quality of experience working with the firm on green building projects.

2. Firms need to display *operational excellence* in terms of meeting building program requirements, budgets and schedules, while achieving specific LEED goals. Creating high-performance buildings on a conventional budget should be the goal in this area.

3. Firms that have a "signature" technological approach can often attract clients who are willing to try new firms who exhibit *product leadership* in key areas of sustainable design.

In her book, *Marketplace Masters*, Suzanne Lowe outlined key differentiation activities for professional service firms.[13] Her Top 10 approaches that work for design and consulting firms are those in which the firm:

1. Conducted an advertising campaign (to establish/maintain positioning).
2. Added new (to the firm) services that blend into the services of another industry (e.g., a consulting engineering firm adding facilities management services).
3. Implemented a formal relationship management program to strengthen the bonds with current clients.
4. Merged with another firm, to strengthen the firm's capabilities and reach.
5. Managed a public relations campaign (to highlight achievements/reinforce positioning).
6. Extended the firm's services via joint ventures, alliances or referral networks.
7. Added new services to the firm within the currently served client base.
8. Created a new visual identity (yes, this does work!).
9. Hired specialized, key individuals.
10. Improved or evolved the firm's current services.

Within this list, design and construction firms can find one or more approaches to immediately differentiate their services in the green building industry. Leading firms are particularly adept at using differentiation strategies 1, 5, 8 and 9. Improving or evolving the firm's services typically takes place over the course of multiple green building projects and several years.

COMPETITIVE STRATEGY

Most businesses use some variant of the theory of competitive advantage first introduced by Michael Porter about 25 years ago. His classic work, *Competitive Strategy*, first set forth the basic building blocks of competitive strategy used today. In his work, Porter outlines three approaches to winning in the marketplace: differentiation (mentioned earlier in this chapter), low cost and focus (which can be combined with the other two).

A larger firm can also tie to these three basic strategies: a variety of strategic thrusts, including pre-emptive moves and seeking synergy with other activities of the firm (such as cross-selling to an existing client a new service or product). The strategic vision's goal is to develop and maintain a "Sustainable Competitive Advantage."

Examples of *pre-emptive moves* would come from larger firms making a major effort to get half or more of their professional staff to become LEED APs, thereby establishing presumptive expertise in the design of green buildings. Table 9.5 shows the top 10 firms with LEED APs as of mid-2007. From this

Table 9.5 LEED APs at leading professional service firms, 2007[14]

Firm Name	LEED APs	Percentage of Total Staff	Industry Rank in Category (2006)
Perkins+Will (A)	753	60.9	3
Gensler (A)	575	23.2	1
HOK (A/E)	456	21.1	1
Stantec (E/A)	277	4.6	6
The Turner Corp. (C)	260	–	–
SmithGroup (A/E)	243	29.7	7
HDR Architecture (A/E)	192	17.3	3
DPR Construction (C)	185	27.4	–
CUH2A (A)	161	43.5	–
HKS (A/E)	155	13.5	4
Mithun (A)	137	69.5	36
LPA (A)	126	59.2	–
Skanska USA Building (C)	125	–	–
Leo A Daly (A/E)	123	11.4	9
DLR Group (A/E)	120	21.6	–
Gilbane Building Co. (C)	118	6.6	–
Cannon Design (A/E)	115	15.4	10
JE Dunn Construction Group (C)	110	3.3	–
Skidmore, Owings & Merrill (A/E)	110	8.6	2
NBBJ (A)	109	15	4
Arup (E)	105	1.2	–
Swinterton Inc. (C)	103	8	–

A = Architect, A/E = Architect/Engineer, E/A = Engineer/Architect, C = Contractor

table, one can see that only 2 of the top 5 firms in terms of percentage LEED APs to total staff are pure architectural firms, while 14 of the top 20 in total numbers are firms that combine architecture and engineering; these firms tend to be larger and have a more diverse client base that is likely to demand LEED expertise. One can also see that, 16 of the top 20 firms with the most LEED APs also ranked in the top 10 of their industry category. This still leaves room for firms that make having LEED APs a priority, but they must start thinking of getting more than half of their total technical staff LEED Accredited to achieve reasonable parity with the larger firms.

Examples of *synergy* would include a mechanical engineering firm opening a building commissioning or energy modeling division, an electrical engineering firm adding capabilities in on-site energy production, PV systems or lighting design, or an architectural firm opening a green building consulting division independent of its regular practice.

In differentiating services, a business seeks to create a difference in the mind of a buyer, with attributes that make *a* difference to that person or organization. For example, we might want to be thought of as the "leading edge" firm or product category; that will limit our market, but sharply define us to buyers who value that attribute, namely the innovators. In today's commercial world, a major task for service firms and for specific technology solutions is to create a *BRAND* that will incorporate those key differences.

Of course, we can create differences for each market segment that we choose to address, since some might value innovation, others low cost, others specific technological choices such as PV or roof gardens. Without a leading brand (and with due apologies to the major companies involved in this business), the average client will not want to make a purchase. Even in commercial situations, the lack of a brand can have drawbacks (e.g., imagine the confusion in the commercial air-conditioning market without major brands such as Trane® and Carrier®).

Low cost of operations gives a firm pricing flexibility. The ability of design and construction firms and green technologies to compete on price (with low cost) is a business asset. These costs may be based on prior project experience, accurate product knowledge, good research, local or state incentives, or a willingness to "pay to get the experience."

Low-cost advantages might be more sustainable than even branding as a way to compete in the marketplace, but most firms don't have the discipline to operate in this fashion. As a good example of the competitive advantage of lower cost of operations, one can examine the almost unblemished success record of Southwest Airlines. For Southwest, the low prices made possible by lower operating costs have become their primary brand, along with "fun." Consider that many of the successful newer airlines such as Jet Blue, Frontier and Air Tran have even lower costs of operations (expressed as cost per seat mile) than Southwest, by being very focused in their routes, not trying to be all things to all people, but offering simple air transportation to budget-conscious business and leisure travelers.

Focus is a key competitive strategy, knowing which markets to compete in and which to shun, knowing which clients a firm wants and which it doesn't. Very often, a firm will try to serve too many clients, not really satisfying the clients it really wants by being too unfocused. For most professional service firms (and I have run the numbers for one engineering firm), 80 percent of revenues come from 20 percent of the clients served in a given year.

To devise an effective strategy, marketers should consider combining focus with either low cost or differentiation. For example, points of *focused* differentiation can include:

- Regional vs. national firms (many smaller design firms compete nationally by narrowing their focus to one target market, such as museums, libraries, zoos and the like). One large commercial PV contracting firm I called in mid-2004 for a quote really impressed me by saying that my job was too small, that they only considered jobs at 100 kilowatts (about $750,000 installation price) or larger. Here is clearly a firm that understands its profitable customer profile and has instructed its salespeople about its decision to serve only larger projects.
- Client types, which can include smaller clients, psychographic profiles (such as early adopter) or those distinguished by strong cultures and values of sustainability. Architects who focus on winning design competitions, for example, clearly seek out projects that embody a community's or institution's highest aspirations, while others serving the same project types (quite well) do not bother with such open competitions.
- Building or project types (or vertical markets) such as office buildings, public service facilities (police, fire, jails), secondary education, higher education, healthcare, laboratories, cultural centers, retail, hospitality or industrial. Those building types likely to be impacted in the future by far higher peak period electricity rates (up to $0.40 per kilowatt hour in some of the larger metropolitan areas in the Eastern United States), such as office buildings and institutional buildings (colleges, public agencies, etc.), might be very good candidates for solar power or high levels of energy efficiency, particularly in states or utility service areas with significant incentives to offset the higher initial costs of such systems.[15]
- Signature green measures, such as PV or green roofs that a firm commits to bring into play on each project. While it can be dangerous as engineers or architects to "always" bring certain technologies to its projects, *it is more dangerous not to be known for anything in particular*.
- Project size can also be a focus, allowing smaller firms, for example, to compete with larger and more capable competitors. For smaller projects, many of the larger firms in architecture, engineering and construction are simply uncompetitive in their pricing, since these projects tend to be very budget challenged.

There is no single competitive response to the growing green building market that is right for every firm, because much has to do with the strategic clarity, capability, capital and character of the firm. Nevertheless, a conscious choice among strategies is vastly preferable to having none, for that assures only a steady diet of "crumbs" from the table of more decisive firms.

PARTICULAR ISSUES FOR MARKETING GREEN BUILDING SERVICES

Marketing green building services in the design and construction industry is inherently different and more difficult than marketing green products. Services are unique from products in four ways.

Perishability

Services cannot be inventoried as products can; one lost "man-hour" can never be recovered. Hence firms are always balancing work load with head count. Given that most service firms have very little capital, it is hard to staff up and hope that demand materializes; instead, most firms active in green building design have to carry out a balancing act between having the right people available at the right time, against losing money if demand doesn't materialize to make use of these people's time. This often means that key personnel are assigned too many projects, often in superficial roles.

Inseparability

Services are produced and consumed typically at the same time. In other words, having a firm's associates working on a design at any given time *is* the service purchased by the client. Because of this, star performers are often asked for by name by savvy clients and, of course, the star's time is inherently limited. Therefore, *a worthwhile marketing strategy is to make the firm the star*, rather than key individuals. This strategy often requires extensive training to succeed, as well as good internal systems for technology transfer from successful projects to new projects. Since the star performers in most professional services firms tend also to be the leading marketers, there is added pressure for them to stay active with projects after they're sold, which is why the design industry is often referred to as a "seller-doer" business, because the seller also has to do the work.

Intangibility

Services are intangible. The quality of a set of green building plans is only discernible to a few, and often not until the building is finished, and all the change orders accounted for. The quality of an integrated design process cannot easily be smelled, tasted, touched or seen, and yet it is critical to the success of projects that have aggressive green goals. To take advantage of this situation, many firms try to create something tangible to point toward the quality of their intangible services, such as a quality headquarters building (often involving a LEED-certified renovation or tenant improvement, or even a LEED-EB project registration); special background studies or signature approaches to projects; marketing communications and marketing collateral materials that consistently emphasize commitment to sustainability; and participation in green building industry associations and events.

Variability

There is no such thing as totally consistent service; good firms have instituted strong quality management programs to try to produce consistent results, but it is always a struggle, because the people in an organization vary greatly in their intelligence, experience, communications skills and commitment to client satisfaction. In this respect, hiring, training and retaining the best people is a key marketing strategy for any service organization. Getting and keeping professional staff, particularly in the "Gen X" cohort, has become a critical problem in professional services; current demographic shifts in the availability of project personnel in the 35 to 44-year-old age range will affect firms' abilities to deliver green building services in years ahead.

Therefore, green design services need to be marketed in a way that differentiates them from other companies' offerings in these four important ways: perishable, inseparable from the key individuals, intangible and variable in quality. It is no wonder that green building marketers often throw up their hands at the inherent complexity of this task, given how difficult it is to get all of a firm's professionals to execute the company's game plan. The following chapter indicates how firms might use successful marketing tactics to create competitive advantage from basic strategic guidance.

NOTES

1   Rogers, E. (2003) *Diffusion of Innovations*, 5th edn. New York: Free Press.
2   Fichman, R.G. and Kemerer, C.F. (1999) The illusory diffusion of innovation: an examination of assimilation gaps. *Information Systems Research*, 10(3), 255–275.
3   Rogers, E. (2003) *Diffusion of Innovations*, 5th edn. New York: Free Press. (Also 1995, 4th edn., p. 314.)
4   Moore, G. (1999) *Crossing the Chasm: Marketing and Selling High-Tech Products to Mainstream Customers*. Revised edition. New York: HarperBusiness.
5   Gladwell, M. (2000). *The Tipping Point*. New York: Little, Brown.
6   Seth Godin (2003) *Purple Cow: Transform Your Business by Being Remarkable*. Dobbs Ferry, NY: Self-published.
7   US Green Building Council data furnished to the author, April 2007. State populations from US Census Bureau [online] http://factfinder.census.gov/servlet/GCTTable?_bm=y&-geo_id=01000US&-_box_head_nbr=GCT-T1&-ds_name=PEP_2006_EST&-_lang=en&-format=US-9&-_sse=on (accessed July 7, 2007).
8   Kotler, P. (1998) *Marketing Management*, 9th edn. New York: John Wiley & Sons, p. 295.
9   American Institute of Architects, Committee on the Environment, www.aia.org/cote.

10   After D.A. Aaker (2001) *Strategic Market Management*, 6th edn. New York: John Wiley & Sons, p. 209.
11   Michael Porter (1980) *Competitive Strategy*. New York: Free Press.
12   M. Treacy and F. Wiersma (1995) *The Discipline of Market Leaders*. Reading, MA: Addison-Wesley.
13   S. Lowe (2004) *Marketplace Masters: How Professional Service Firms Compete to Win*. New York: Praeger Publishers.
14   LEED AP numbers from Building Design + Construction, July 2007, Copyright 2007 Reed Business Information. All rights reserved. Industry rank from: Dave Barista, "25,000 LEED Professionals and Counting," *Building Design & Construction Magazine*, July 2006, p. S5.
15   In Oregon, for example, the state's Business Energy Tax Credit, worth a net 25 percent of the initial cost of PV systems, can be "passed through" from an institution or government agency to a for-profit tax-paying entity, on a dollar for dollar basis, making it available for all projects in the state.

10 SUSTAINABLE DESIGN MARKETING TACTICS

As we have documented earlier, the green building revolution is well underway in the US and Canada. To understand the current market situation, let's review what has happened since the introduction of the LEED system in April of 2000:

- Membership in the US Green Building Council, the primary industry association has increased 14-fold in six years, from about 600 corporate members at the end of 2000 to more than 8,400 members as of April 2007, representing tens of thousands of design and construction professionals, as well as public agencies, environmental groups, building owners, property managers and developers.[1]
- The LEED for New Construction green building rating system has certified more than 500 completed projects, as of December 2006, with another 300–400 certifications expected during 2007.
- Nearly 4,000 projects were registered at the end of December 2006 for certification under LEED-NC, representing 50 states and 13 foreign countries, including Canada, Spain, India and China. Thousands of other projects are using the LEED evaluation system without formally registering with LEED. (As shown in Table 2.3, 27 percent of the LEED-registered projects are in California, Oregon and Washington, making the West Coast the hot spot of national green building activity.)
- More than 45,000 professionals have taken the all-day LEED Intermediate Workshop covering the basics of the LEED system.[2]
- More than 36,000 building industry professionals have passed a national examination and become "LEED APs".[3]
- The USGBC's fifth annual *Greenbuild* conference and trade show in Denver, Colorado, in November 2006, attracted more than 13,000 attendees.

By anyone's reckoning, LEED is the fastest growing voluntary program to affect the design and construction industry in many years. Understanding LEED and how to use it effectively in marketing a design or construction firm has become more important in the past few years. As clients' knowledge of, and comfort with, the LEED system grows over time, they will increasingly demand that designers and builders understand how to use the system and how to achieve LEED results with little or no incremental design or construction cost. In effect, LEED has raised the bar for all building industry professionals. Not being up to speed on LEED, not having successful LEED projects in one's portfolio, will put firms increasingly at a significant disadvantage in this hyper-competitive marketplace.

WHO IS USING LEED?

The USGBC has documented the uses of LEED by public, private and nonprofit organizations. As of the end of March 2007, the total size of LEED-registered projects could be categorized by end-user as follows:

* Corporate   48% (the for-profit market)
* Local Government   14%
* Nonprofit   16%
* State Government   8%
* Federal Government   6%
* Other/Individual   8%

These data show that government agency buildings represent nearly one third the total project area, with government and nonprofit corporations together comprising about half of all project area. Corporate projects tend to be larger projects (typically for major corporations), with a smattering of local small companies with significant environmental goals or missions. *For marketers, the clear focus at this time can be either governmental and institutional or nonprofit projects, if their firms have experience in these sectors or it can be private sector projects alone.*

Another way to look at the LEED-registered projects is by end-use, as of March 2007. This is a much more diverse assortment; the largest uses, in descending order are:

* Commercial offices (including government and nonprofit clients) – 13%
* Multi-use (such as office/retail) – 19%
* Higher education – 7%
* K-12 education – 6%
* Public safety (police, fire, courthouses) – 5%
* Multi-family residential – 5%
* Industrial – 3%
* Healthcare – 3%
* All other – 39%

Just about every conceivable project type has been LEED registered, including a mostly underground Oregon wine-making facility. What marketers should understand from this brief rendition of the growth of LEED is that many public projects are likely to carry requirements either for a firm's having either LEED project experience or LEED APs on staff. Large adopters of LEED such as state and federal governments are beginning to consider having LEED-registered projects as 10 percent or more of the evaluation of a prime designer's qualifications.

Given that it often takes two years or more for projects to move from design to completion (and certification can only take place after substantial completion of a project), marketers should be pressuring their firms and their clients now to step up and participate in the certification of existing or upcoming projects. Some firms are even taking the step of providing the LEED project certification documentation (which can take from 100 to 200 hours of professional time) "pro bono" to valued clients, just to make sure that they can certify the project and have at least one on their resume. Considered as a marketing expense, such pro bono time is not large in the overall marketing budget of mid-size (30–50 people) or larger firms.

As of the end of April 2007, the 599 projects certified under the LEED-NC versions 2.0 and 2.1 certifications had attained the following levels. (There were also 19 LEED-NC version 1.0 certified pilot projects, but since these are "ancient history," we do not deal with them in our analysis, although firms do include them in their profiles.)

The 242 LEED-NC version 2.0 projects were certified at various levels, as follows:

- Certified: 89 projects   (36.7%)
- Silver: 72 projects   (29.8%)
- Gold: 73 projects   (30.2%)
- Platinum: 8 projects   (3.3%)

By the end of April of 2007, 357 projects LEED-NC version 2.1 projects had achieved the following certification levels:

- Certified: 147 projects   (41.2%)
- Silver: 115 projects   (32.2%)
- Gold: 83 projects   (23.2%)
- Platinum: 12 projects   (3.4%)

The most surprising result from this analysis is that the number of higher-level certifications has declined between LEED-NC version 2.0 (the earlier version that was in effect for projects registered from 2000 through 2002) and LEED-NC version 2.1 (in effect since 2003), from 33.5 to 26.6 percent, indicating teams are either settling for lower ratings, or that many new teams are doing their first project and are happy just to be at the Certified or Silver certification levels.

The 156 LEED-NC 2.0/2.1 Gold project certifications have included such varied building types as:

- Renovation of a 100-year-old warehouse in Portland, Oregon.
- A developer-driven technology park in Victoria, British Columbia.
- An elementary school in North Carolina.
- An office/warehouse building in Gresham, Oregon.
- A nonprofit office building in Menlo Park, California.
- Two projects for Herman Miller Company in Zeeland, Michigan.
- A public office building leased to the Commonwealth of Pennsylvania.
- A very large state office building in Sacramento, California.
- An environmental learning center in the Seattle, Washington area.

ROLES OF BUILDING PROFESSIONALS

Each professional discipline has a role to play in a typical green building project. Coordinating all of these professionals to produce a green building is often a formidable task, especially for a firm's first few sustainable design projects. However, each of these types of professional service firms has a strong interest in gaining credentials in sustainable design, so that they can do their own marketing in the future. Therefore, architects and owners need to appeal to their self-interest in this regard, especially if it's everyone's first green building project:

- **Architects** naturally have the task of coordinating overall building design and of dealing directly with the building envelope, daylighting, materials selection, window and roof specification, etc.
- **Interior designers** are responsible for materials selection for furniture and furnishings and specifying low-VOC paints, carpets and similar low-toxicity items. They may also be asked to assist with specifying elements of under-floor air distribution systems, such as carpet tile.
- **Mechanical and electrical engineers** can contribute between 25 and 50 percent of the total points required for LEED certification, focusing on water use, rainwater reclamation and gray water reuse systems, energy efficiency, lighting design, commissioning, indoor air quality, carbon dioxide monitoring and thermal comfort.
- **Civil engineers** have to deal with stormwater management, provide input on rainwater reclamation systems, prepare erosion and sedimentation control plans, and sometimes advise on constructed wetlands, bioswales and on-site waste treatment systems.
- **Landscape architects** need to consider water efficiency of landscaping design, provide input to design of detention ponds, bioswales and constructed wetlands, and also oversee site restoration programs.
- **Structural engineers** are asked to consider the relative benefits of wood, steel and concrete in structural systems, given their different effects

on sustainable design. Often projects that use passive thermal conditioning require heavy mass structural components such as concrete. Structural engineers also have a role to play in green roof technology, since weight is added to the structure.

- **Cost management consultants** have a significant role to play in assessing the costs of innovative green building systems, such as eco-roofs, solar power and stormwater retention systems, as well as advising clients on the overall costs of green buildings.

- **General contractors** have to provide for recycling of construction debris (often at a 90 percent or better level) and document the costs of all of the materials that go into a building. They oversee the construction indoor air quality management plans and activities, and they play a vital role in documenting the costs of the project. Contractors are also responsible for appropriate construction staging and erosion control plans.

- **Subcontractors** are often asked to work with unfamiliar or hard-to-obtain recycled-content materials and to document the costs they incur. Mechanical and electrical subcontractors often have to interact with the building commissioning process as well.

- **Environmental consulting** firms also have a role to play in sustainable site selection practices and assessment of the potential for on-site storm water management, brownfield redevelopment and site restoration, for example.

CASE STUDY: GREEN BUILDING ROLES FOR STRUCTURAL AND CIVIL ENGINEERS

It's easy for marketers of mechanical and electrical engineering services to see how their firms play a role in sustainable design projects, because of the clear connection with such topics as energy use, indoor air quality, daylighting integration, solar energy systems and similar green building measures. For marketers of structural and civil engineering services, the challenge is to identify and then publicize the importance of their contributions to attaining LEED certification.

As water conservation gains increasing importance in green building projects, so will rainwater harvesting and stormwater management systems, along with topics such as permeable paving in parking lots to allow infiltration of stormwater directly into local groundwater. Civil engineers can help design detention ponds in many areas that can collect rainwater on-site and use it for water features and landscape irrigation during dry periods. These ponds can also be designed to improve the quality of stormwater runoff from a site, helping to gain a LEED-NC water quality point. In some cases, by retaining all rainfall from a "100-year storm" on-site for reuse in a building, engineers have been able to eliminate the need for new storm drainage systems from a site, saving enough money to pay for the rainwater collection and treatment system.[4]

Graywater treatment systems can involve both the civil and mechanical engineers teaming up to collect and treat such wastewater for reuse in the building, cooling tower makeup, or even landscape irrigation or hardscape washing. Civil engineers can also look for opportunities to reuse existing concrete or asphalt for various fill and sub-base applications in project site work, thereby helping to achieve LEED credits for salvaged or recycled-content materials.

Often, the integration of all water conservation measures with stormwater management can lead up to eight points in the LEED-NC system. Marketers of civil engineering systems should look for projects where some or all of these green design elements are present and should actively challenge their technical staffs to put forward such contributions early in the conceptual design phase of a project with sustainability goals.

Structural engineers work hand-in-hand with architects to select appropriate structural systems for projects. Structures that use a lot of steel can contribute greatly to the recycled-content and (possibly) locally-sourced materials credits in LEED-NC projects. For projects with a lot of concrete use, structural engineers can help with recycled-content credits by specifying up to 50 percent fly-ash replacement for Portland cement and other cementitious materials in concrete mixtures.[5] Choices of structural systems can also reduce floor-to-floor heights (and therefore materials use and cost) in office buildings, if structural engineers coordinate locations for HVAC distribution systems with the mechanical engineer.[6]

In large-span structures such as arenas and concert halls, appropriate structural systems can reduce volumes that need to be conditioned, reducing the required size and cost of mechanical systems. Projects that want to use passive solar design measures often prefer to use thermal mass (concrete and stone) for radiant space conditioning; therefore, structural systems can often become part of the finished architectural design. Other projects want open ceiling systems that will expose the structural systems; in those cases, attention to their esthetic appearance is important.

As the attention of green building projects turns more to life cycle assessment of materials choices, it will become more important for structural engineers to provide input data on the environmental attributes of various structural systems.

These brief examples show how civil and structural engineers can play significant roles in promoting integrated design, sustainable site design, energy savings, water savings and use of recycled materials in green building projects. Therefore, marketers for such firms should make sure their technical staffs are present at early-stage design charrettes and actively engaged in project discussions with architects and other engineering consultants. Stressing the importance of these collaborative roles will help structural and civil firms differentiate their services for green building projects.

Greening a design firm

Building sustainable design capabilities at architectural and engineering firms engaged in green buildings can take many forms. Responding to an in-depth survey, firms reported seven major areas of activity, similar to our own survey data reported elsewhere in this book:[7]

1. An in-house Green Team that will offer internal consulting to projects.
2. Internal training and education, including staff-led and vendor-led in-house sessions and support for attending conferences and outside trainings.
3. Management of green building information, including a library and development of in-house specifications for green projects.
4. Tools for designers to use, including energy modeling tools and metrics for determining "shades of green," such as LEED.
5. Include expertise from outside (this is one of the most effective, but least favored measures, in my experience, owing to cost and the perception that "we can't do it ourselves"), or use capable consultants (in the case of architects, this would include mechanical, electrical and civil engineers).
6. Set goals for green projects, including LEED for client projects and internal assessments using LEED for all projects. Some firms start every project with an intent to "green" it as much as possible, regardless of budget or expressed client interest.
7. Green your own offices. Many design firms show their interest in sustainable design by crafting a LEED-CI, LEED-NC or LEED-EB project for their own offices. Figure 10.1 shows the offices of one firm, Opsis Architects, in Portland, Oregon, a simple 20,000 square foot (1836 sqm) building renovation that received a LEED-NC Gold certification that added an exclamation point (!) to the firm's already strong reputation for green design.

Assessing sustainable design marketing strategy

Certainly for most firms, the key marketing strategy of our time is "focus and differentiate." Most firms know their areas of focus fairly well, so the issue becomes how to differentiate a firm's capabilities in sustainable design from other firms'. Here are some suggestions for marketers of design and construction services.

Strategic assessment

Often a firm needs first to conduct a strategic review of its capabilities and opportunities using a "SWOT" (Strengths, Weaknesses, Opportunities, Threats)

▲ **10.1**   Originally used as a warehouse, office and stables, Opsis Architecture designed the upper 10,000 square foot floor for use as their own office space in the 75-year-old Lovejoy Office Building which is LEED-NC Gold certified. Courtesy of Opsis Architecture.

analysis, a well-known tool for assessing the following areas of concern:

- **Strengths:** Internal, including staff skills, project history, client relations, cost structure, competitive position within its market sectors, knowledge of green design, interest in green design, knowledge of specific building types, financial strength, etc.
- **Weaknesses:** Typically include lack of experience with green design projects, strong local and regional competitors who are advanced in such experience, lack of resources to hire the people they need to buttress their expertise, etc.
- **Opportunities:** External, including market trends, growth in various market sectors, new laws and regulations favoring green buildings, new financial incentives for green buildings, actions of competitors, industry dynamics, profitability of various market segments, new developments in green technology, etc.
- **Threats:** Changes in client policies to favor firms with green design expertise and completed projects, stronger competitors opening offices in a firm's home markets, etc.

Using this SWOT analysis, a firm can better assess its areas of maximum opportunity and direct its marketing efforts in a more cost-effective manner.

The sustainable design world changes fast and we need to assess the environment to make intelligent plans, so one of the key aspects of marketing planning is the situation analysis, environmental assessment or SWOT analysis. Identifying new opportunities in sustainable design should be one of the main goals of your marketing plan, both by client type and market sector. The SWOT analysis links your current situation with your vision, to generate an action plan for the coming one-to-three year period.

The SWOT analysis should be done at the beginning of each year, identifying internal strengths and weaknesses in sustainable design (e.g., getting or losing key people with track records in green buildings), as well as changes in the external environment that could create opportunities (e.g., you do university work and the president of the university you're closest to just announced that it will mandate LEED Gold for all upcoming projects) or threats (e.g., a firm with substantial expertise in green design just opened an office in your city). An accurate assessment of the competitive environment is critical for planning your marketing efforts.

INTEGRATING SUSTAINABLE DESIGN INTO MARKETING PROGRAMS

How should marketers advise their firms to take advantage of market opportunities in sustainable design? First of all, marketing plans have to explicitly promote sustainable design as a major focus of the firm; second, market research has to yield profitable opportunities in selected market segments and among targeted clients.

Marketing plans

Marketing plans are by nature speculative. They take what we know, add what we don't know but can guess at, and then come up with a game plan for the future that we intend to follow. Design firms are by nature opportunistic; I've yet to encounter very many that have the discipline and cohesion to follow a plan over the course of even 12 months, let alone multiple years. Those that stay on plan and "on message" often reap the rewards of gaining better projects, because there is an opportunity cost to not having a plan (and just pursuing any project opportunity that lands in front of you), just as there is a cost to having a plan and having to spend to implement it.

Yet the exercise of marketing planning is essential, for several reasons. As the old saying goes, "if you don't know where you're going, any road will take you there." Without a plan, it's impossible to make intelligent choices as to how to spend your budget, your time and the time of the key people in your firm – your number one marketing resource. Focusing most of your resources on a few key positioning strategies is the essence of good planning.

Marketing planning helps leverage your core capabilities, which include what your firm has already accomplished in sustainable design and green buildings, including LEED-certified projects in the past year and total of firm-wide LEED APs, as well as what you are capable of doing, but haven't yet found the right project to demonstrate.

Just as we leverage new prospects and our knowledge of upcoming projects, we need to have a marketing plan that clearly spells out "go/no go" decision criteria for sustainable design, development and construction opportunities. In fact, if you've done a good job of market segmentation, targeting and relationship management, you'll clearly know which projects *not* to pursue so that you can save your energy and resources for the project proposals that will move your firm forward in the world of green building.

Marketing planning is an essential ingredient in guiding marketing communications budgeting and execution, especially if a firm plans to open up a new line of business and wants to get the client and prospect base to look at the firm in a new light. Once you are clear about your firm's positioning in the world of sustainable design, then you'll know what the key messages need to be to reinforce your positioning.

A marketing plan provides a clear roadmap, in terms of both wayfinding and destination, against which you can assess your performance. Client needs are always changing, new competitors emerge, and your own project experience adds new dimensions of client satisfaction (or dissatisfaction) that will help (or hinder) your marketing efforts. Assessing the marketing environment and your performance in securing the work that you want is an essential element in marketing planning.

The marketing budget is a primary tool for pursuing new opportunities. Late in 2004, I convinced management of an engineering firm where I worked to spend more than $60,000 (a large amount for them) to prepare a detailed case study of a project still in design that we expected to be our first LEED Platinum project (and the largest in the world). This project was certified Platinum in early 2007. In the meantime, the firm has reaped enormous rewards (prior to project completion) from sending out more than 9,000 copies of the case study around the world. As part of a larger marketing communications program, this case study elevated the position of the firm in the minds of architects to one of the leading sustainable engineering firms on the West Coast. As this case illustrates, sometimes the marketing budget has to be viewed as an investment in a five-year strategic plan, rather than just a tactical expenditure for the coming year.

Market research

Given the rapid growth of the green building industry, it is clear that every firm is going to have to come up to speed on sustainable design and green construction, or risk falling behind its competitors. Some of the market research issues around creating sustainability marketing plans include:

- data gathering
- using sources of information
- designing formal research surveys
- analyzing qualitative and quantitative data
- forecasting trends.

Where should you get started? There are a growing number of trade magazines (and their online versions) that deal with sustainable design for the built environment. Probably the most useful for marketing professionals are the more general trade and professional publications with regular coverage of green buildings and green developments, described in Appendix 1.

You will easily see that there is way too much to read on a regular basis! Obviously there are online newsletters of every variety. Instead of subscribing to every one, I recommend trying Google Alerts; use such search terms such as "green building," "green development," "green construction," "sustainable design," and your inbox will get a good digest every morning of four to six news articles and two to four blog entries on the topic. This is a great way to get current information and an easy way for marketers to impress a firm's professional staff that they're on top of this issue.

You also need to understand the terminology of sustainability, especially LEED. I recommend taking a LEED Technical Review workshop as soon as possible to get better acquainted with the broad dimensions of the field, especially if your firm is an architect, engineer or builder. There are nearly 100 such workshops offered each year, so there should be one near you at least once a year. Also, make sure your firm is a member of the USGBC and attend some of the local chapter or branch meetings to learn more of the terminology and what's hot in your area at the present time.

I also recommend some serious market research, first of all with your clients. How much are they changing their focus toward sustainable design and construction? For example, the AASHE is a new umbrella group formed early in 2006 to coordinate architects and planners, business officers, facilities staff, administrators, faculty and students around the topic of sustainability on campus.[8] At the beginning of 2007, nearly 200 universities were dues-paying members. Simply put, sustainability is the hottest issue in higher education right now, and the student, faculty and university presidents' interest in this topic is putting pressure on college facilities staff to be as green as possible. That usually means achieving at least a LEED Silver rating for each project.

Research how many LEED APs your competitors have, and make sure you have a significant number of professional staff who are LEED APs and can respond to this new demand from established or prospective higher education clients.

DPR Construction is a major California-based firm with 185 LEED APs, 27 percent of its total staff of 665, a very strong showing for a construction firm and the highest percentage I know of that industry group. DPR's own 52,000-square foot (4775 sqm) regional office in Sacramento, California, shown in Figure 10.2, is a LEED-NC Silver-certified project. DPR also received LEED-CI

▲ **10.2**   DPR Construction gained an even greater understanding of the development process from an owner's perspective when they pursued (and received) LEED-NC Silver certification for its own 52,000 square foot Sacramento office building. Courtesy of DPR Construction, Inc.

Gold certification for the commercial interiors portion of the project, owned in conjunction with ABD Financial and Insurance Services, Inc. Their demonstrated corporate commitment ("we exist to build great green things") goes a long way toward selling institutional clients on their services, particularly in a world where contractors are chosen on qualifications, rather than just on price. As a construction firm interested in advancing its own capabilities, DPR used the project as an opportunity to further enhance its unique "LEED Preconstruction Cost Analysis Tool" to evaluate first costs vs. potential life cycle savings, making informed decisions regarding which credits to pursue and estimating the anticipated ROI. For example, DPR determined that the additional $85,000 outlay (1.4 percent of capital cost) for the new building would be recovered within 2½ years through water and energy savings, with an anticipated overall return of $359,758 by 2013.[9]

Take a look at upcoming local and state government projects; more than 15 states and 60 major cities have substantial policies requiring sustainable design certification for their own projects. Many public and institutional projects are incorporating five percent, 10 percent or higher weightings for sustainable design experience in their requests for qualifications (RFQs). (A good source for information on local government policies is the USGBC web site.)[10] More than 25 states offer incentives for renewable energy; a directory of incentives can be found online.[11] Your firm needs to know which such incentives are offered, for which types of projects, in each location where you do business.

Each market sector involved with building and development is moving quickly to incorporate LEED or other sustainable design standards in their projects: secondary education, healthcare, high-rise residential, affordable housing, cultural and recreational facilities, fire and police stations and corrections. Wherever your firm is active, you need to start tracking green-certified projects in that market area, by segments such as geographic, project type, project size and public/private.

Finally, there is still a role for qualitative research. For example, a firm should interview clients on a regular basis and find out where your firm is positioned (in their minds) relative to other firms offering similar services. Find out what sustainable design services they want that no one is yet offering; understand their level of experience and offer to update them from your own firm's projects.

If you've completed green design projects, there is a "one question" survey that can be easily administered and the results tracked, yielding surprisingly good data and trend lines. It is this question: "Based on your experience with this project, on a scale of 0–10, with 10 representing 'extremely likely,' how likely would you be to recommend our firm's green building services to a friend or colleague?"[12] The "promoters" give your firm ratings of 9 or 10. The "detractors" give your firm ratings of 0–6. Most marketers would consider 7 and 8 scores to be more or less neutral or "passively satisfied;" they are unlikely to give strong recommendations to others. Subtract the number of detractors from the number of promoters, to get the "net promoter score," and you'll get a more accurate picture of who is singing your praises and who is telling the world not to use your services. Tracked over time, the results of this simple question can lead to a revolution in client loyalty, as well as spurring your internal training and education efforts. The lifetime value of a client is realized fully only from truly loyal clients who recommend your services to others. Says Harvard Business School Professor, Frederick Reichheld, "The only path to profitable growth may rest in a company's ability to get its loyal customers to become, in effect, its marketing department."[13]

BUSINESS DEVELOPMENT

In a 2007 interview, Russell Perry of SmithGroup spoke of his major business development goals for the sustainability focus at that firm: be considered equal or better than all major competitors by desirable clients and to be shortlisted in all major design procurements.[14] Perry said, "we want to get to a place where sustainability as a firm focus and our experience with completed projects will give us an advantage among our clients and prospects. My assessment is that we're there right now." In addition, the firm has a specific numerical goal: be among the top five design firms in the percentage of LEED Accredited Professionals on staff. As Perry said, "That will tell me and our clients that we care deeply about sustainable design and that we're ready to deliver on our commitments with each project opportunity."

If you're not considered equal or better than the competition, you aren't going to be able to grow the firm or even hold onto some existing clients. In addition, you won't be able to hold your own in the recruiting battles for top talent either. After all, if someone has a passion for sustainability, why would they want to go with a second-tier firm in that field?

And if you're not shortlisted for desirable projects, it's like not getting up to the plate in baseball: if you're not swinging, you can't get a hit. (I also like this baseball analogy: if you hit one out of three times up, you're a cinch for the Hall of Fame; if you're always on the three-name shortlist and get one of three, you should consider that a noteworthy accomplishment!)

In professional services marketing, current and future clients look at a firm differently depending on their own commitment to sustainability. In early 2002, I took on the task of developing a sustainability reputation for a midsize consulting engineering firm in the Northwest, serving mainly architects as clients.

A younger generation of managers had taken over at the firm, and they wanted to move it in this direction. At the time, the firm had completed two LEED-certified projects, but was primarily regarded as a rather ordinary firm doing pretty straightforward commercial and institutional projects.

Many of our more desirable clients/prospects were beginning to show strong interest in sustainable design and green buildings, but we faced three similar sized, reasonably progressive engineering competitors who had been building good reputations in the green building field. So, we had to adopt a systematic approach to this marketing problem.

Early on, we adapted our Customer Relationship Management (CRM) system to track all of our work in the sustainability field, for use in future RFPs and RFQs. That took a bit of work, because no one had marked any of the 2,500 existing data entries with sustainability tags. We also had to write a number of sustainability project case studies (ultimately numbering more than 50) and develop standard proposal/qualifications language that we could use in the future.

But the bigger problem was how to convince prospective architect clients that not only were we serious about green design, but had the background, project experience and capabilities to be a good project partner for them, often in competitive situations. So we embarked on a threefold business development program.

First, we just asked for meetings with their principals and senior staff, so we could discuss our interests and find out theirs. These meetings sometimes included presentations of specific green building projects or those with green elements. It turns out that architects were actually interested in how we might approach a particular green building issue and eager to expand their own knowledge base. Whenever we were able to present an approach that the architect's current engineering consultants hadn't thought of or had dismissed, we could see a light go on and observe the nods between the client's principals and senior staff.

Second, we ramped up the internal training efforts on sustainability and green design, with a special effort to grow the number of LEED Accredited Professionals in the firm, to at least stay equal with local competitors. This effort was particularly important to the marketing group, because we didn't want to sell a client on our interests and capabilities in sustainable design, then have our people not appear knowledgeable (or even interested) in the subject at the first project meeting! As most marketers know, if you sell a project and your people don't deliver what you said they would, you're toast! In most cases, it can take 2–3 years (or more) to recover from a client's bad experience with your people.

Third, we decided to become more visible in the green building industry. We joined the USGBC and began to hang out with the local chapter as well as attend meetings of the AIA Committee on the Environment. In fact, the goal was to become ubiquitous among architects and to cultivate the reputation as engineers who "got it," as far as green design was concerned.

As an adjunct to the first effort, we began to share our knowledge, not just in one-on-one client meetings, but in as many industry forums as we could find. This had the benefit of showcasing our skills as green engineers and building a cumulative positive impression in the minds of our architect–clients and prospects (and their clients, the ultimate decision-makers). Prior to this effort, the firm had the reputation of being competent, with lower fees than most competitors a key competitive advantage. Now the goal was to stay competitive on fees, but bring a much higher level of skill to our projects. In addition to local- and regional-speaking engagements, we also published as much as we could in the national building (and engineering) trade magazines, as way to introduce ourselves to as many clients and building owners as possible.

The result: as of early 2007, the firm had more than 12 LEED-certified projects, including one Platinum, and more than 60 LEED projects underway. Many of the original target prospects have become regular clients, and the firm is quite competitive in attracting talented engineers with strong green building interests. As an unexpected benefit, we also began to attract developer–clients who would ask us to be the engineers on a project team.

One final note: every client likes to be asked for feedback. When introducing or emphasizing a new service like sustainable design, it's really important to get client comments during the design phase, rather than waiting for a completed project. For example, if the client had high expectations that a particularly skilled person would spend more time on its project than s/he is actually doing, that early feedback enables corrective measures. I remember dropping off Christmas gifts about six months into a really important and high-profile green project and casually asking the principal-in-charge at the architectural firm how we were doing. The negative feedback, fair or not, was that our lead design principal wasn't being responsive enough for what was a highly important project for the architect. After I delivered that feedback, our lead engineer really stepped up his efforts to put this project first on his priority list. The end result: two years later, a really satisfied client, an enhanced reputation and an award-winning project.

MARKETING TACTICS THAT WORK

Firms are beginning to focus on a series of measures that will ensure success in sustainable design. As with most good ideas, the first test is commitment. In the competition for a firm's time and resources, sustainability must be given adequate attention and priority.

Make a major firm commitment to sustainability

Many design firms have been proactive in promoting a commitment to sustainability. To organize its sustainability efforts in the early 2000s, one Portland architectural firm, BOORA Architects, set up three internal committees that address first, sustainability at home (for all firm members); second, building up the firm's internal sustainability activities and third, examining each project for its success in incorporating sustainable design elements.[15] Still other firms have hired sustainability coordinators to set up and manage internal information and to provide expertise and resources to each project. Other firms have set up separate internal profit centers to offer their sustainability expertise as consultants to both their own projects and to external clients. Finally, some architectural and engineering firms have taken advantage of planned moves of their own offices to experiment with green design, participate in LEED-CI pilot projects and to show everyone that they can "walk the talk."

Sustainability is not a destination, but a journey. By making a strong company commitment to sustainable design and operations, many firms are beginning to walk the talk, in an open way. Clients appreciate working with firms that share their values and that are willing to experiment with new technologies and processes. This is true contemporary marketing: *building relationships based on shared values.*

DEVELOPING A SUSTAINABLE DESIGN FOCUS

Marketing professionals are in a good position to assess a firm's strengths and weaknesses and to know what the client base is looking for. The first rule of good professional service marketing is "don't oversell." Show clients what you have done and tell them what you'd like to do, specifically, to help them green their next project.

Capabilities

Know what your principals and senior level people are doing in the area of sustainable design and learn what they are hearing about the need for these services among your client base. Incorporate all sustainable design projects into the firm's standard capabilities statements (SOQs) and proposals. (Many projects have sustainable design elements that can be used without necessarily being LEED registered; my estimate is that less than half of all projects with some form of sustainability commitment register with LEED, owing to cost considerations.) Make sure you're familiar with the language of sustainable design for your professional area and, if you're the firm's chief marketer, push the technical types to "clue you in" where your own knowledge base might be a little weak.

Competitors

Know the strengths and weaknesses of the competition in this area of design and construction, so that you'll be prepared to match their strengths and exploit their weaknesses in the proposal and interview stage. You may even decide not to respond to a solicitation from a client asking for sustainable design, if you think your firm can't yet stand up to the competition for a certain project type or for a client that is already experienced in LEED projects.

Differentiate services

Of course, the major focus of green design marketing has to be some form of service differentiation. Make sure clients know how your firm will approach the project differently from major competitors by showcasing your team's design tools and understanding of sustainable design. One North American mechanical engineering firm showed its commitment to the LEED system in the early 2000s, for example, by certifying more than 60 percent of its staff as LEED APs, including some not directly involved in design, and by eagerly embracing and introducing new technologies in its area of expertise. As a result, this firm was able to establish strong connections in new geographic territories with innovative green architects.

People

Make sure that at least 20 percent of your total staff becomes LEED APs. As of mid-2007, only 13 of the top 50 firms ranked by number of LEED APs had achieved this level. More importantly, the firm needs to realize that there is a huge commitment required to training and education, as well as to acquire specialized expertise and tools, to compete effectively in the green building marketplace.

Publish results

Build a portfolio of LEED-registered and LEED-certified projects as quickly as possible. Look for other projects that have sustainability elements and try to incorporate them into your case studies as quickly as possible. One firm hired a writer to craft more than 30 case studies profiling its successful project experience in sustainable design that it uses to market these services and provide to the media to help in profiling the firm's expertise.

Press

Tell your story aggressively to as many media outlets as you can. Successful sustainable design projects are still rare enough in many areas of the country and in specialized market niches (even large market segments, such as K-12 schools, had less than 50 certified projects nationwide as of early 2007). Publications in all vertical markets are publishing articles on sustainable projects on a regular basis. These are one of the main vehicles for new clients to become aware of your firm.

USGBC activities

Membership "has its privileges," to borrow a phrase. Make sure your company joins the USGBC and uses its logo on proposals, stationery and brochures. Joining the USGBC and becoming active in the local chapter or branch signals to clients that you have the interest and knowledge they are seeking. The cost is minor, and it is probably the best investment a firm can make to establish credibility with clients.

External marketing

It is essential for your principals and key staff to share their knowledge and enthusiasm for sustainable design with potential clients on a regular basis. You will find out what your clients know and want, and what your people don't know and should learn. Prepare to offer sustainability services as an extra service on all major proposals to your clients (but be prepared soon to include most of these design services in the base fee, as clients learn what is and isn't required for LEED projects). Be prepared to explain to them why this approach will not only benefit the project directly, but could also result in major marketing benefits for their project, company or organization. I advocate sharing knowledge in the form of talks, articles, classes, seminars and one-on-one discussions; leading professional firms can successfully differentiate themselves by sharing knowledge with clients and the larger green building community in an appropriate way. This often leads to "casual marketing" through word-of-mouth referrals, improved relationships and team building. It is also a way to attract new talent without having to pay fees to professional recruiters!

Narrow the focus

A final cautionary word: not every client is a candidate for green marketing at this time. Not every client wants to be the "first kid on the block" to have a "new toy" or to be a technology leader. While many building owners and institutional facilities managers trust their architects and are willing to follow the architect's lead in pursuing a green building agenda, most corporate and building owners are more cautious, and speculative developers, for the most part, are still in the "wait and see" stage. So, focus most of your marketing efforts on the more adventurous owners, the innovators and early adopters.

INTEGRATING GREEN DESIGN AND MARKETING ACTIVITIES

Once a firm secures a sustainable design project, the marketing work has just begun, for a successful effort is always the best marketing tool, and one cannot wait for a project to be finished (which might take two to three years) to start generating enthusiastic client support for referrals and testimonials. Early design activity, such as eco-charrettes and green forums, should also have a clear presentation of the areas of uncertainty in the project and should develop explicit strategies for dealing with them.

These strategies might include:

- Literature research and site visits to similar green projects; look at the LEED scorecard from similar projects in other parts of the country and discuss with those designers what worked and what didn't.
- Early design modeling of daylighting, energy efficiency and natural ventilation opportunities, to confirm costs and technical feasibility.
- Early design interaction with materials and equipment vendors, to confirm availability, suitability for the project and approximate cost.
- Careful attention to early design decisions so that they do not preclude effective green building measures from consideration during later stages of design. (One school project that I encountered had a client demand – from the inception – for air conditioning. This school was located in a very mild coastal Northwest climate, and natural ventilation strategies were quite appropriate for the intended use. By giving in to this demand early, the designers added cost to the project and precluded some more elegant design approaches.)

USING DIFFUSION THEORY TO FOCUS YOUR MARKETING EFFORTS

The theory of "diffusion of innovations" gives powerful insight into this behavior (see Chapter 9 for a more detailed presentation). Less than three percent of clients are likely to be *innovators* and willing to pursue a new design trend or technology development before seeing how others have done with it. Another 13 percent or so are called *early adopters* who are likely following these trends and developments closely and are willing to try them once they see a few successful experiments or case studies. The remaining population of clients will not generally embrace change or take much risk, without clear evidence of benefit and a clear track record to examine. They are the "wait and see" crowd and at this time, generally represent a waste of time for marketers at this stage.

This analysis suggests that architects and engineers need to be selective about which clients they pursue for green building projects and how they approach them. Your past successful (and documented) experience will be a powerful selling point in convincing clients to pursue LEED-registered projects with you. Additionally, designers should do research on other innovations the client has embraced in the past, what forces – internal and external – are driving the client to consider green design, and in which areas of technology and operations the client is likely to have greater tolerance for the risk and ambiguity inherent in taking new approaches.

CASE STUDY: MITHUN

Based in Seattle, Washington, Mithun shows how a leading sustainable architecture, urban planning, interior design and landscape architecture firm applies these principles. The firm's President and CEO, Bert Gregory, emphasizes that firms must invest in efforts like extensive staff training, conference and event speaking engagements and in opportunities that encourage collaboration and team effort – all while pursuing internal research and development using the firm's money and not the clients'. Without these efforts, firms will eventually fall by the wayside as more aggressive and savvy businesses pass them by.[16] With Mithun since the mid-1980s, and as president and CEO for some time, Gregory has been instrumental to the firm's ongoing focus on sustainable design, beginning with the landmark Seattle Recreational Equipment Inc. flagship store in the 1990s.

The firm takes a proactive approach to marketing sustainable design through both its internal programs and external visibility. Remarking on Mithun's speakers' presence at various events, Gregory says, "These talks always help make people aware of our firm. Proactivity means working toward this awareness; making sure that we're establishing relationships and investing in our community."

Collaborative efforts have complemented Mithun's sustainable design practice by emphasizing strategies that rely upon a diverse team from the outset of a project. According to Gregory, such strategies have changed the firm and brought its leadership onto a number of complex projects. "These days we are spending more time sitting on the same side of the table as our clients, helping them understand the long-term economic impact, ROI and choices they can make that will establish a higher value for their project or their portfolio," says Gregory. "The distinguishing feature of our practice has been our ability to incorporate design excellence with sustainable strategies – all while collaborating across disciplines."

In terms of competitive strategy, Gregory believes sustainability is the cost of entry for the most interesting assignments. Research and development is an important aspect of the firm's sustainability practice, because it helps the firm remain a leader. Most design firms do very little unpaid research and development, but Mithun's example indicates that dedicating even as little as a half-percent of revenues can help a firm lead the way.

Leading the way with other endeavors, Mithun is a member of the Chicago Climate Exchange, a voluntary, legally binding, rules-based system for reducing and trading greenhouse gas emissions. Carbon-neutral since 2004, Mithun is also an associate of the Bonneville Environmental Foundation, a nonprofit corporation funding watershed restoration programs and clean, environmentally preferred renewable energy projects. Initiatives of this kind and the firm's known leadership in green design help bring talented employees from throughout the world to Mithun. Demand for green design has doubled the firm's size between 2002 and early 2007.

In terms of actual practice, Mithun has completed a number of LEED-certified projects and many studies of urban sustainability, including two important studies of entire urban districts, profiled in Chapter 6.[16] The "Resource Guide for Sustainable Development in an Urban Environment," focusing Seattle's South Lake Union neighborhood and the "Lloyd Crossing Sustainable Urban Design Plan," focusing on Portland, Oregon's Lloyd District, are both landmarks in green urban design and can be downloaded from Mithun's web site.[17]

As an example of the firm's approach to sustainable design, consider the Zoomazium project in Seattle.[18] The first LEED Gold-certified zoo building in the world, Zoomazium demonstrates a new paradigm for interactive exhibit space that is sustainable, adaptable and flexible. Nestled in the zoo's lush vegetation, the building is not a backdrop; rather, it is an integral part of the learning experience.

An integrated design process combined the architectural, exhibit, landscape, interior design teams with structural, mechanical, electrical and civil engineers and the zoo's experts in botany, interpretation, construction and marketing. This collaboration reinterpreted the project's sustainable principles (natural ventilation, daylighting, flexible space, views from adjacent exhibits and trails, and a vegetated roof) as powerful environmental teaching tools for children.

Zoomazium is designed specifically to conserve energy, reduce pollution, and improve building performance and comfort. For example, the building is powered 100 percent by purchased green power to reduce reliance on fossil fuels. It consciously departs from the "black box" exhibit model that relies entirely on artificial lighting, and instead reaches out to the surrounding Pacific Northwest forest as an extension of the interior space. Mithun refers to this marriage of LEED values and "black box" infrastructure as the "green box" approach. Durable materials, easy maintenance and adaptability are the key to buildings that will be used for more than 50 years. Designed with these qualities, Zoomazium is destined to become an integral part of Woodland Park Zoo.

NOTES

1   USGBC data provided to the author, April 2007.
2   US Green Building Council, LEED Faculty Newsletter, April 2007.

3   Ibid.

4   From Gray to Green: Sustainability and the Engineer, 2003, R.C. Field and D. Hun, Moore Facts, available from Walter P Moore Inc., www.walterpmoore.com.

5   A Designer's View of Fly-Ash Concrete, 2007, J.A. Vargas, *Concrete International*, February, pp. 45–48.

6   Green Design for the Structural Engineer, 2002, R.C. Field, available from Walter P Moore Inc., www.walterpmoore.com.

7   *Environmental Building News*, Vol. 13, No. 5, May 2004, www.buildinggreen.com.

8   AASHE [online], www.aashe.org.

9   DPR Construction, project case study [online], www.dprinc.com/projects/project.cfm?ID=287 (accessed April 25, 2007).

10 US Green Building Council [online], www.usgbc.org.

11 Directory of State Incentives for Renewable Energy [online], www.dsireusa.org (accessed April 19, 2007).

12 Frederick F. Reichheld, "The One Number You Need to Grow," Harvard Business Review, December 2003 [online], http://harvardbusinessonline.hbsp.harvard.edu/b02/en/common/item_detail.jhtml?id=R0312C&referral=2340 (accessed April 19, 2007).

13 Ibid., p. 7 of article.

14 Flying with Eagles, *Marketer*, April 2007, Vol. 26, No. 2, pp. 12–15, www.smps.org.

15 Oregon Natural Step Network, Case study of BOORA Architects, January 2002 [online], www.ortns.org/documents/boora_001.pdf (accessed April 19, 2007).

16 Original Interview with Bert Gregory, Mithun, *Marketer*, April 2004 [online], www.smps.org. Updated in April 2007 for this publication.

17 Mithun [online], www.mithun.com.

18 Information supplied by Mithun.

11 CHALLENGES TO THE FIRM POSED BY GREEN MARKETING DYNAMICS

In this chapter, we discuss how a firm needs to reorganize itself to promote sustainable design in both its marketing and the rest of its operations. In itself, this is no simple task, as most firms have gone through several iterations of responding to the sustainable design opportunity and imperative, sometimes lasting five years or more. The most important thing in 2007 and 2008 is to get started, if you haven't already, and to take the next steps, if you're already on the path.

J. Rossi of Burt Hill, ranked 26th among US architecture and engineering (A/E) firms based on 2005 revenues, says this about the challenges facing her firm, going forward.[1]

> It's going to be tough to remain competitive. I think one of things that distinguishes our firm is that we have not just recently started doing this. Sustainability has been part of our ethic for a long time; however, getting that message across is the challenge. We incorporate that in our marketing materials, proposal responses website, etc. We haven't just jumped on the bandwagon in the past couple of years. We've honestly been aware of and conscious of sustainable practices since the '70s but the competition is stiff in every single way. I think we just have to keep getting our message out there.

The firm has responded by creating the position of "director of sustainable design," reporting to the CEO and the board. Rossi says, "We formed a firm-wide committee of individuals from each office that meet regularly and are responsible for leading the sustainability effort in each office. We've developed a philosophy, a plan for education and an operations plan that is being executed. It's a dedicated effort that's happening within Burt Hill."

MARKETING REQUIREMENTS FOR SERVICE FIRMS

Figure 11.1 depicts three interrelated forms of marketing by service firms, including those in the green building industry. Marketing for service firms is

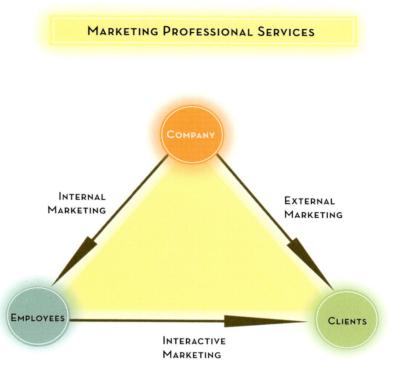

MARKETING PROFESSIONAL SERVICES

COMPANY

INTERNAL
MARKETING

EXTERNAL
MARKETING

EMPLOYEES

CLIENTS

INTERACTIVE
MARKETING

▶ **11.1** Marketing professional services.

very different from marketing for products, because of the amount of client trust and professional competency involved. In the building industry, each "product" is a "one-off" prototype, never exactly repeated, whereas in the sale of products, a manufacturer might make a million copies based on the same prototype, thereby assuring quality control.

First, service firms carry out "external marketing" to their clients. Typically, it is only this activity that has been considered as "marketing." In external marketing, key people at a firm make contact with current or potential clients to secure future business. Service firms make a considerable effort to develop marketing collateral materials, place advertising, carry out public relations campaigns, develop client relationship management systems (CRM) and practices, engage in direct mail, newsletters, etc., all to appeal to a client or prospect, with the purpose of securing an assignment.

However, the service that is being marketed is actually delivered by individual associates and project teams to the client; this form of marketing can be called "interactive marketing" since the quality of the interaction between client and project team (leading to a successful project in the client's mind) is decisive in determining the success of future marketing efforts. A leading academic marketing text puts it this way:[2]

> Interactive marketing describes the employees' skill in serving the client. Because the client judges service quality not only by its technical quality (e.g., Was the surgery successful?), but also by its functional quality (e.g., Did the surgeon show concern and inspire confidence?), service providers must deliver 'high touch' as well as 'high tech.'

The third aspect to professional service marketing is "internal marketing," in which the firm trains and indoctrinates its associates in how it expects them to perform for clients, for example, using an *integrated design process* to carry out sustainable design on a given project. This third form of marketing is most often neglected in the architecture, engineering and construction industry. Typically, everyone is too busy to invest much quality time in training and professional education; by contrast, some firms have made an aggressive commitment to this form of marketing by making sure that most of their professional staff involved studies for and passes the test to become a LEED Accredited Professional.

Case study: Developing a sustainability focus at an engineering firm

How should firms market their capabilities to the audience of decision-makers? What results should they anticipate? The following is an example of how my former employer, Interface Engineering, Inc., approached the challenge over a five year period from 2002 through 2006. Headquartered in Portland, Oregon, with four other offices, Interface Engineering emerged as a leader among Northwest mechanical and electrical engineering firms in promoting and executing sustainable design. This resulted from increasing attention to energy engineering and other aspects of sustainable design, as well as a change in management philosophy and marketing perspective, with a clear commitment to promoting sustainable design and operations.[3]

An integrated mechanical/electrical consulting engineering firm, with about 150 employees, Interface ranks approximately 50th to 60th in size nationally among similar firms and one of the top five in its primary market area of northern California, Oregon and Washington. Two fundamental principles have anchored this evolution. They are very similar to those enunciated by Bert Gregory of Mithun Architects, Seattle, profiled earlier in this book.

1. Do the work well that's in your area of professional responsibility, with a passion for achieving high-performance results.
2. Make it clear to staff and clients alike that there is a major firm commitment to sustainability. (This principle is discussed later in this chapter.)

Do the work well

Without good design execution, all good intentions are for naught. In 1997, Andy Frichtl, PE, a young engineering principal with a passion for energy efficient design, helped Interface design the first thermal-energy storage system in the Portland area, using ice as a storage medium. The principle of these systems is simple: buy cheap power during the night to make ice, and then use the ice for cooling (in place of more expensive electricity) during the day. In 1997, this project won an Architecture+Energy design award (the firm's first) from the Portland Chapter of the AIA.

In 2000 and 2001, Frichtl was the lead mechanical designer for the Interface team for the Ecotrust Building (now known as the Jean Vollum Natural Capital Center) in Portland's Pearl District. In this case, the team was faced with converting an 1895 brick warehouse into a modern office building for a nonprofit owner. Andy's team came up with a design estimated to be 22 percent more efficient than the Oregon Energy Code, in effect updating the building by 100 years without changing its 22-inch-thick brick walls. With an emphasis on low cost/no cost energy-efficiency measures such as occupancy sensors, low-emittance glazing, daylighting controls, CO_2 monitors to control ventilation rates, and a first-rate building automation system to control all the various sensors and energy-using systems, the project also incorporates operable windows and a wonderfully daylit atrium. Interface's design effort was instrumental in the project's LEED Gold rating, the first in the western US and only the second in the country.

At the LEED Silver-certified Clackamas High School, inaugurated in April 2002, Interface Engineering provided electrical engineering, daylighting design and controls, and building commissioning. The daylighting design is fairly sophisticated and represents the first commercial use of an effective, but complex new lighting control system. The building commissioning program was able to work out many of the performance bugs in the building control system prior to occupancy. However, the commissioning of the complex lighting controls took much longer.[4]

Make the commitment to sustainable design clear

The Interface Engineering team is also involved in more than 60 LEED-registered and soon-to-be-certified projects (with 12 LEED-certified through early 2007), including the Courthouse Square public building in Salem, OR (a LEED 1.0 Bronze-certified project), the Eagle Creek Elementary School in Jackson County, OR and a new middle school in The Dalles, OR with LEED Silver-certification aspirations. Other projects use similar skills: at Portland (OR) State University's new Epler Hall Student Housing project (LEED Silver certified); the Interface team designed an innovative rainwater recycling system for on-site use in toilet flushing. A project in central Oregon, the Mid-State Electric Cooperative headquarters in La Pine, OR, received a LEED Gold Rating (see Figure 5.3).

In 2003, the firm competed for the engineering design of the $145 million *Center for Health and Healing* at Oregon Health & Science University in Portland. Spending a considerable time with an internal design charrette, the firm's innovative proposals for high-performance results, using less than the original budget, won the assignment from an experienced local build-to-suit developer. In 2005, the firm completed design on what has become the world's largest LEED Platinum-certified building (certification granted in March of 2007). This project received the 2006 ARC national "Project of the Year" award from *Consulting-Specifying Engineer*, a national engineering trade magazine.[5] A strong and multi-faceted public relations effort, coupled with high-performance results (61 percent energy savings and 54 percent water savings) achieved at 10% less than the original budget for mechanical and electrical systems, has brought the firm considerable attention and new business.

As a result of doing the work well, Interface Engineering is now receiving regional recognition for its expertise in energy engineering, indoor air quality, daylighting controls, natural ventilation, building commissioning, rainwater harvesting and water conservation design. It is also a good business, as an increasing number of architects are including the Interface team as their sustainable design consultants for green building projects.

CHANGING THE DNA OF A DESIGN FIRM

Figure 11.2 shows the five major areas in which a design or construction firm needs to change its character, its competitive DNA, to successfully pursue sustainable design as a major business element. The five areas are:

1. Leadership
2. Communications
3. Knowledge management
4. Education and training
5. Operations.

Leadership

Leadership is always the first element in catalyzing change in any organization. Leadership in sustainable design means putting that emphasis forward as a major new direction for the firm, then convincing partners, senior associates, technical staff, engineering consultants, vendors and clients that this is what they should also be doing. As is often said, "without vision, the people perish" (Proverbs 29:18). With clear and decisive leadership, a firm's opportunities in sustainable design may pass without anyone prepared to grasp them.

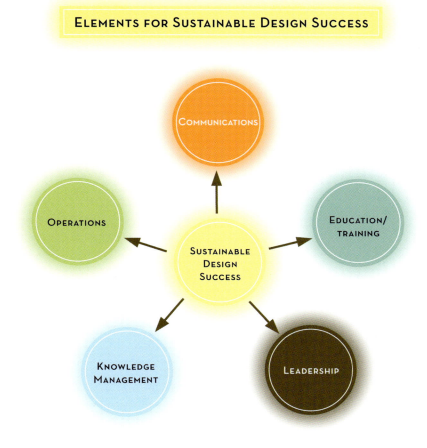

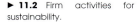 **11.2** Firm activities for sustainability.

In late 2005, Russell Perry was hired as a Vice President and Director of Sustainability for SmithGroup, an integrated A/E firm with about 800 employees and 2005 revenues of about $120 million.[6] In 2006, Perry secured a commitment from the firm's 160 principals that every one of them would become LEED Accredited by the end of 2007.[7] He feels that this sends a message to the rest of the professional staff about what management considers important and will spur them to complete their LEED accreditation as well.

As another example, a 230+ person A/E firm based in Sacramento, California, *Lionakis Beaumont Design Group* has 14 principals, all LEED APs. One principal,

David Younger, describes the firm's commitment to sustainability as "leading by example." All of the principals in the firm have made this commitment by becoming LEED accredited. This top-down approach serves as an example to the staff demonstrating the firm's commitment to sustainability. It is this leadership that has been instrumental growing the firm over the past five years, to secure a reputation for excellence in sustainable design.[8] The firm began its sustainable journey in 1999, as the result of losing a major competition with sustainable design goals and realizing they needed to learn this new approach to design. By 2002 the firm had 10 LEED APs out of 115 total staff.[9]

Communications

Internal and external communications need to reinforce a firm's commitment to green design and sustainable practices. Perry says it was hard on SmithGroup's marketing staff to "tell our story because we really didn't know what it was."[10] As a result, the firm decided that a key focus for 2007 was to develop coherent statements about its approach to sustainable design, with a compelling story about commitment, process and achievements. Once a firm makes a strong commitment to communicating its interest in and commitment to green design, it is amazing how many opportunities arise to present them to current and prospective clients. People inside the organization are also eager to hear this message, so it is important that the company Intranet also be used as a communications vehicle, with frequent postings of interesting news links about sustainable design as well as the firm's own achievements.

Knowledge management

Many larger design firms have hired sustainability coordinators in the past five years, people whose main job is to maintain all of the information flowing through the firm about green products, green specifications, green design methods, new building systems and similar items. Often these coordinators have technical backgrounds, but sometimes they do not. One key aspect of knowledge management is capturing the lessons learned from each project, whether or not the owner or client decides to pursue a LEED certification. Some firms keep a LEED scorecard internally for each project and ask design teams to prepare documentation, so that they can judge how well the firm is doing in its commitment to sustainable design. That way, it becomes easier to move the entire firm along and to present clients the cost and performance implications of their proposed project, for example, for a LEED Gold science laboratory. In a large firm, of course, this process can also set off a healthy internal competition to be the most sustainable design studio. The key with knowledge management is to capture the institutional learning so that future projects can benefit from discoveries or errors on current projects.

Education and training

Every design firm budgets for education and training. But how many have thought that sending several talented younger designers to Europe or Japan to observe sustainable design projects can be beneficial to the entire firm? Some larger design firms do this, sending younger associates out for four to six weeks, with a mandate to report back on new developments in other countries that the firm can use in its work. Of course, with more design and construction work moving overseas to places like Dubai and Shanghai, it makes good business sense to begin internationalizing the firm's experience.

Internal education is essential at every design firm. For an architect, it often means vendor-sponsored "lunch and learns" as well as inviting in key consultants to present their perspectives. It means an intensive commitment to senior and more knowledgable staff teaching those with less experience. It often involves extensive case studies of the firm's first few sustainable design projects, so that everyone can learn from mistakes made and also from things that went well. Training in integrated design process, typically using outside facilitators and instructors, will become more prevalent as firms realize that a strong commitment to integrated design is the only way to achieve high-performance results on conventional budgets. Once mastered, it is also a great selling point to clients, who themselves are struggling to come up with new methods of delivering green design projects.

For most firms, education and training also means attending more green building trade shows, conferences and seminars; it means sending everyone who would ever be at a project meeting (recall Figure 11.1) to a basic LEED workshop, so that they'll understand what people are talking about when LEED enters the discussion. Of course, it means getting all of the senior staff and much of the junior staff to take the examination for becoming a LEED AP and honoring that achievement with both internal and external communications. In many firms, education will also mean attending the proliferating green conferences focused on a special areas of expertise, such as higher education, laboratories, healthcare, K-12 schools, government projects and similar market segments.

Operations

Describing the many methods for greening a firm's operations could take an entire book. Typical sustainable operations involve such areas as recycling, transit subsidies, purchasing policies, analyzing overall use of paper products, green housekeeping and using the office as a laboratory for practices that can be brought to clients' projects. More adventurous firms also have begun contributing their new expertise to the community, by serving on advisory boards and commissions, getting involved with local schools and similar activities.

And, as mentioned earlier, committed firms also seize on opportunities to green their own offices, either with a LEED-CI or a LEED-EB project.

But a firm can always do even more, if the leadership and senior staff are committed. For example, look at what one design firm, SERA Architects in Portland, Oregon has done. Through a commitment to The Natural Step principles for sustainability, the firm has engaged in a decade-long internal study of how to make their own operations conform to these principles.[11] Beginning in 2003, the firm's action plan encompassed nine major areas: energy, chemical use, materials use, travel, paper, food, furniture/finishes/equipment, the firm's design library and human resources. Choosing to pick the "low hanging fruit" made the actions more understandable to the firm's staff and led to early "wins" that encouraged the process to continue.

CHANGING THE DNA OF A MAJOR CONSTRUCTION FIRM: SWINERTON BUILDERS

For this book, we interviewed Mark Gudenas, National Marketing Director of Swinerton Incorporated, an employee-owned general contractor headquartered in San Francisco.[12] In 2005, Swinerton ranked 18th among general contractors in the US with about $1.2 billion in revenues.[13] Gudenas spoke of the long evolution at Swinerton toward becoming focused on green building. This story can be used by any design, development or construction firm to accelerate their progress toward embedding sustainability in the fabric of the company, as Swinerton has done.

Swinerton Builders constructed what can arguably be called one of America's first green buildings in 1970 – the Weyerhaeuser headquarters campus in Federal Way, Washington. With extensive green roofs, natural daylighting and a man-made lake created for passive heating and cooling, this was a pioneering effort that turned out great. Swinerton went on to build the Pacific Bell campus in 1985 in San Ramon, California that featured the same green building features as the Weyerhaeuser headquarters. Then in 1997, Swinerton Builders worked with William McDonough+Partners architects to create the Gap Inc. campus in San Bruno, California. This project put green building in the spotlight – and firmly rooted green at Swinerton Builders.

Swinerton started attracting new employees because of what they heard about the company's green building projects, the new techniques that it was introducing into the building process and the growing interest of their clients in pursuing sustainable practices in building their projects.

In 2001, Swinerton took out its checkbook to demonstrate a corporate commitment to green practices. Having long recognized the importance and value of construction and design practices that conserve energy, water and other resources, reduce waste and promote healthier (and more productive) built environments, it was only natural for the company to apply these principles to our new corporate headquarters at 260 Townsend Street in San Francisco. Swinerton decided to pursue LEED Gold certification for the building as a pilot project under the USGBC's new Existing Building category.

Design decisions enabled Swinerton to beat Title 24 (California's stringent commercial building energy code) by more than 12 percent on a 20-year-old building. A state-of-the-art, digital building management system continuously monitors temperature, CO_2 and humidity, maximizing outside air and running the HVAC systems only to meet actual rather than anticipated demand, thus saving over 30 percent on utility bills. New high-efficiency light fixtures with motion sensors were also installed.

Swinerton received a LEED-EB Gold certification from the USGBC, and the greening of the *260 Townsend* office become an exemplary case study for LEED-EB, with tours coming in on a weekly basis. Above all, the true benefits are not only in the conservation of resources and energy savings but in the healthy environment that Swinerton and the architect created for the employee–owners who work in the building.

Gudenas says, "We now have a formal Swinerton Green Board of Directors, a full-time Corporate Sustainability Manager, extensive green training programs active in every single office and a huge competition between Division Managers to see who can boast the largest increase in their number of LEED APs by June 1st each year. Our chairman, Gordon Marks, has set the goal of having 250 LEED APs on board by our next Green Building Summit in April 2008 [up from about 50 in early 2007]."

"Green building and sustainable design permeates virtually all of our markets and we bring it to the table at every opportunity. I think that it's how it affects the owners within specific market segments. As we evolve our intelligence in sustainable design and green building – and can then present that intelligence to our colleagues and clients – we witness growing interest, understanding and adoption. For example, we are finding that clients in the hospitality market are extremely interested as it favorably positions their property. We just completed the new Orchard Garden Hotel in San Francisco, and it's become the first LEED-certified hotel in California. As a result, the hotel has received tremendous acclaim in the travel press both locally and internationally. We're now working with the owner to green their existing Orchard Hotel [also in San Francisco] to LEED standards."

Education is another market that is very active in green building. Swinerton is active at the new University of California, Merced campus; the Los Angeles

Community College District (a $2.1 billion Green Building Program); Humboldt State University and others currently in preconstruction.

In terms of winning new business, Gudenas says, "since we have been building green for nearly four decades, we have an impressive resume of green buildings – and the reviews from our green clients are great, with many of them repeat clients".

> We work hard on an ongoing basis to increase our intelligence in green building techniques and practices, and share the lessons learned and new data throughout all of our offices. That makes every one of us smarter and faster and enables us to bring that to our RFQ (request for qualifications) and RFP (request for proposals) responses. Our Green Team participates in the client sales presentations, and clients recognize the expertise that we bring to their projects.

On the firm's green focus being rewarded by existing clients, Gudenas says, "We found that after we built Gap's San Bruno campus with William McDonough + Partners, Gap awarded Swinerton the contract to build their corporate headquarters on the Embarcadero in San Francisco, and we recently completed the tenant build-out of their new Old Navy offices in the new Mission Bay neighborhood in the city."

In terms of future growth, Gudenas says that the firm believes that "the faster that we can educate the owners and developers who are looking at new projects in the environmental and economic benefits of building green, the greater the increase we'll see in sustainable projects. The data is here. We just need to distill it down so that we can deliver the appropriate information on increased building performance, including LCA, increased worker productivity and healthier living environments, and increased valuation of spec offices built green in a manner that address the specific requirements of each individual client."

In terms of new marketing materials, the firm published the *Swinerton Green Book*, featuring comprehensive project case studies of all of its green buildings. They're gearing up for a third printing, as demand has been tremendous, and they will add 20 new case studies in the next edition.

One marketing innovation stands out. For Gudenas, "more than anything else, our Swinerton Green Building Summits have positioned the company as a leader within the industry. The Green Building Summit in 2003 brought together thought leaders who were pioneering the sustainable design and green building movement with owners and developers who were either building green or considering it. Clients who attended that first Summit took away valuable, new intelligence that they actually applied to projects that Swinerton built for them.

The second Swinerton Green Building Summit in 2006 brought back many of the speakers who delivered great insight during the first Summit, plus new participants who brought intelligence on New Urbanism, green building valuation and case studies that illustrated the monumental progress that had taken place in just three years. We created a DVD of the 2006 Swinerton Green Building Summit to share all of the great presentations with those who did not attend. As a bonus only found on the DVD, we interviewed eight of the top presenters in a fireside chat setting. Those interviews provided personal insight and vision, entertaining stories and have proven to be the most popular – and watched – feature of the DVD." The firm plans to host a third Swinerton Green Building Summit in April 2008. For those clients and associates who missed the 2006 summit, the firm hosted a pair of one day Swinerton Green Building Forums in May 2007 in Southern California.

Firm leadership has been strongly engaged since at least 2001, when the company committed millions of dollars to green its corporate headquarters, a move sent a louder message than anything else. At the beginning of 2007, the Swinerton Inc. Board of Directors voted to create the Swinerton Green Board of Directors and officially create the position of Corporate Sustainability Manager. They issued a mandate to reduce the company's carbon footprint by 15 percent, and issued mandatory green housekeeping practices for all of their offices. The Swinerton Board of Directors made the *2007* Swinerton Green Initiative the company's top priority.

After 10 years of activity and commitment, Swinerton is not resting on its laurels. Their business is too competitive for that. The firm is evolving how it deals with sustainability and has now made it the top priority for actions in 2007. Each design, development and construction firm can see in this brief rendition of Swinerton's path toward sustainability some actions it can take to become and stay competitive in this very dynamic marketplace.

THE PEOPLE PROBLEM

No discussion of green building marketing strategies would be complete without a fuller discussion of the "people problem." Without talented people committed to sustainable design, most firms can't grow and can't take full advantage of their opportunities in this growing segment of the design and construction industry. I have heard many times in the past few years from principals at design firms that "we have the business, but just can't hire the people to perform it."

So, most design firms are experiencing the best of times and the worst of times right now: after a brief recession in the early 2000s, in 2007 commercial and institutional business is booming in most market sectors and most parts of the country, but some companies are turning away profitable work because they can't hire enough good people. This situation has been developing over the past 10 years, alongside the tech-boom-fueled growth and then recession of the US economy, but most firms have not responded with a comprehensive strategy to address the people problem (one reason, because the brief construction recession of 2002 and 2003 made it easier to hire and keep designers).

What's going on? Most design firm principals today are Baby Boomers, those born between 1946 and 1964, making them 43 to 61 years old in 2007. For most Baby Boomers, the salient fact of their working lives has always been "more people than jobs." Baby Boomers have been competing with their age cohorts for most of their working lives for a relative scarcity of jobs. As a sign of this, real wages in the US did not increase for most of the period from 1973 (when the Boomers first began to be a major presence in the workforce) until well into the early 1990s, despite the prosperity associated with the 1980s.

During the late 1990s, the record-breaking US economic expansion created far more jobs than there are people to fill them. One reason for this is the Generation X cohort, born between 1965 and 1978, between 29 and 42 in 2007. Not only does this group have vastly different expectations for employment, but it is much smaller than the Boomer group in absolute numbers. As a result, real wages for this group have started to rise again, for the first time in a generation, and the balance of power between the workforce and firm management will continue to shift dramatically, even though there were layoffs in many design firms during 2002–2003 building industry recession.

Consider the demographic changes afoot, shown in Table 11.1. By the year 2005, the population in the 25–34-year age groups (mostly Gen X), which in 2000 had already fallen 9 percent in absolute numbers from 1995 levels fell another 2.4 percent. This is the group of workers on which professional firms depend to "grind out" the daily work. The next age group, 35–44 years old, the group which manages most of the work in a professional firm, and which rose from 1995 to 2000 (reflecting the last of the Boomers), fell 5.6 percent by 2005 and an additional 8.8 percent by 2010 compared with 2005 levels.

Let's make some sense out of these dry statistics: By 2010, the people available to manage the creative daily work of a firm (35 to 44 year-olds) will fall to a level six percent below that of 2005, 2.5 million fewer people. However, by 2010, the cadre of people available to perform the daily work of a firm (25–34 years old) will increase only by 2 million people over 2005 levels.

One might think: OK, we can make up a 10% shortfall in senior technical workers and project managers. But look at what's happening to the economy at the

Table 11.1 Demographic changes, 2000–2010 (millions)[14]

Year/Age Group	2000 Number of Workers	2005 Number of Workers vs. 2000	2010 Number of Workers vs. 2005
18–24	26.3	28.3 (+7.6%)	30.1 (+6.4%)
25–34	37.2	36.3 (−2.4%)	38.3 (+5.5%)
35–44	44.7	42.2 (−5.6%)	38.5 (−8.8%)

same time. Compounded annual growth rates of 3–4 percent make the requirement for workers even greater than today. Consider a 3.5 percent growth rate, with 1.5 percent increases in productivity, leaving a need for 2 percent more workers each year, or 10.4 percent more between 2005 and 2010. In comparison with 2005 staffing levels, by 2010 that growth means that *our worker shortage will be potentially be 19 percent in the 35–44-year-old range and 4–5 percent in the 25–34-year-old range.* Yet the average annual amount of work will increase by at least the rate of growth of the gross domestic product.

What are the issues for firms? There are three major ramifications:

1. Business strategy will have to focus more on profits and less on internal growth.
2. Marketing strategy will become hostage to the people problem.
3. Human resources will become the most strategic issue for professional services firms.

Business strategy cannot be predicated solely on organic growth by adding more people. More growth will take place via acquisitions and mergers. Businesses will have to continue the early 2000s trend of focusing on key customers and aiming at profitable long-term relationships, with fewer clients and fewer markets covered. In an era of project-type specialization, the "we do it all" small firm may be headed for the "dustbin of history." Business strategy will also rely on outsourcing more and more services. Engineers and designers in less developed nations such as India and China and in work-short economies of Eastern Europe may do the CAD work each evening, after US-based designers have marked up the drawings earlier that day. With this happening, we'll move to the 16-hour and maybe even 24-hour design work day, all enabled by computer technology and the Internet. When outsourcing comes to professional services in a big way, it will change how firms are organized, with today's leaders much more in the role of account executives and project coordinators than project designers.

Marketing professional services is highly dependent on bringing outstanding people to work on the client's problems. With fewer people in the key age ranges, marketing strategy will have to focus less on increasing revenues and more on targeting long-term relationships that have a strong lifetime value associated with each client. Marketers will have to become even more involved in creating and selling the image of the firm, since that image will be part of the new employee recruiting effort. There may be a way to bring technological improvements and systems to bear on design and construction problems in place of people, but these typically take more than a half-decade to develop, test and bring into general practice. One example is the work of some architects to move directly from CAD-generated designs into shop drawings for construction, leaving out the blueprint stage of design entirely, as well as the move toward building information modeling (BIM) systems that will leverage design resources.[15]

Human resources will become elevated as a strategic and management issue. I foresee firms adding an Executive Vice President, Corporate Development role that will have command over and responsibility for both marketing and human resources. Every possible means will have to be used to recruit, retrain and retain key people. In my view, these are the "3R's of the New Economy": recruitment, retraining and retention. Keeping and continually retraining a firm's good and average performers is the only viable alternative to constant recruitment. *A strong commitment to sustainable design will be one of the primary ways of attracting and keeping these employees.*

The good news: if a firm can hold on for the next 5 to 10 years, there is a new generation of people, Generation Y, that is nearly as large as the Boomers, and just coming of age. Called by demographers the "Echo" of the Baby Boom, these "Echo Boomers," now under 29, will begin to swell the ranks of younger workers over the next 5 years, as the numbers of those in the 18–24 age group will rise by 14 percent by 2010, compared with 2000 levels. This group is going to be even more focused on their careers than the Gen X group, but paradoxically will demand even more flexibility in scheduling, lifestyle and workstyle. They are completely Internet-literate and have more information at their fingertips than any of us ever had. In addition, they are passionately committed to the environment and will want to work for firms that elevate sustainability to a core strategic value.

To summarize: our economy and our professional service firms are facing unprecedented people shortages, and executives must begin to commit significant amounts of management time to preparing design and construction firms to look a lot different 5–10 years from now.

The 3R's of the New Economy will become a mantra for all professional service firms: recruit, retrain and retain as many good people as possible.

Notes

1   Interview with J. Rossi, Burt Hill, April 2007; ranking based on "Giants 300," *Building Design & Construction Magazine*, July 2006, p. 59.

2   Philip Kotler, *Marketing Management*, 9th Edition, 1998, New York: Wiley, p. 473.

3   Interface Engineering, Inc., www.ieice.com.

4   For a fuller discussion, see the author's article in *Environmental Design & Construction Magazine*, March 2003, www.edcmag.com.

5   *Consulting-Specifying Engineer Magazine* [online], www.csemag.com/article/CA6426830.html?text=2006+and+ohsu (accessed April 18, 2007).

6   "Giants 300," *Building Design & Construction Magazine*, July 2006, p. 43.

7   "An Interview with Russell Perry," *Marketer*, published by the Society for Marketing Professional Services, www.smps.org, April 2007, pp. 12–15.

8   Interview with David Younger, Lionakis Beaumont Design Group, www.lbdg.com, March 2007.

9   Jennifer Wehling, "*The Sustainable Design Firm: Floor Plans to Business Plans*," Presentation to *EnvironDesign 10*, Toronto, April 26, 2006, furnished by the company.

10   Russell Perry Interview, op. cit.

11   Oregon Natural Step Network, www.ortns.org/documents/seracasestudyfinal_000.pdf, document prepared in January 2005 (accessed April 18, 2007).

12   Interview with Mark Gudenas, San Francisco, by email, April 2007.

13   "Giants 300," *Building Design & Construction*, July 2006, p. 59.

14   US Census Bureau, P25-1130, Middle Series, www.census.gov (accessed April 19, 2007).

15   Cadalyst [online], http://aec.cadalyst.com/aec/article/articleDetail.jsp?id=133495 (accessed April 28, 2007).

PART 3

THE FUTURE OF GREEN BUILDING MARKETING

12 SEVEN KEYS TO SUSTAINABLE DESIGN MARKETING

There is no single competitive response to the growing green building market that is "right" for every design firm. Your firm needs to consider its response in the light of the "4 C's" – the *clarity* of its strategic vision, your *capability* to execute the vision, the *capital* available for marketing and sustainability initiatives, and the *character* of the firm's principals – their willingness to "walk the talk" of green design. Nevertheless, a conscious choice among strategies and a clear focus on one dominant approach, are vastly preferable to having none or just improvising responses to opportunities.

Industry surveys and diffusion of innovation theory (see Chapters 8 and 9) contribute to an understanding of what the marketplace for green development wants and needs. Green building design firms, contractors and consultants marketing sustainable design services and projects should incorporate the following information and techniques in their marketing strategies and marketing communications programs:

- Case study data from finished projects, accompanied by solid cost information, including initial cost increases for various green building measures and post-occupancy surveys of occupant satisfaction (the latter is almost guaranteed and the survey itself garners an additional LEED NC 2.2 credit point at little additional cost).
- Comparative cost information, within and across building types, as to the full costs of LEED certification, including documentation, for the firm's various projects.
- Demonstrable information and marketplace feedback on the benefits of green buildings beyond well-documented operating cost savings from energy and water conservation. In particular, gathering information on how clients have realized some of the business-case benefits, such as a rent premium, increased occupancy, faster lease-up and faster permitting, or greater employee retention, are essential to build credibility for green buildings.
- Clear evidence of usefulness of various green building measures, including the business-case benefits such as marketing and public relations, but also

independent studies of consumer and corporate demand, including willingness to pay for specific levels of LEED achievement, as evidenced, for example, by preferential selection of green buildings as a matter of corporate policy.

• Use of a growing cadre of LEED APs who can provide certainty about the LEED-certification process. The new LEED version 2.2 goes a long way toward providing more certainty through an end-of-design-phase review of applicable LEED credits, instead of having to wait until construction completion to begin the certification process.

• Stronger use of multimedia approaches and other modern sales tools to increase the connection with green building goals and methods by stakeholders and decision-makers, including the use of BIM design approaches for communicating the costs and benefits of key green building measures much earlier in the design process.

This chapter describes seven good ideas for developing a marketing strategy, explores the motivations that drive clients who are the target markets for green buildings and addresses some key points in selling green buildings.

THE SEVEN KEYS

In today's environment, a company must be remarkable in the eyes of its clients and the media just to get some attention. Finding points of differentiation and new ways to tell the sustainability story is the perpetual task of the marketing arm of the design firm.[1] Looked at in this fashion, the marketing function assumes strategic importance, as firms struggle to both retain clients and key employees in the face of an increasingly competitive global marketplace for design and construction services and people.

The seven keys to marketing green buildings are a combination of two familiar principles of marketing presented in Chapter 9: the STP formula – *segment* your market, *target* key segments and *position* your company; and the building blocks of competitive strategy – differentiation, cost and focus. Table 12.1 presents the seven keys. Most of them can be combined, but even a clear focus on one will yield results.

Segment markets

Marketers try to understand and segment markets in order to focus on the most profitable or available segments. As discussed in Chapter 9, segmentation variables can include demographics, geographics, firmographics and psychographics.

As for *demographics*, there is little evidence that this approach to segmentation is useful for marketing green buildings.

Table 12.1   Seven keys to green design marketing

Key	Rationale
1. Segment your markets	It is difficult for a firm to focus on more than four market segments
2. Choose competitive targets	Many firms spend their resources chasing unattainable clients
3. Position your firm as a leader	Most clients prefer to choose known leaders in their business
4. Differentiate	Find a difference that makes a difference!
5. Become a low-cost provider	Low cost attracts many clients
6. Focused differentiation/relationship management	Focus on "lifetime value" of clients
7. Build a brand image	Brands facilitate choices in a complex world

Geographics – where people are locating and building – is certainly a prime variable to consider in deciding where to market green building services and products. Evaluating the number of LEED project registrations by state is one way to evaluate the impact of geographic location on the availability of clients for green design services (see Table 9.3). Within each state with a large number of LEED registrations, one can then "drill down" in the data and find out which cities are the most amenable to LEED-certification projects at any given time. Typically, green building activity is more prevalent in the largest metropolitan areas in each state.

Firmographics, a business-to-business marketing analog of demographics for individuals, helps marketers understand the nature of the client base. Here the focus is on the size of the client company or organization; whether it's a private, public or nonprofit entity; building (office, library, lab, classroom, etc.) type; and other pertinent data. Project type is also a type of firmographic segmentation and reflects the fact that most clients prefer to hire firms with prior experience in their type of project. This could include such specialized project types as new acute-care hospitals, biotech research laboratories, college and university student unions and high-rise condominiums, to name a few.

Psychographics refers to segmenting by psychological orientation. In segmenting the market for green buildings, a marketer would look for industry leaders and innovators in early-stage segments. Some people are just more welcoming to new ideas and new technologies than others. Knowing who the industry leaders are in given segments allows marketers to target them with new ideas such as green buildings, knowing that the vast majority of decision-makers want to see experimentation done successfully before committing to a green project.

Choose targets

Targeting is a process that marketers must use when deciding to focus on one or a few segments. Targeting is a critical component in setting marketing strategy because it limits the number of competitive targets in order to focus on those most likely to be successful. Most design firms specialize in one or a handful of client types (public, private, nonprofit), project sizes (under $10 million, over $100 million) and market segments (K-12 education, cultural, fire stations, commercial offices, retail, hospitality, healthcare), so the choice of targets is necessarily limited by the company's prior experience, financial capability and the project resumes of key individuals. Some marketers aim to increase market share in a given industry or extend their geographic reach in tackling a certain type of project, but most focus on increasing revenues from current relationships to grow their businesses. Designers who have built a reputation in a particular market segment and a history of successful projects are often invited to compete for projects far from home, often as associated architects with a local design firm, and they are often successful in this endeavor. Most clients want the best design firm for their green project.

Prime targets for green building marketing share these characteristics:

- They are *early adopters* of new technology, or in some more mature segments, in the early majority.
- They may be *potentially significant users of a new approach* (e.g., they control multiple properties or represent a large campus).
- They may be *opinion leaders* (able to sway others, both inside the organization and in a larger community of peers).
- They *can be reached at relatively low cost* (e.g., already are clients of a firm or interested in new green approaches).

Since few prospects share all of these characteristics, marketers must choose targets by considering each of these factors along with some intangibles, which might include the quality of existing relationships, stakeholder activity pushing the prospect to choose green buildings and market forces pushing local entities to keep up with innovative companies.

Position your company as a leader

Positioning is the third activity of the STP formula. It takes segmentation and targeting analyses and turns them into messages designed to influence clients and prospects. Positioning is something you must do or it will be done for you (and to you). In marketing, we learn from hard-won experience that "perception is reality."

Positioning is a strategic and tactical communications activity that aims at changing a target prospect's perception of a firm, to create a "difference that makes a difference." These differences should be important, distinctive, superior to others, communicable, not easily copied and affordable to the client. Architects, engineers and builders seen by the client base as green building experts because of their project successes, find it possible to maintain their "top of the market" positioning even as more competitors come up to speed in sustainable design.[2]

Positioning, then, is what a company does to take real facts and position them as reality in the minds of the targeted prospect; positioning deals with creating lasting perceptions. In marketing green buildings, positioning is an essential component of a design firm's communications strategy and serves to reinforce a single powerful message. Because green buildings are a new industry, they offer the positioning strategy of seizing the high ground and occupying a new, position that clients and prospects will value. For example, a company could claim the most LEED-registered projects in a given industry or location, or the most LEED APs, or the most LEED Gold projects with a certain technology.

Differentiate your green development offerings

Differentiation is an approach to marketing strategy that takes decisions regarding segmentation, targeting and positioning variables and focuses them on particular markets (see Figure 9.3). This approach must be coupled with a specific project type, owner type, geographic or other focus. *Focused differentiation* is the main marketing approach used in professional services. The main green building differentiators for design firms are:

- successful projects (especially LEED-certified buildings),
- satisfied clients,
- high levels of LEED project attainment (Gold and Platinum ratings),
- demonstrated ability to deliver green building projects on conventional budgets,
- number of LEED APs.

A design firm usually needs to show high levels of attainment on several of these key variables to secure major new projects in highly competitive situations.

As discussed in Chapter 9, each design firm needs to excel in one of three key disciplines of market leaders: customer intimacy, product leadership and operational excellence, while providing at least good service in the other two areas:[3]

1. Prospective clients expect *intimacy* in the form of high-quality relationships between them and the design firm. Successful projects are seldom one-shot affairs. Rather, the continuing relationships among clients, design

teams, builders, public officials and owners yield the most successful projects in each major urban area.

2. Companies show *operational excellence* in terms of meeting building program goals, budgets and schedules while achieving specific LEED certification goals. For designers, this means getting a project finished within specific market windows and meeting cost and quality goals set by the client.

3. Companies that have a signature technological approach such as green roofs or solar power often attract clients who value *product leadership* in the area of sustainable design. Design firms focused on such unusual project types as brownfield redevelopment, moderate-income or affordable housing, and complex urban infill, mixed-use projects can excel in this area.

Five of the top ten differentiation activities for professional service firms are most often used by design firms to assist with their green building marketing efforts:[4]

1. Advertising campaigns to establish or maintain positioning (done in less than 20 percent of the firms, according to one survey).
2. Improved relationship management programs to strengthen bonds with current clients (this is by far the most common, cheapest and fastest way to get results, in my professional experience).
3. Manage a public relations campaign to highlight achievements and reinforce green market positioning.
4. Hire specialized individuals, often with control of key relationships (this is done in less than 25 percent of firms, according to one survey).
5. Improve or evolve a firm's current services, particularly in setting up a separate green building consulting division (this is done in less than 10 percent of the firms, according to one survey).[5]

Design firms can find one or more approaches on this list that will differentiate their services over a two to three year period in the green building industry. Research shows that the leading companies are particularly adept at using differentiation strategies such as advertising, public relations, new visual identities and attracting key people. Improving or evolving the company's services typically takes place over the course of several green building projects.

When embarking on a program of focused differentiation, remember that existing clients already know your firm and appreciate its strengths. Communicating a new message about green building should not be at the expense of these relationships, and the message needs to reinforce current positive perceptions of your firm as a cost-conscious, schedule-conscious, client-focused organization. Key relationship managers need to meet with existing clients and explain how the new people you're hiring, the newly accredited LEED APs, and the new green building focus of the firm will benefit them and their projects. In turn, this requirement implies a need for strong internal communications before embarking on new green building marketing initiatives.

Become a low-cost provider of green design and construction services

Many building projects are budget-challenged. Projects are exposed to rapid increases in materials and labor costs in many urban areas. The ability of design and construction firms and green technologies to compete on price is valuable. Low cost of operations does not necessarily mean low profitability; instead it gives a firm more flexibility to negotiate profitable fees for green building projects, even in a very competitive environment.

For example, the ability to be creative with green building engineering for energy and water savings, along with high levels of indoor air quality, might help an engineering firm create far more valuable green buildings for the same fee as a more conventional competitor. The ability to specify building-integrated PV systems would fall into the same category, both for an architectural firm and for an engineering firm. Knowing the costs and the engineering details for PV systems would help an engineering firm convince owners to move forward with these systems.

One example of a developer focused on low cost as a basic competitive strategy is Workstage, LLC, which is focused on the corporate build-to-suit market, primarily in the Midwest. Based in Grand Rapids, Michigan, Workstage aims to wring out costs of doing green buildings by standardizing every element of the design and construction process. They use interchangeable modules ("a kit of parts") and like-minded architect–engineer teams for each project.[6] Workstage's corporate and institutional clients want green buildings, but they do not want to spend an extra penny to get this benefit. Workstage's approach is not to change architects or engineers, but to work with the same designers on the same project types, as a means to "wring out" costs from the system. If a design firm wants to engage such clients, it needs to understand how to produce standard designs that can quickly be customized for each location and specific program requirements.

Focused differentiation/relationship management

The essence of marketing wisdom is knowing in which markets to compete in and which to ignore, which clients a company wants to keep and which it does not. Often by being unfocused, a design firm will try to serve too many clients, at the expense of not satisfying the clients it really wants. To derive an effective strategy, marketers need to combine a laser-like focus on market segments and key targets within those segments, with either low cost or differentiation.

One of the most effective tools for differentiation is to connect with the clients' value systems. After all, how many design firms take the time to really connect with a client's deep-seated mission and purpose? Kirsten Sibilia, Marketing Director for FXFOWLE Architects in New York City, says:

A lot of our marketing involves trying to connect with our clients' value systems. If you look at the mission statement of most of the Fortune 500 companies, for example, it includes something about sustainability or environmental responsibility. So we try to get them to understand the impact that the built environment has on the natural environment and illustrate that their new building can really be a symbol of their corporate goals. It's similar for our education clients. Their mission is to educate, to nurture, to protect; and we demonstrate that the building can represent that and be an educational tool in myriad of ways. We designed the School of Management building at Syracuse University where they train future business leaders. Part of what those future business leaders need to understand is the role that built environment plays and the power of architecture and sustainability together.[7]

Points of focused differentiation can include:

- *Regional vs. national focus.* Firms that are very focused locally are often able to compete against much larger national firms or else to team with them to secure larger projects.
- *Client types.* Architects focused on winning design competitions, for example, clearly seek out adventurous decision-makers for projects that embody a community's or an institution's highest aspirations. When the City of Seattle chose the Dutch firm, Office of Metropolitan Architecture (OMA), to design its dramatic new main city library in 2002, it consciously decided to place this building on the world stage, much as it had done with the Space Needle for a World's Fair 40 years earlier. For OMA, it was worthwhile to go after such a high-profile design competition, since *avant-garde* architecture is its main business, and it teamed with a local architect to win the commission.
- *Building or project types* such as office buildings, secondary education, higher education, healthcare or laboratories. Likely to be affected in the future by higher electricity rates, these building types, including office buildings and institutional buildings (colleges, public agencies), might be good candidates for energy-efficiency investments, particularly in states or utility service areas with significant incentives. Therefore, a green design firm can identify such clients, make energy-efficient buildings its major marketing focus and direct most of its communications to their needs.
- *Signature green measures.* While it can be risky for developers and designers to always include green technologies to their projects, it is riskier *not to be known for anything in particular.* Branding a company in the green building

arena with specific technology solutions for particular building types and sizes can be an effective marketing measure, allowing such companies to at least make the "short list" for interviews.

- *Project size.* An example might be a focus on maintenance and operations facilities for public works; that is a type of project that is typically smaller than most office buildings, but can occasionally exceed $10 million in construction cost.

Build a brand image

In today's commercial world, a major task is to create a brand that incorporates the key differences in a design firm that make a difference in the mind of a buyer. A design firm might want to be thought of as a leading-edge technology innovator (think of Frank Gehry or Thom Mayne of Morphosis in this context) or as dominating a large product category (such as HOK Sports in arenaa or Skidmore, Owings and Merrill in large complex office buildings) in order to limit its market but sharply define itself to buyers who value that experience or approach.

To understand the branding opportunity, consider the following statement: "All marketers are liars."[8] One way to read this statement is to understand that we create stories about projects, capabilities, values and interests for ourselves and our clients on a regular basis. The story about the green building project you just finished is already manifesting in the minds of all project participants, readers of new stories about the project and the general client base ("It's only a LEED Silver project, what's the big deal?"). And it will continue to be permuted, just like a message in the game of Rumor, if you don't proactively shape it. Therefore, you must tell a story about your project: if it is significantly different from the contractor's experience and the owner's experience and the occupants' experience, then one of you is a liar! The point is that green building branding is best done when it is a story about project successes and lessons learned.

The essence of a brand is incorporated in how you deliver your services, in your firm's personality and core values (which in turn determine who you hire and who you let go), your culture (collaborative or confrontational, or something in between) and all the promises you want your client to believe (clear and frequent communications, for example, on each project; the highest level of expertise and technological competence, etc.). A brand is something that creates a strong personal and professional relationship between your people and the client's staff, that builds loyalty and fosters lasting relationships.

The marketing benefits of branding are multiple. It can shorten the decision cycle of a client and reduce your cost of marketing. If you're always "short listed" by certain clients and client types, you have a brand. It gives you some pricing flexibility; after all, if they really want you, they'll pay for all the special things you bring to the project, within reason. It helps you attract the kind of people that in turn reinforce the brand.

This point deserves the strongest emphasis: *Marketing and recruiting are two sides of the same coin.* The same values and branding attributes that attract clients also attract good people, and a professional service firm is nothing if not a "talent agency." Without the talent, you have nothing to sell, and you will never be a market leader. You can see, therefore, that this is a "positive feedback loop." The clearer you are about your market positioning and values, the more likely you are to attract the talent that will help you grow market share and dominate various green building niches. The successful execution of your brand promises generates loyal clients, which in turn builds your business. Since many clients perceive design services as a commodity, and since many design firms deliver them as a commodity, a brand differentiates your services in a significant way from those of "also ran" firms.

What makes a brand in the green building marketplace?

- *A brand is a story told between marketer and consumer, between architect and client, between developer and tenant or buyer.* The story must resonate with the client or buyer to be effective. The storytelling focuses on the features of the project, but translates those features into benefits that the recipient can clearly appreciate.
- *A brand sells an experience or a series of benefits to the consumer.* People must be led from understanding the value of the features to understanding how they will benefit from them. Think of Starbucks: it sells a commodity product you can buy in thousands of locations in any big town, and at a significant price multiple. Starbucks has managed to create more than 5,000 permutations for the basic "cuppa java" to give you a unique taste experience.
- *A brand delivers on its promises.* For example, in my own LEED Gold-certified apartment building in Portland, the presence of a trash room with recycling bins, just down the hall and on every floor, and the enforcement of the required "no smoking" policy, both reinforced daily the promise that the green building experience was something different and valuable.
- *A brand walks the talk.* Consumers expect sellers to live by the values of what they are selling. A green design firm should have offices in a green building. A green firm should craft a LEED-EB or LEED-CI certification for its own offices. A green design firm should be promoting sustainability in all its activities, not just in an isolated design project now and then.
- *A brand communicates its differences effectively.* A common observation is that the average adult is subjected to about 2,000 commercial messages daily. Getting through the "fog" with an effective communications program is a

great art. Most savvy design firms engage a strong public relations firm to tell their story and support a continuing dialog with the marketplace as an integral part of their marketing effort.

Of course, one can create differences for each market segment that one chooses to address: some might value innovation, while others value low cost or specific technological choices, such as geothermal heat pumps, PV or roof gardens. *Almost without exception, there are few established brands in the green building marketplace today.* Without a leading brand (and with due apologies to the major companies involved in this business), the average client will not have a basis for making a purchase. In commercial situations, the lack of a brand can have drawbacks. While a home builder can sell Energy Star, GE or Whirlpool appliances to residential buyers, the lack of name recognition for most green technologies forces the design firm or the developer to become the brand. This is a heavy burden for a service firm, but one well worth the effort, even if it takes five years or more.

MARKETING AS AN EVOLVING STRATEGY

Practitioners need to understand how their marketing must evolve in order to compete effectively:

- They must choose a strategy that incorporates *high levels of differentiation or lower overall costs*, with explicit focus on particular market segments that might include geographic, project type, owner type, psychographic profile, project size, specific technological approach or signature green measures.
- This strategy must be *reinforced internally and externally* so that it becomes recognizable as a brand identity. Internal reinforcement includes incentivizing people to get educated and accredited as green building professionals and offering small bonuses for those who do. External reinforcement includes activities to increase the visibility of the firm and its key professionals in the chosen niche markets.
- Larger design firms should consider developing their own *proprietary tools* for managing sustainability goals in their projects, as part of a branding approach. Along with these tools, firms should develop methods to successfully execute LEED projects without additional design fees.
- Design firms must form *close working alliances* with contractors and clients to ensure that their green building projects will actually get built within prevailing budget, time, technology options and resource constraints.

UNDERSTANDING DEMAND FOR GREEN BUILDINGS

Now that we've presented how a design firm should market sustainable design, it's important to recognize also that a clear analysis of current and potential clients and future project opportunities is critical to refining the marketing message. This said, how should companies think about marketing and selling high-performance buildings and developments? In all cases, the answer comes down to:

- Who is the buyer?
- What are their characteristics, motivations and unmet needs?
- What elements of green buildings do current and potential buyers value most?
- What are they really buying?
- How do various customer segments differ in their priorities?
- What changes are occurring in these priorities?
- Do the customers for high-performance green buildings fall into any logical groups based on needs, motivations or characteristics?

Client characteristics

At this stage of market development for green projects, the *private-sector buyer or owner* will be an innovator or early adopter (in diffusion of innovation terms) and somewhat of a risk taker who is willing to balance the strong case for financial and organizational gain against the risk and possibly higher costs of this new approach to building design and construction. Innovators tend to be high-status individuals with higher education levels than later-stage adopters. This type of buyer will respond well to a factual presentation of benefits, will see the longer-term picture and will likely have done considerable homework before considering the green building approach.

The *institutional- or government-sector buyer* is more likely to be an early adopter of new technology driven largely by policy considerations, supplemented with the perspective of a long-term owner–occupier–operator of buildings. These owners typically are more risk-averse than innovators and tend to rely more on social networks for information. They want to see solid cost data and preferably local examples of successful projects. They will not be the first to act. Even though they are not spending their own money, they are willing to take only carefully calculated risks.

Motivations for green building

The top triggers to green building among building owners reflect the current focus on reducing energy costs (see Table 1.6). How can we translate these triggers into a consistent set of buyer motivations? How do owners, developers, designers and builders see the market benefits of green buildings, and how do these benefits work with the motivations of the various classes of buyers or decision-makers?

Securing a direct financial return

This motivation can take several forms. For example, a public agency can view financial return in terms of long-term ownership cost, typically using life-cycle cost (LCC) analysis, with 5 percent discount rates reflecting today's low cost of public borrowing. A private-sector owner could be attracted by the return on investment (ROI) on energy-efficiency investments, using a corporate weighted average cost of capital or some other criterion such as internal rate of return (IRR), but may have to deal with a prescribed minimum return level for this type of discretionary investment. Within a company, extra expenditures on green buildings still have to compete for scarce capital resources, so the financial and business case for extra investment must be convincing. Other companies use a simpler approach, requiring payback of discretionary investments in relatively short periods of 18 to 36 months. Green building investments for energy efficiency often can provide paybacks of two to four years, with an ROI or IRR exceeding 15 to 25 percent.

Reducing market risk

Risk reduction benefits to private developers may increase as more projects achieve a quicker lease-up due to their green certifications. The Brewery Blocks project in Portland, Oregon completely leased up its flagship commercial office building and they sold out the highest-price condominiums in the city nine months ahead of opening. One third of the apartments in the Louisa, a LEED Gold-rated project, among the highest priced in town, were leased before construction completion.[9] The developers report that energy savings and healthy building features were a factor in the purchase decision for about one-third of the condominium buyers and a determining factor for about 10 percent of buyers. For the office and retail units, the green building characteristics of the development were a deciding factor for some key tenants, such as a large local law firm and the Whole Foods grocery chain, which opened its first Pacific Northwest store in the Brewery Blocks.

Enjoying public relations benefits

Many public agencies and large corporations see public relations benefits from green building certifications. For example, responding to a strong public sentiment for environmental responsibility, the city of Seattle mandated in 2001 that all new public buildings larger than 5,000 square feet had to achieve at least a LEED Silver certification. Vancouver, British Columbia, passed a similar ordinance in 2004 requiring LEED Gold status. In 2006, San Jose, California mandated LEED Silver certification for all new public building projects above 10,000 square feet (900 sqm).[10]

In New York City, the Four Times Square project by the Durst Organization garnered widespread publicity during the late 1990s for its variety of green features and was able to lease up the 48-story office building in 2000 primarily to just two anchor tenants, a large law firm and a major publisher. Another Durst project in New York City, the 2.1 million square foot, 52-story Bank of America Tower at One Bryant Park, is aiming to be the world's largest LEED

Platinum-rated building when it is completed and occupied in 2008. Because of the high-performance features and high-profile nature of this project, Durst was able to enlist Bank of America as a 50 percent development partner and 50 percent occupier of the office space.[11]

Improving risk profile

Many large corporations and most public agencies are self-insured, all or in part, so it makes sense for them to invest in green building features for risk management purposes. For this reason, they may want to achieve high levels of energy efficiency while exceeding code requirements for ventilation and moisture control. They should also be concerned about future large increases in energy prices, especially during peak summer periods. Such owners are meeting these concerns with measures as lower overall energy use, lighting and occupancy controls, off-peak energy generation from thermal energy storage systems and, in some cases, from on-site generation using combined heat and power technologies such as microturbines and cogeneration systems.

Securing an indirect financial return

Green buildings offer the prospects of increased productivity, reduced absenteeism and reduced employee turnover, an advantage in a service economy in which people costs often constitute more than 70 percent of an organization's total operating costs. It makes sense to maximize productivity, health and morale with higher-performing buildings, employing such techniques as daylighting, improved lighting levels, greater indoor air quality, operable windows, views to the outdoors, natural ventilation and underfloor air distribution systems. Higher levels of indoor air quality or energy efficiency can be marketed to tenants and employees through the LEED-certification award or local utility certification programs and through project-specific marketing and communications channels.

Doing the right thing

Many developers are leading the way into high-performance buildings because they feel it is the right thing to do and the wave of the future. They hope to create a market advantage, in effect "doing well by doing good." The Hines organization, which builds speculative offices for long-term ownership, has expressed its view in many green building forums that a LEED Silver-certified building would provide a long-term market advantage in terms of lower costs of ownership and a better story to sell to prospective tenants. The buildings owned and managed by Hines professionals strive to maximize efficiency and minimize energy use in creative and pioneering ways.[12] Another major developer, Jonathan F.P. Rose, says simply, that his company aims to repair "the fabric of communities ... by creating environmentally and socially responsible real estate." Rose is a strong proponent of transit-oriented green development, because of the lowered energy costs from not commuting by car.[13]

Unmet needs

The marketing task for architects and facilities professionals is to respond to clients' unmet needs by designing high-performance buildings for their next project. In many cases, however, these needs are not articulated well enough to compete with other priorities. It makes sense to use something like the LEED or Energy Star rating system to evaluate a project design and elevate these concerns to the same level as esthetic or functional criteria.

It often happens that, during the course of design and construction, high-performance measures are often "value engineered" out of the project owing to budget reductions or higher initial cost projections. Many LEED projects have found that the client's strong requirement to achieve a certain level of LEED certification has forced the design team toward an integrated design approach that places the desired LEED rating at the same level as other budgetary concerns. As a result, the team looks for cost savings in areas other than energy efficiency, water efficiency or indoor air quality, effectively preserving those investments. Often, early-stage eco-charrettes or visioning sessions can help to articulate key stakeholders' unmet needs.

DESIGNING MARKETING MATERIALS

Designers and facility professionals need to sell their choices to others. Often it is necessary to make a convincing business case to those who hold the purse strings before embarking on the design and construction of a high-performance building. But as most salespeople know, they have to keep selling even after a contract is signed, or run the risk of *buyer's remorse* after the initial sale.

Speculative developers in the world of commercial real estate use the services of real estate brokers, whose main task is to facilitate transactions for their clients. Architects and designers need to equip these brokers with an understanding of the green features of the project, communicate why they are important and specify what benefits they create, so that they will be able to present them to prospective clients or tenants. Brokers specialize in negotiation and communications, so some thought has to be given to integrating the green features into the marketing and sales materials for the building, especially if the developer is trying to recapture some of the investment in energy efficiency with higher rents or a faster sales/lease cycle, for example. Since brokers are not going to become specialists in green buildings anytime soon, these marketing materials have to be straightforward and readily understandable by those without technical training.

The best approach is to make the literature about the features of green buildings fit in with the marketing literature for the project. In some ways, this is uncharted territory, especially in the "speculative" commercial building world. Nonetheless, the basic tenet of sales remains: "Sell the sizzle, not the steak." For technical features of green buildings, this means spelling out and selling the benefits rather than the features. For example, if a project is saving 40 percent more energy than a commercial building, then the pitch to a CEO or COO is that you have just made one-third of the building's operating costs 40 percent cheaper. This investment also has a high return and offers some protection against future uncertainties in energy prices. If the buyer is a tenant, then the healthier indoor air quality or daylighting needs to be marketed in terms of reduced absenteeism due to illness or disease; if the tenant pays the energy bills, then part of the sale is the reduced total operating cost for rent and utilities. Convincing a tenant is a harder sell in terms of risk that the tenant will not value the benefit appropriately, so some form of certification such as LEED or Energy Star is helpful.

Then marketers need to use all available sales tools:

- A project or building web site with full explanations of the green features and benefits and links to favorable newspaper and magazine articles about the project.
- Email newsletters or blog entries about the building features, along with links to other sites.
- Streaming video testimonials from the designers and builders (or current tenants), along with "360-degree" fly-arounds of the prospective building and walk-arounds of the interior.
- Attractive signage and explanations in the project's sales office.
- Radio and TV coverage.

ENSURING CLIENT SATISFACTION AFTER PROJECT COMPLETION

In the institutional setting, the facility manager and design professionals often share the responsibility for occupant satisfaction. Many stakeholders in a high-performance building (from top executives down to the file clerk) need to know what they are getting in their new building, how it works, what the expected benefits are to them and to their organization and, in some cases, how to make it work.

Without a strong pre- and post-occupancy sales effort, it is entirely possible that the benefits of the building will go unrealized and unappreciated or under-appreciated. For example, in a building with operable windows, who will actually operate the windows? In humid climates, how will people learn when they are allowed to open the windows? When people work side by side, disagreements happen about such matters. Research suggests that people will often tolerate greater temperature swings from "normal" if they have the ability to control the environment. In the case of natural ventilation, employees need to be prepared to dress cooler in the summer and warmer in the winter. In one LEED Gold project in Portland, Oregon, the Jean Vollum Natural Capital Center, the building owner (an environmental nonprofit organization) included in its leases a provision that allowed the temperature range for the building to be 68F to 76F degrees, putting tenants on notice to dress for the season.

LEED NC version 2.2 provides one point for committing to a "post-occupancy survey" of building occupants to find out their satisfaction with thermal comfort. Wouldn't this survey be a good marketing tool for a design firm to use, in securing future business? The key point here: *marketing is a continuing process, even for completed projects*! Getting users engaged in praising a project provides ongoing testimonials for marketers to use.

NOTES

1   Seth Godin (2003) *Purple Cow: Transform Your Business by Being Remarkable*. Dobbs Ferry, NY: Do You Zoom.

2   "New Tricks for Old Dogs," *Building Design & Construction*, December 2005, p. 48.

3   Michael Treacy and Fred Wiersema (1995) *The Discipline of Market Leaders*. Reading, MA: Addison-Wesley.

4   Suzanne C. Lowe (2004) *Marketplace Masters: How Professional Service Firms Compete to Win*. New York: Greenwood.

5   "Green Buildings and the Bottom Line," *Building Design & Construction Magazine*, November 2006 Supplement, p. 7.

6   Workstage, LLC. Information from www.workstage.com (accessed April 18, 2007).

7   Interview with Kirsten Sibilia, FXFOWLE Architects, April 2007.

8   Seth Godin (2005) *All Marketers are Liars: The Power of Telling Authentic Stories in a Low-Trust World*. New York: Portfolio Hardcover.

9   Personal communication, Dennis Wilde, Gerding Edlen, March 2007.

10 US Green Building Council, "San Jose to Require LEED Silver" [online], www.usgbc.org/News/PressReleaseDetails.aspx?ID=2812 (accessed April 18, 2007).

11 US Green Building Council, "Facilities Building 'Green' Saves Banks Green" [online], www.usgbc.org/News/USGBCInTheNewsDetails.aspx?ID=2721 (accessed April 18, 2007).

12 Personal communication, Jerry Lea, Senior Vice President, Hines, March 2007.

13 Charles Lockwood, "Q&A With Jonathan Rose," *Urban Land Magazine*, March 2007, p. 102, published by the Urban Land Institute, www.uli.org.

13 THE FUTURE OF GREEN BUILDINGS

In December 2006, the largest advertising agency in the US, JWT Worldwide, published a list of 70 trends to watch in 2007.[1] In seventh place was "sustainable construction/green buildings." This trend is unmistakable. In 2006, just about every major business magazine and most large newspapers published cover stories and multiple articles on the "Green Trend," many of them focusing on green buildings. In 2006, Lowe's completed its first LEED-certified project in Austin, Texas. PNC Bank, a large Mid-Atlantic financial institution, has LEED-certified nearly 40 bank branches. Private businesses all over the US and Canada are beginning to see the value of "greening" their buildings.

GREEN BUILDING GROWTH RATES BY MARKET SECTOR

A recent survey conducted for the USGBC projected market growth for various building sectors, shown in Table 13.1.[2] (Note that the "education" sector includes both the higher education and K-12 sectors.) What's notable about the table is that the projected fastest-growing sectors are those that have seen the most activity so far: education, government, institutional and office. Other market sectors such as healthcare, residential, hospitality and retail are still finding their way into green buildings. But when Starbucks announces that it plans to build 10,000 stores over the next four years, it won't be long before the company decides that its customers and employee associates want them to be green buildings.[3]

Wal-Mart has already made a major green commitment, in the form of a pledge to invest $500 million in energy-conservation improvements; in early 2007, Wal-Mart began a move to become the largest seller of compact fluorescent lamps in the country.[4] According to Wal-Mart's "Earth Day" 2007 pledge: "Through deep investments and efficiency innovations in our stores and trucking fleet, we plan to reduce our overall greenhouse gas emissions by 20 percent over the next eight years. We will also design a store that will use 30 percent less energy and produce 30 percent fewer greenhouse gas emissions than our 2005 [standard] design within the next three years."[5] The same holds for other

Table 13.1   Projected annual growth rates for green buildings, by market sector

Market Sector	Projected Growth Rate in Green Construction (%)
Education	65
Government	62
Institutional	54
Office	48
Healthcare	46
Residential	32
Hospitality	22
Retail	20

Source: McGraw-Hill Construction. Green Building SmartMarket Report, 2007. Education Green Building Issue. Reprinted with Permission.

major retailers, hotel chains, healthcare providers and large homebuilders. For these market segments, the green building revolution is just getting started!

COMMERCIAL GREEN BUILDING GROWTH RATES

First, the commercial and institutional green building market continues to grow at more than 50 percent per year (see Figure 13.1). In 2006, cumulative LEED-NC-registered projects and project area grew by 41 percent, and cumulative LEED-NC-certified projects grew by 55 percent. LEED statistics indicate considerable growth potential ahead for commercial green buildings as well as high-rise and mid-rise residential projects (a dozen or more of the LEED-NC-certified projects in fact are mid-rise to high-rise multi-family residential units, both rental and for sale). The growth of the market tends to feed on itself; as more green projects are built, costs are reduced, leading to more cost-effective projects, which tips the scales in favor of building even more projects. Greater publicity for green buildings leads to more pressure on companies to specify green design for their next building project. For these and many other reasons, I expect the exponential growth of the green building market, which began in 2000, to continue for the foreseeable future, at least through 2012.

In 2006, the USGBC's LEED-NC green building rating system registered 1,137 new projects (see Table 2.2). As shown in Figure 13.1, using "diffusion of innovations" theory, I predict that the total number of LEED-NC-registered projects will increase from the end of 2006 more than threefold through 2010, continuing to increase at more than 30 percent each year, even through 2012.[6]

Growth in LEED-certified projects means that people everywhere will continue to see more information about green buildings in their cities and towns. This information should translate into significantly increased activity in both the

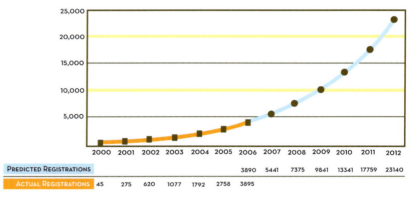

▲ 13.1   Long-term projection of cumulative LEED registrations to 2012.

commercial and the residential green building markets, both for new homes and energy and water-conservation retrofits.

The USGBC believes that we are on the cusp of an "explosion" in green building activity that could increase these estimates dramatically within the next three to five years. In November 2006, USGBC CEO Rick Fedrizzi set a "stretch goal" of 100,000 LEED green building certifications at the end of 2010, a 150-fold increase from the end of 2006! He also set a stretch goal of 1 million new LEED home certifications, number that would exceed green home certifications of about 20,000 homes in 2006 by more than 50 times. Such growth would represent far more "revolution" than "evolution."[7]

Whatever growth rate occurs, just about everyone agrees that green building expansion will far outpace the general growth of the building industry over the next five years. For example, in 2007 commercial construction is predicted to increase 12.7 percent, after a 13.5 percent increase in 2006, but new green building registrations in our model are predicted to increase 35 percent in 2007 over the 2006 total, with the addition of more than 1,500 new projects. Residential construction (including both new housing and remodels) in 2007 is predicted to decrease 7.8 percent, after a 1.8 percent decrease in 2006.[8] Contrast this with green building home growth of 40–50 percent expected in 2007.

The new reality of energy is that it's a "seller's market," and prices will climb as new supplies become harder to find and extract. Over time, this will likely translate into higher electricity and gas prices for residential use and more interest in investing in conservation. For example, market studies for the King-Snohomish Master Builders Association (Seattle area) in 2003 (well before the current rise in energy prices) showed a willingness by homebuyers to pay 1 percent more, about $2,500 on a $250,000 new home with an energy-efficiency package. Isn't it likely that the willingness to pay will increase to more like $5,000, especially with the new $2,000 homebuilders' tax incentive?

THE RAPID RISE OF THE GREEN RESIDENTIAL SECTOR

What people learn from working in green office buildings will also translate to their choices at home. The rise of the "Creative Class," first chronicled by Richard Florida in 2002,[9] has the potential to change American demographic geographic patterns as dramatically as the rise of Levittown and the suburban lifestyle did after World War II, a pattern that has just begun to reverse itself. People want connectedness, they want the amenities of urban living, and they don't want to commute for hours each day.

In particular, with an array of new state and federal solar power incentives look for a rapid rise in small 1.0 to 2.5 kilowatt solar electric systems, as the most visible way to show that a homeowner is doing something to save energy. The strong role of Governor Arnold Schwarzenegger's solar initiatives in California has played a role in "kick starting" the solar industry in California, the nation's largest market. In 2007, the state of New Mexico passed a major green building tax credit, and the state of Oregon increased its 35 percent solar energy tax credit to 50 percent.[10]

Residential green building is also poised for a rapid growth in the 2007–2010 period. In 2006, nearly 175,000 new homes were Energy Star certified, representing 12 percent of the new home market.[11] The LEED-H program, now in its pilot phase or "beta test," with 300 projects and about 6,000 homes, will roll out a standard version in the summer or fall of 2007.[12] Given the success of the LEED-NC program and the growing recognition of the LEED brand name, LEED-H should begin to affect the residential market significantly in 2008–2010. Other local programs such as the homebuilders' associations' "Built Green" (in seven states now) and local utility programs, as well as the National Association of Home Builders' (NAHB) voluntary certification program should also keep the new home energy-efficiency market growing rapidly.

More cities that have subscribed to climate change initiatives will begin to require green buildings from residential projects, especially large developments with major infrastructure impacts. In 2004–2006, many states, large universities and many cities began to require LEED Silver level (or better) achievements from their own building programs.[13] In 2006, Washington, DC, required all new commercial buildings over 50,000 square feet to meet the LEED standard by 2012.[14] Also in 2006, Boston announced it would put green building standards into its building code.[15] These requirements and policy directions for commercial buildings will spill over into the homebuilding market throughout the next half decade.

The increasing attention given in 2006 and 2007 to the dramatic energy-use reduction position of a new nonprofit, Architecture 2030,[16] will also affect green building in the next five years. By showing the dramatic contribution of the building industry to carbon dioxide emissions, Edward Mazria, the architect who founded Architecture 2030, has escalated the discussion about green buildings from a "nice idea" to a planetary imperative. Through his influence, the entire architecture profession was put on notice that energy-efficient, green buildings are no longer just one option among many for a new building or renovation, but must become a "front and center" priority.

The burden of more socially responsible activities increasingly falls on public companies, major commercial developers and homebuilders. For example, just to get projects permitted, built and sold, companies will increasingly have to build green buildings. To recruit top talent, the source of growth in revenues and profits, green buildings will form an integral part of a company's sustainability "story." Look for the corporate governance and socially responsible investing movements to influence how large homebuilders (the top 10 builders now account for more than 25 percent of all new homes in the country) plan, design and market their homes. More capital is flowing into socially responsible real estate investment funds, and these will in turn influence how commercial green projects are conceived, developed, leased and sold.

The slowdown in the homebuilding market in 2006 and 2007, likely to last for several years, may spur more builders toward building green homes as they attempt to find a point of differentiation that will resonate with an increasingly educated, socially conscious and environmentally concerned consumer base. People are already responding to the idea of low-energy-use homes, both for economic and social reasons. It won't be long before major homebuilders start retooling their models to be more energy-efficient, and to be certified as such by some reputable national organization.

THE LARGER PICTURE: CARBON REDUCTION

Reducing carbon dioxide emissions from the buildings sector is critical to our ability to combat global warming. Energy-efficient design and operations of buildings, along with on-site renewable energy production, are a strong part of the answer to the challenge to Americans to reduce their "ecological footprint." Figure 1.6 shows the divergence between carbon dioxide emissions between now and 2050 with a "business as usual" scenario and a strong carbon release mitigation program.

Jim Broughton is a business development manager in Houston with a manufacturer that focuses on energy efficiency in buildings, power generation and industrial processes. From his vantage point, he sees a dramatically altered future for property holdings:

> *The asset value of buildings that are not energy efficient will get hammered if owners do not build or renovate for low energy use – particularly as energy costs rise. Buildings are responsible for about 40% of our nation's carbon emissions primarily because of consumption of electrical power. Given this fact, carbon dioxide emissions regulations will be focused on power producers who may, in turn, force building owners to conserve by linking power rates to the building's carbon footprint. In addition to present tax incentives for reducing energy consumption, there is a strong possibility that regulators will consider a carbon tax as disincentive to stimulate renovation of high energy-use buildings. As owners and property managers realize carbon dioxide regulations are likely and buildings will be a prime target, renovations of existing buildings for energy-use reductions should accelerate dramatically.[17]*

CONTINUING BARRIERS TO GREEN BUILDINGS AND GREEN DEVELOPMENT

Still, there are barriers to the widespread adoption of green building techniques, technologies and systems, some of them related to real-life experience and the rest to perception in the building industry that green buildings add extra cost (see Chapter 4). In a 2005 survey, senior executives representing the entire construction industry[18] said that they believed green features added 13–18 percent to the cost of a project.

A 2006 survey of more than 800 senior people in the building industry revealed similar findings: 56 percent said green buildings add significantly to first cost, and 52 percent said the market was not willing to pay a premium.[19]

Jim Goldman is a Project Executive with Turner Construction in Seattle and was co-chair of the national committee for LEED-NC. He has had a front-row seat at the green building revolution the past seven years, delivering green projects to institutional and commercial building owners. Goldman says cost is always a barrier, both construction cost and the costs of services for studying green options and for certifying the projects. Nevertheless, he says, "in five years green building will be ubiquitous."[20]

Triggers to green building

While currently energy savings are the major trigger for green buildings, over the next few years, it is not hard to see that securing competitive advantage and gaining access to good investors will move up to the top of the list for many developers and design firms. As Hines development's Senior Vice President Jerry Lea says, "We were the first to create an investment fund for green buildings. We had investors approach us and ask if we would participate in such a fund. We created the fund with CalPERS (in 2006, for $120 million), the California state employees pension fund. It's been very successful and we anticipate another green fund will follow it, simply because the first was so successful."[21]

FUTURE LEED VERSIONS

There are many groups working right now within USGBC and other stake-holder groups such as the AIA and ASHRAE on the next generation of LEED, the so-called version 3.0. Realistically, one can expect it to emerge in 2008 as a pilot program, with more stringent requirements in a variety of sections and with an ability to "customize" LEED for particular geographic and climatic locations. This system could have a lengthy evaluation period, if it is very different from the current system. This means that projects started before the effective date of future LEED versions, can plan on being allowed to use the current system for at least five more years. However, some projects may want to switch immediately to the more flexible LEED version 3.0 once it becomes available.

Significant changes in LEED will focus more heavily on reducing carbon dioxide emissions from buildings, moving away from a "one-size-fits-all" system toward one more appropriate to bioregional issues, and taking into account the life-cycle assessment of building systems and building materials. While I do not expect the LEED system to disappear anytime soon, I do expect that it will become more flexible and even more embedded in building codes and standard practices of architects, engineers and builders. In that way, the USGBC's goal of market transformation of the building industry will see its full realization.

To hazard a guess at this point, without having any particular "insider" information, I expect the following changes to appear in future LEED versions. Firms might want to begin planning for these changes by looking for project opportunities to implement them, to accumulate experience with new ways of doing sustainable design:

- LEED will adopt a "bookshelf" of credits that projects will be able to select from, allowing them to "customize" a rating system to meet particular project needs.
- LEED will adjust its requirements and raise its minimum standards for energy efficiency, with goal of ensuring that "carbon neutrality" is a core value of the rating system. Zero net energy buildings will be especially rewarded in the new system.

- LEED will become *more stringent* in its requirements, to meet its goal of continuing its *market transformation* orientation; this means that, for example, one LEED credit point for water efficiency is likely to be awarded at the 30 percent savings level vs. 20 percent today.
- *Relative weightings* of credit categories will likely change a little, with more points likely being awarded to water efficiency and indoor environmental quality, particularly if LEED follows the "customizing" approach, so that projects in the arid regions could use, say, 10 water efficiency credits instead of just 5 in the present system.
- The *total number of points* available in LEED-NC is unlikely to exceed 75. Compared with today's 69-point system, such a change will not be significant.
- There will be more focus on *absolute levels of energy and water use* vs. *today's relative comparisons.* For example, energy use will likely gravitate to the *Energy Star* system of comparing a building's energy use against all other similar buildings in a region. This change will clear up certain anomalies in the current system that, for example, make it difficult to get all 10 energy efficiency points in a naturally ventilated building with no HVAC systems and no net energy use (because there's nothing to compare it to). Similarly, water use will be measured as total gallons per square foot (or liters per sqm or kilogram per sqm) of a building, perhaps for different building types, compared with merely achieving percentage reductions against today's code.
- There will be more focus on LCA of materials used in buildings, including the energy and environmental impacts of producing, distributing, using and disposing of them. These tools are under active development and aim to provide a more comprehensive way to choose the materials used in a building, considering all environmental impacts over the life cycle of a building.
- The "bar" for a certified system could be raised from 40 to 50 percent of the available points, reflecting the low initial cost of creating a certified building and the increasing sophistication of owners and design teams. That would push up the levels for Silver and Gold certifications, from 50 and 60 percent, respectively, to 60 and 70 percent.
- *Controversial issues* such as reducing PVC and vinyl use, elimination of chemicals alleged to be "persistent, bio-accumulative or toxic" may be somewhat addressed in the next version, but this is not certain, owing to potential legal and political complications and, in some ways, the peripheral nature of these issues to many in the design and construction business.
- *Certain prerequisites will be dropped* that represent standard practices in most of the US, and don't add anything but extra documentation to the LEED system: erosion and sedimentation controls; a ban on CFC use in HVAC systems; and requirements for recycling spaces in buildings, basic ventilation performance and a smoking ban in buildings.

- The next version of LEED will likely adopt *an additional commissioning point,* to stress the importance of design-phase commissioning, acceptance testing, performance verification and training of building operators. There may be a requirement for *certified commissioning professionals* to commission a building.
- Competing standards for the same credit category are likely to be recognized in the next version of LEED, ranging from certifying green power, to indoor air quality, to a large number of industry-specific product certifications, to requirements for third parties to certify green claims. Certifying green products that help meet LEED standards is an area that will acquire far more importance in the next LEED version.
- *Ventilation and indoor air quality will likely increase in importance.* The need for credits that deal more adequately with health, comfort and productivity issues in buildings will likely increase over the next two years and be incorporated in LEED. There is considerable technological progress being made at this time in building space conditioning, and the next version of LEED will address these changes with more sophistication and recognition of emerging design practice.
- A number of *current "innovations,"* such as 95 percent construction waste recycling, will likely become addressable LEED points, as more projects demonstrate their feasibility. This is clearly anticipated by the inclusion of four credit points for innovation included in the current LEED version 2.2 standard.
- There may be a move to allow certification by professional auditors and by local government agencies, rather than having only a few national certification review teams. This would be similar to the requirements for certification under the ISO 9000 and ISO 14001 standards for quality management and environmental management.

How should marketers be positioning themselves to take advantage of these changes in LEED? Those at the leading edge of the green building industry are likely already participating in making the changes in LEED postulated here and will be well positioned to capitalize on them if they do occur. USGBC now allows all its members to take part in "corresponding committees," to stay abreast of proposed changes in the LEED system. Market-savvy companies should make sure that someone on their staff is monitoring the changes that would affect their role in building design and construction.

Bert Gregory of Mithun in Seattle is part of the new generation of sophisticated sustainability thinkers. In Chapter 10, we profiled how sustainability helped the firm to double in size the past few years. Looking ahead, he says,

> *I don't believe that individual report [the February 2007 IPCC report on human-induced climate change] was a watershed moment. It's part of a huge wave of*

compounding information regarding global systems – energy instability, global align-
ment, health, pollution, population growth – that is raising public consciousness.
This awareness allows thought leaders to instigate action across industries. It's a
paradigm shift. In two to four years, a tremendous movement worldwide to reduce
energy consumption will include tax breaks and other incentive strategies. Cap and
trade systems in the US will dramatically improve the landscape. It's one piece of
information that's helping to raise awareness and spur action, accelerating change.
We won't be entirely green in five years, but we will be moving up the ladder.

William Viehman, Chief Marketing Officer of Perkins+Will shares similar
thoughts:

Knowledge of sustainable design is now the price of admission. Talking about it is
less a point of differentiation than it was 18 months ago. With virtually every com-
petitive selection process, you going into it expecting to have some conversation
about sustainability and you know all of your competitors will too. The differentiat-
ing point now is clearly on result. Before it was somewhat theoretical – you could
talk about theories and design concepts and ideas. But now we're getting more and
more results, so it's easier to talk about how our clients are actually benefiting from
sustainable design. I think the point of differentiation in the future will be to dem-
onstrate clearly the social and financial results to our clients.

Firms should be thinking about how to incorporate certain elements of the
"new wave" of sustainable design into current projects, without waiting for
them to be incorporated into a new LEED standard. This may be a hard sell to
a client concerned only with meeting current LEED requirements, unless it is
couched in a larger "sustainability context" and shown to be relevant to stakeholder concerns. An example could be a carbon dioxide emissions mitigation
plan (or the purchase of "green tags" for carbon offsets) as part of the energy
system planning for a new university building, since many colleges and universities are responding at this time to student and faculty concerns about global
warming. Finally, companies should be continuing to fund the staff training and
promote the hiring necessary for them to have qualified people on hand to
handle all of the changes likely to occur in green building techniques and strategies in the next five years.

BEYOND LEED

Many leading voices in the green building industry are beginning to look at
how to move beyond LEED requirements, toward buildings and neighborhoods that are "restorative" or "regenerative" (or "biophilic"[22]) providing all
of their own power (on an annual average, if not moment by moment) and
most or all of their water, along with restoring habitat and in some cases,
restoring natural stream drainage patterns. Many of these projects aim to use

renewable energy systems to achieve some of their goals. At least through the end of 2008, the solar energy tax credits contained in the EPACT should facilitate many more projects with integrated PV, solar water heating and similar approaches to using "free" on-site resources.[23]

The *Living Building Challenge* of the Cascadia Green Building Council, a USGBC chapter in the Pacific Northwest and British Columbia, is an example of this trend.[24] The Living Building approach contains no points, only prerequisites based on the absolute performance of a building against 16 environmental attributes that taken together constitute a living building. In other words, if a project doesn't meet all the prerequisites, it can't even be considered a "living building." This is obviously a trend that will acquire increasing importance as more adventurous clients want to design buildings that truly go beyond LEED, without that being just an empty slogan.

As to the merit of going beyond LEED, architect Gail Lindsey says, "Much of the green development that's going on now is at the most basic level; it is really about doing *less bad*; attempting to slow down the damage. We need to move on to the restorative and regenerative levels, ultimately make the place better than it was before."[25]

The need to start thinking beyond LEED is also driving many design firms to look at ways to add sustainable features beyond the requirements contained in the LEED system. Principal Leland Cott of Bruner/Cott (Cambridge, Massachusetts) believes that institutional clients will drive the future of sustainable design because they look at their buildings as long-term investments and are receptive to advanced ideas:

> Our sustainable design expertise has helped us win new business on college campuses more than anything. This is true both for rehabilitation and new construction projects. At Harvard and Dartmouth specifically, we have proven that we can take a building to any level of sustainability the client can imagine. Our first LEED Platinum project just received certification and achieved the highest LEED score of any renovation in the country. We bring new things to the table [on every project], especially when it comes to issues of light and daylighting, ventilation, materials selection, water use, and heating/cooling approaches.[26]

Many projects are beginning to experiment with going beyond LEED by creating LEED Platinum buildings and then adding regenerative or restorative features to them. A current example is the Kirsch Center for Environmental Studies at DeAnza College in Cupertino California, a two-year institution, shown in Figure 13.2. Taking a client's project that already calls for a Platinum LEED rating and then adding restorative features such as 100 percent reliance on rainfall or a "net zero energy" on-site production system will not only

▲ **13.2** Kirsch Center for Environmental Studies, designed by VBN Architects in association with Van der Ryn Architects, is a virtual laboratory for DeAnza College's environmental curriculum. Its LEED Platinum features include natural ventilation, extensive daylighting and native landscaping.

qualify for LEED innovation credits, but will also call attention to the future direction that green buildings will take.

Notes

1   Media   Post   [online],   http://publications.mediapost.com/index.cfm?
    fuseaction=Articles.san&s=53075&Nid=26151&p=401551 (accessed March
    21, 2007).

2   "Green Building Smart Market Report," McGraw-Hill Construction, Novem-
    ber   2005,   44   pp.,   www.construction.com/SmartMarket/greenbuilding/
    default.asp, p. 12.

3   Remarks of Chairman Howard Schultz at Starbucks Annual Meeting,
    March   20,   2007,   as   reported   in   http://online.wsj.com/article/
    SB117448991525244165.html?mod=index_to_people.

4   Wal-Mart [online], www.walmart.com/green (accessed April 22, 2007).

5   Wal-Mart   [online],   http://walmartstores.com/GlobalWMStoresWeb/
    navigate.do?catg=347 (accessed April 22, 2007).

6   This is a far more conservative estimate than that of the USGBC's CEO Rick Fedrizzi, who announced a goal of 100,000 registered projects by 2010, at the organization's annual conference in November 2006.

7   US Green Building Council [online], remarks at *Greenbuild 2006* plenary session, www.usgbc.org/Docs/News/openplenaryrick.pdf (accessed April 22, 2007).

8   *Building Design & Construction Magazine* [online], www.buildingteamforecast.com/article/CA6421650.html?industryid=44206 (accessed March 22, 2007).

9   Richard Florida (2002) *The Rise of the Creative Class: And How It's Transforming Work, Leisure, Community and Everyday Life*. New York: Perseus Books Group.

10 Personal communication, Clark Brockman, SERA Architects, March 2007.

11 Energy Star [online], www.energystar.gov/index.cfm?fuseaction=qhmi.showHomesMarketIndex (accessed March 30, 2007).

12 US Green Building Council data as of April 10, 2007, provided to the author.

13 Sarah Karush, "D.C. Council Passes Green Building Rules," Washington Post [online], www.washingtonpost.com/wp-dyn/content/article/2006/12/06/AR2006120600165.html (accessed April 28, 2007).

14 Architectural Record [online], http://archrecord.construction.com/news/daily/archives/070216boston.asp (accessed April 28, 2007).

15 Association for the Advancement of Sustainability in Higher Education (AASHE) Digest [online], www.aashe.org (accessed April 28, 2007).

16 Architecture 2030 [online], www.architecture2030.org (accessed April 28, 2007).

17 Interview with Jim Broughton, TAS, March 2007.

18 Turner Construction Company. Survey is available at: www.turnerconstruction.com/greensurvey 05.pdf (accessed March 6, 2007).

19 Rob Cassidy, "Green Buildings and the Bottom Line," *Building Design & Construction Magazine*, November 2006 Supplement, www.bdcmag.com, p. 8 (accessed March 6, 2007). Reprinted with permission from Building Design & Construction. Copyright 2006 Reed Business Information. All rights reserved.

20 Interview with Jim Goldman, Turner Construction, March 2007.

21 Interview with Jerry Lea, Hines, March 2007.

22 Stephen Kellert and Edward Wilson, eds. (1995) *The Biophilia Hypothesis*. Washington, DC: Island Press.

23 The tax credits and deductions in this act currently are set to expire on December 31, 2008, unless extended by the Congress before that deadline.

24 Cascadia Green Building Council [online], www.cascadiagbc.org.

25 Interview with Gail Lindsey, Design Harmony, North Carolina, March 2007.

26 Interview with Leland Cott, Bruner/Cott, April 2007.

Green Building Resources

BIBLIOGRAPHY

Coburn, P. (2006) *The Change Factor: Why Some Technologies Take Off and Others Crash and Burn.* New York: Penguin Portfolio.

Gladwell, M. (2000) *The Tipping Point: How Little Things Can Make a Big Difference.* New York: Little, Brown.

Godin, S. (2003) *Purple Cow: Transform Your Business by Becoming Remarkable.* Dobbs Ferry, NY: Do You Zoom.

Godin, S. (2005) *All Marketers are Liars: The Power of Telling Authentic Stories in a Low-Trust World.* New York: Penguin Portfolio.

Kats, G.H. et al. (2003) *The Costs and Financial Benefits of Green Buildings: A Report to California's Sustainable Building Task Force.* Sacramento, CA. Available from www.cap-e.com.

Kotler, P. and Keller, K.L. (2006) *Marketing Management,* 12th edn. New York: Prentice Hall.

Lowe, S. (2004) *Marketplace Masters: How Professional Service Firms Compete to Win.* Westport, CT: Praeger.

Mendler, S.F., Odell, W. and Lazarus, M.A. (2005) *The HOK Guidebook to Sustainable Design,* 2nd edn. New York: Wiley.

Moore, G.A. (1999) *Crossing the Chasm: Marketing and Selling High-Tech Products to Mainstream Customers,* Revised edition. New York: HarperBusiness.

Porter, M.E. (1980) *Competitive Strategy: Techniques for Analyzing Industries and Competitors.* New York: Free Press.

Rogers, E.M. (2003) *Diffusion of Innovations,* 5th edn. New York: Free Press.

CONFERENCES

US Green Building Council, Greenbuild International Conference and Exposition, typically early November.
The 2007 show will be held in Chicago, Boston is scheduled to host the 2008 show and Phoenix the 2009 event. The world's largest green building conference, this is definitely a "must" if you are in the commercial design world. For further information: www.greenbuildexpo.com. Mostly an "industry" show, it is open to the public, especially valuable for the exhibits and the educational program.

West Coast Green, San Francisco.
Covers both residential and commercial green buildings, includes a few hundred exhibit booths. For further information: www.westcoastgreen.com. Typically held in late September in San Francisco. Public invited.

American Solar Energy Society.
Conferences are typically held in the summer; they provide an annual update on solar energy. For further information: www.ases.org. Open to the public.

Ball State University, Muncie, Indiana, Greening the Campus Conference. Biennial.
Greening of the Campus VII: Partnering for Sustainability: Enabling a Diverse Future, was held September 6–8, 2007. This biennial conference has been held since 1996 and focuses on a broad range of campus topics. For further information: www.bsu. edu/provost/ceres/greening. Ideal for students and faculty.

Society for College and University Planning.
Annual conference typically held in July. Strong sustainable design program. For further information: www.scup.org. A must for architects and engineers marketing to the higher education sector.

BOOKS

Most books are outdated shortly after they are published in this fast-changing field. Nevertheless, there are a few that have good shelf life, even now. You might find them interesting, perhaps life-changing.

Anderson, R. (1998) *Mid-Course Correction*. Atlanta, GA: Peregrinzilla Press.
This is a classic book that chronicles the successful beginning of a corporate paradigm shift through a personal transformation by the CEO. Ray Anderson writes as he speaks, straight from the heart, with experience, passion and eloquence.

Frej, A. (ed.) (2005) *Green Office Buildings: A Practical Guide to Development.* Washington, DC: Urban Land Institute.
An excellent guide to broad-scale thinking about green developments.

Gore, A. (2006) *An Inconvenient Truth*. Emmaus, PA: Rodale Press.
The instant "classic" on why we need to make a wholesale change in our energy-wasteful habits; though long on analysis and passion, it is short on prescription. Gore's book (and movie) have had a revolutionary, paradigm-shifting impact.

Hawken, P., Lovins, A. and Lovins, L.H. (1999) *Natural Capitalism: Creating the Next Industrial Revolution*. Boston: Little Brown.
This book is a respected treatment of how much we can learn from natural systems and how little we are applying what we already know. This book will reward anyone who wants to understand how to take the next leap into whole systems thinking and sustainable design.

Kiuchi, T. and Shireman, B. (2002) *What We Learned in the Rain Forest: Business Lessons from Nature*. San Francisco: Berrett-Koehler Publishers.
An excellent guide to the rationale for using sustainability principles in every organization, as a means of ensuring its evolutionary success.

Mau, B. (2004) *Massive Change*. London and New York: Phaidon Press.
Massive Change is not about the world of design, it's about the design of the world for long-term success.

McDonough, W. and Braungart, M. (2002) *Cradle to Cradle: Changing the Way We Make Things*. New York: North Point Press.
Not printed on ordinary book paper, this book "walks the talk." The authors take us step-by-step through their reasoning for advocating a new industrial paradigm and give great case studies of how they've begun that process for a number of companies.

Steffen, A. (ed.) (2006) *World Changing: A User's Guide for the 21st Century*. New York: Harry N. Abrams, Inc.
It's hard to know what to say about this nearly 600-page compendium of everything we know about green solutions, except that you need a copy in your library for reference.

US Green Building Council (2003 and 2005) *LEED-NC Reference Guide. Versions 2.1 and 2.2*. Washington, DC: US Green Building Council. Available from www.usgbc.org.
A comprehensive guide to the LEED rating system's current version and an excellent contemporary one-volume resource on sustainable design.

Van der Ryn, S. (2005) *Design for Life: The Architecture of Sim Van der Ryn*. Salt Lake City: Gibbs Smith.
An overview of the present situation and future potential of sustainable design from a master practitioner.

Whitson, B.A. and Yudelson, J. (2003) *365 Important Questions to Ask About Green Buildings*. Portland, OR: Corporate Realty Design and Management Institute. Available from www.squarefootage.net.
Practical questions to ask at each design phase when considering viable green design options.

Yudelson, J. (2006) *Developing Green: Strategies for Success*. Herndon, VA: National Association of Industrial and Office Properties. Available from www. naiop.org with CD of case studies attached.
This is the best introduction to the business case for green buildings, written primarily for developers and building owners. Includes case studies of green developments submitted for the NAIOP Green Development of the Year award in 2005.

PERIODICALS

It's hard to keep up with the proliferation of green building magazines and related publications. Here are a few publications I read on a regular basis and find valuable for staying in touch. Most of these are available both in hard copy and electronic versions, so if you're averse to having too much paper around, you can keep up with the news via the electronic editions and related online newsletters.

Architectural Products, www.arch-products.com
This monthly provides coverage of green products on a regular basis.

Architectural Record, http://archrecord.construction.com
This is an excellent source of green building information for the mainstream architectural community and a good way for engineers to keep up with the evolving discussion of sustainability among architects.

Building Design & Construction, www.bdcmag.com
BD&C is one of the authoritative voices in the industry. Written primarily for "Building Team" practitioners, it is eminently accessible to anyone.

Buildings Magazine, www.buildings.com
Buildings Magazine provides a good introduction to the practical side of building design, construction and operations. Good coverage of specialty topics in the industry.

Consulting-Specifying Engineer, www.csemag.com
A monthly trade magazine for mechanical and electrical engineering management.

Eco-Structure Magazine, www.eco-structure.com
Eco-structure is the most illustrated of the trade magazines covering the green building industry. Good case studies and a broad selection of topics make it a good read for keeping up.

Environmental Design & Construction, www.edcmag.com
Now 10 years old, ED&C provides first-class editorial coverage of the relevant issues, along with well-written case studies of leading green building projects.

Green Source Magazine, www.construction.com/greensource
Started in 2006 by the publishers of Engineering News-Record and Architectural Record, the most authoritative publications in their field, the quarterly Green Source is edited by the team at Environmental Building News. The case studies are the best written you will find anywhere.

HPAC Magazine, www.hpac.com
Monthly trade magazine covering technical aspects of heating, plumbing and air conditioning for commercial buildings.

Metropolis, www.metropolismag.com
If you want to know what's going on in the broader world of sustainable design, the monthly Metropolis is a "must read." Outstanding coverage of all aspects of design, it has sharpened its focus on green buildings in recent years.

Solar Today, www.solartoday.org.
The official publication of the American Solar Energy Society, but written for a general audience; you can even find it at the checkout counter of natural foods stores.

WEBSITES

Association for the Advancement of Sustainability in Higher Education (AASHE), www.aashe.org
Subscribe to the "AASHE Bulletin" for a comprehensive overview of sustainable programs and activities in American higher education.

Better Bricks, www.betterbricks.com
This is an excellent resource of energy-efficient and green building design from the Northwest Energy Efficiency Alliance (www.nwalliance.org), a utility-funded organization that offers hundreds of articles, interviews and technical resources for sustainable design.

Clean Edge, www.cleanedge.com
The self-described "clean tech" market authority; a nice newsletter keeps you up to date on renewable energy and related companies and venture capital activity in this fast-paced industry.

Efficient Buildings, www.efficientbuildings.org
This site covers the 2005 federal energy tax law's commercial energy efficiency tax deduction. Another site, www.energytaxincentives.org/tiap-gen-info.html, from the Tax Incentives Assistance Project, covers the law more broadly.

GreenBuzz, www.greenbiz.com
A good web site for a continuous read of the sustainable business movement.

IGreenBuild, www.igreenbuild.com
This is a good overview web site of the business and product side of the green building movement.

Renewable Energy Incentives, www.dsireusa.org
State incentives for renewable energy can be found at www.dsireusa.org. Renewable energy incentives in federal tax law are analyzed at a number of sites, including the Tax Incentive Assistance Project (www.energytaxincentives.org).

Royal Institute of Chartered Surveyors, www.rics.org/greenvalue
The source for the major UK–Canadian–US report on the asset values of green buildings, released in late 2005.

US Green Building Council, www.usgbc.org
The USGBC web site is the premier web site not only for the organization but for news and happenings in the broader field of green buildings. If a trend that "legs," you'll find it here. You can download copies of all LEED rating systems and also search for LEED-registered and certified projects.

World Changing, www.worldchanging.com
Emerging innovations and solutions for building a brighter green future; an essential site if you want to know what's going to be a mainstream concern in short order.

SELECTED ARTICLES

Building Design & Construction Magazine (2003 and 2004) Progress report on sustainability Cassidy, R. (ed.) *Building Design & Construction*, Supplement to November issue. Available at www.bdcmag.com

Building Design & Construction Magazine (2005) Life-cycle assessment and sustainability Cassidy, R. (ed.) *Building Design & Construction*, Supplement to November issue, 64 pp. Available at www.bdcmag.com

Building Design & Construction Magazine (2006) Green buildings and the bottom line Cassidy, R. (ed.) *Building Design & Construction Magazine*, Supplement to November issue. Available at www.bdcmag.com

ORGANIZATIONS

- *US Green Building Council* (www.usgbc.org) is the largest (8,500 members) and most significant group in the US. Publishes the *LEED Reference Guides*, the definitive resources for the LEED system and for green building design in general.
- *Sustainable Buildings Industries Council* (www.psic.org) focuses on schools and residential new construction.
- *Canada Green Building Council* (www.cagbc.org) covers the same territory for Canada as the US Green Building Council does for the US.

- Building industry web sites include the *American Institute of Architects Committee on the Environment* (www.aia.org/cote_default), the *American Society of Heating, Refrigeration and Air-Conditioning Engineers* (www.ashrae.org) and the *Construction Specifications Institute* (www.csinet.org). See also the annual AIA Committee on the Environment Top Ten awards for a sense of the state of the art in green buildings, www.aiatopten.org/hpb.
- *Collaborative for High-Performance Schools* (www.chps.net) has published an excellent set of design resources in four manuals for designing green school buildings.
- *BioRegional Development Group* (www.bioregional.com) is working in the UK and Portugal on zero-energy developments.
- *New Buildings Institute* (www.newbuildings.org) publishes the *Benefits Guide: A Design Professional's Guide to High-Performance Office Building Benefits*, aimed at helping architects and engineers talk to their clients about the multiple benefits of sustainable design for smaller office buildings.
- *Green Guide to Health Care* (www.gghc.org) publishes a "best practices" system for health care design, construction and operations.

LEED Rating Systems Comparison

This appendix provides a comparison of all four major LEED rating systems, including the most often-used of the USGBC's, LEED-NC, which represents 75 percent of registered projects and 77 percent of all certified projects, through the end of March 2007. Table 1 shows how each of the four major systems, LEED-NC, LEED-CI, LEED-CS and LEED-EB, shares the same credit structure and many of the same credits.

Additional USGBC rating systems not included here are LEED-H and LEED-ND, both of which are still in a pilot evaluation phase. The healthcare best practices guidance document, *Green Guide for Healthcare*, is not really a rating system but a collection of best practices and so is not presented here. We believe that green building marketers need to know what's in each rating system, to understand what's feasible in a given marketing situation and to appreciate how to market accomplishments from certified projects.

All systems are presented in their April 2007 version and all are publicly available from the USGBC web site, www.usgbc.org. Readers should note that the specific requirements of these systems change on a periodic basis. They should make sure they are using the most current versions available on the USGBC's web site. Please also note that I have only presented the subject of the credit requirements (and in some cases have abbreviated them); each credit has additionally specified requirements and submittals that must accompany the certification application, but these are too detailed for our purposes here.

Table 1 Comparison of LEED credits among the four major rating systems

LEED Credit Category (Excludes prerequisites)	LEED-NC Points	LEED-CS Points	LEED-CI Points	LEED-EB Points
Sustainable sites				
1. Site selection	1	1	3	
2. Development density/community connectivity	1	1	1	1
3. Brownfield redevelopment	1	1		
4. Alternative transportation				
Access to transit	1	1	1	1
Bicycle storage	1	1	1	1
Low-emitting/fuel-efficient vehicles	1	1	–	1
Parking capacity	1	1	1	–
Carpooling/telecommuting	–	–	–	1
5. Site development				
Protect/restore habitat	1	1	–	1
Maximize open space	1	1	–	1
6. Stormwater design				
Control runoff quantity	1	1	–	2
Control runoff quality	1	1	–	
7. Heat island effect				
Nonroof	1	1	–	1
Roof	1	1	–	1
8. Light pollution reduction	1	1	–	1
10. Green site/building exterior management plan	–	–	–	2
Total sustainable sites	**14**	**15**	**7**	**14**
Water efficiency				
1. Water-efficient landscaping				
Reduce potable water use 50%	1	1	–	**1**
Eliminate potable water use	1	1		**1**
2. Innovative wastewater technologies	1	1	–	**1**
3. Water use reduction: 20%/30%	2	2	2	**2**
Total water efficiency	**5**	**5**	**2**	**5**
Energy and atmosphere				
1. Optimize energy performance	10	8	8	**10**
2. Renewable energy	3	1	–	**4**
3. Enhanced commissioning/building systems maintenance	1	1	1	**3**
4. Additional ozone protection	1	1	–	**1**

(Continued)

Table 1 (Continued)

LEED Credit Category (Excludes prerequisites)	LEED-NC Points	LEED-CS Points	LEED-CI Points	LEED-EB Points
5. Measurement and verification	–	2	2	**4**
6. Green power	1	1	1	–
7. Documenting cost impacts	–	–	–	**1**
Total energy and atmosphere	**17**	**14**	**12**	**23**
Materials and resources				
1. Building reuse	3	3	2	–
Tenant long-term commitment	–	–	1	–
2. Construction waste recycling	2	2	2	**2**
Sustainable materials purchasing	–	–	–	**5**
3. Materials reuse	2	1	3	
Optimize use of low-emitting materials	–	–	–	**2**
4. Recycled-content materials	2	2	2	–
Sustainable cleaning products	–	–	–	**3**
5. Use regionally produced materials	2	2	2	
Occupant recycling	–	–	–	**3**
6. Use rapidly renewable materials	1	–	1	
Reduced mercury in light bulbs	–	–	–	**1**
7. Use certified wood products	1	1	1	
Total materials and resources	**13**	**11**	**14**	**16**
Indoor environmental quality				
1. Outdoor air delivery monitoring	1	1	1	1
2. Increased ventilation	1	1	1	1
3. Construction indoor air quality (IAQ) plan	2	1	2	1
4. Low-emitting materials use	4	3	5	
Documenting productivity impacts	–	–	–	2
5. Indoor chemical/pollutant source control	1	1	1	2
6. Controllability of systems	2	1	2	2
7. Thermal comfort: design	1	1	–	–
Thermal comfort: compliance and monitoring	1	–	2	2
8. Daylighting and views	2	2	3	4
9. IAQ practice	–	–	–	1
10. Green cleaning	–	–	–	6
Total indoor environmental quality	**15**	**11**	**17**	**22**
Total "core points"	**64**	**56**	**52**	**80**

(Continued)

Table 1 (Continued)

LEED Credit Category (Excludes prerequisites)	LEED-NC Points	LEED-CS Points	LEED-CI Points	LEED-EB Points
Innovation and design process				
Innovation in design	4	4	4	–
Innovation in upgrades/maintenance	–	–	–	4
LEED Accredited Professional (LEED AP)	1	1	1	1
Total rating system points	**69**	**61**	**57**	**85**
Certification levels				
(Minimum points)				
Certified	26	23	21	32
Silver	33	28	27	40
Gold	39	34	32	48
Platinum	52	45	42	64

Acronym Reference List

AASHE	Association for the Advancement of Sustainability in Higher Education
AIA	American Institute of Architects
ANSI	American National Standards Institute
ASHRAE	American Society for Heating, Refrigeration and Air-conditioning Engineers
BD&C	*Building Design & Construction* magazine
BEEP	BOMA Energy Efficiency Program
BIM	building information modeling
BIPV	building-integrated photovoltaics
BOMA	Building Owners and Managers Association
BREEAM	Building Research Establishment Environmental Assessment Method (U.K.)
CalPERS	California Public Employees Retirement System
CASBEE	Comprehensive Assessment System for Building Environmental Efficiency (Japan)
COC	chain of custody
CHPS	Collaborative for High-Performance Schools
CHP	combined heat and power
CRM	client relationship management
COPT	Corporate Office Properties Trust
EPACT	Energy Policy Act of 2005 (U.S. Federal)
FEMP	Federal Energy Management Program
FSC	Forest Stewardship Council
GGHC	Green Guide for Healthcare
GSA	U.S. General Services Administration (Federal)
HVAC	heating, ventilation and air conditioning
IESNA	Illuminating Engineering Society of North America
IRR	internal rate of return
LCA	life-cycle assessment
LEED	Leadership in Energy and Environmental Design®

LEED APs	LEED Accredited Professionals
LEED-CI	LEED for Commercial Interiors
LEED-CS	LEED for Core and Shell
LEED-EB	LEED for Existing Buildings/High-Performance Operations
LEED-H	LEED for Homes
LEED-ND	LEED for Neighborhood Development
LEED-NC	LEED for New Construction
LOHAS	Lifestyles of Health and Sustainability
NAHB	National Association of Home Builders
NAIOP	National Association of Industrial and Office Properties
NAR	National Association of Realtors
NRDC	Natural Resources Defense Council
NREL	National Renewable Energy Laboratory (U.S. Dept. of Energy)
PV	photovoltaics
RECs	renewable energy certificates
RFP	request for proposals
RFQ	request for qualifications
RMI	Rocky Mountain Institute
ROI	return on investment
SFI	Sustainable Forestry Initiative
SOQ	statement of qualification
SWOT	strengths, weaknesses, opportunities and threats
TPPA	Total Perceived Pain of Adoption
UF	urea-formaldehyde
VOCs	volatile organic compounds

Author Biography

Jerry Yudelson is a Professional Engineer and one of the leading authorities on green development and marketing green buildings, having already written five books on these subjects. He has been actively involved in the green building industry and in the green building movement since 1999. Prior to that, he spent his career developing new technologies and providing services in the areas of building systems engineering, renewable energy, environmental remediation and environmental planning. As a marketing, technology and management consultant, Jerry worked with state and provincial governments, utilities, local governments, Fortune 500 companies, small businesses, architecture and engineering firms, and building product manufacturers.

 He holds an MBA with highest honors from the University of Oregon and has taught 50 MBA courses in marketing, business planning, organizational development and public relations. A registered professional engineer in the State of Oregon, he holds degrees in civil and environmental engineering from the California Institute of Technology (Caltech) and Harvard University, respectively. He has been a management consultant to more than 75 CEOs of various-sized firms and a marketing consultant to more than 100 companies.

Currently, as Principal at Yudelson Associates, a green building consultancy based in Tucson, Arizona, he works for architects, project developers, engineering firms, building owners, investors and building product manufacturers seeking to make their projects and products as "green" as possible. His work on design projects involves early-stage consultation, eco-charrette facilitation, and LEED expertise and coaching. He works with development teams to develop effective marketing programs for large-scale green projects and with manufacturers and private-equity firms to provide "due diligence" on product marketing and investment opportunities, as well as assisting corporate sustainability efforts.

He is a frequent speaker and lecturer on green building topics, keynoting regional, national and international conferences, and conducting workshops in marketing green building services and developing green projects. During the past 5 years, he has published more than 60 articles on green building marketing in various trade, technical and professional journals.

Since 2001, as a national trainer for the US Green Building Council (USGBC), Jerry has trained more than 3,000 building industry professionals in the LEED rating system. Since 2004, he has chaired the USGBC's annual conference, *Greenbuild*, the largest green building conference and trade show in the world.

Jerry also served on national committees charged with producing the LEED for Core and Shell standard for the development community and updating the LEED for New Construction rating system.

In 2006, the US General Services Administration named him to the national roster of "Peer Professionals," to advise its Design Excellence program for major federal facilities. In 2004, the Northwest Energy Efficiency Alliance named him "Green Building Advocate" of the year.

He serves on the editorial boards of a trade journal, *Environmental Design & Construction*, and *Marketer*, the magazine of the Society for Marketing Professional Services. He is senior editor at the web site, www.igreenbuild.com. Jerry and his wife, along with their Scottie, live on the edge of the Sonoran desert in Tucson, Arizona.

INDEX